POWER
THE STORY OF CHINA LIGHT

POWER

THE STORY OF CHINA LIGHT

NIGEL CAMERON

HONG KONG
OXFORD UNIVERSITY PRESS
OXFORD NEW YORK MELBOURNE
1982

Oxford University Press

LONDON GLASGOW NEW YORK TORONTO
DELHI BOMBAY CALCUTTA MADRAS KARACHI
KUALA LUMPUR SINGAPORE HONG KONG TOKYO
NAIROBI DAR ES SALAAM CAPE TOWN SALISBURY
MELBOURNE AUCKLAND
and associates in
BEIRUT BERLIN IBADAN MEXICO CITY NICOSIA

ISBN 0 19 581326X

*Designed by Format Limited
Published by Oxford University Press, Warwick House,
28 Tong Chong Street, Quarry Bay, Hong Kong.
Filmset in Hong Kong by Asco Trade Typesetting Ltd.
Printed in Hong Kong by Hip Shing Offset Printing Factory*

CONTENTS

Endpapers: Detail from a technical drawing of a boiler much used in the 1930s

ACKNOWLEDGEMENTS

THE most important sources upon which this history is based are the records of the Company. With the exception of that for the year 1908, the records of board meetings from the statutory meeting of 1901 onward have fortunately been preserved, and full use has been made of them.

In terms of the printed word, the various newspapers of Hong Kong during the period of the Company's existence have been of considerable value, especially in providing necessary background relating to the everyday condition of the Colony and its neighbours at certain crucial points, as well as plumping out the necessarily bare facts reported in Company meetings, in which references were often made to events well known to board members present but which are not at once comprehensible today. For considerable assistance in this area I would like to thank Mr. Ian Diamond, Government Archivist, his assistant Ms. Robyn McLean, and the staff of the Public Records Office for their ready help.

Published books and the Annual Reports of the Hong Kong Government have also been consulted, and these are listed in the Bibliography.

Mention should also be made of Mr. H.A. Rydings, Librarian of the University of Hong Kong, and Mr. Peter Yang of the same library for their usual willing assistance.

In the general and also the particular background to the generation of electricity, historically and in practice, I am greatly indebted to Mr. R.W.M. Clouston, Group Archivist, Babcock Power, London. I happily acknowledge his painstaking and friendly assistance, which included finding technical drawings of early steam boilers supplied to the Company, and also taking me through a crash course in the history of boilers.

For similar advice, and documentation on early generating equipment, I am obliged to Mr. Brian M. Feeney of APE-Belliss, Birmingham.

I would particularly like to thank the management of the Guangdong Power Company at Guangzhou, Mr. Chan Hok-ling, deputy chief engineer, and others from the company (including two charming and efficient interpreters from Jiangsu Province, traditionally the home of the most beautiful girls in China), for their invaluable help when I wanted to see the old power station there – which was China Light's first profitable enterprise long ago. Apart from their help, their open friendliness and generosity made the visit memorable.

Some meticulous special research was undertaken by the Rev. Carl Smith in Hong Kong, and much of the basic documentation throughout most of the text was done by Mr. Edgar Laufer, formerly employed by the Company, whose general outline and figures proved invaluable, entirely reliable, and allowed me more time to concentrate on aspects of the broader canvas.

A great deal of information, not by any means all of it used directly but nonetheless invaluable as background, was provided in letters, in conversation, and in interviews with past and present members of the Company in Hong Kong and elsewhere. The author is heavily indebted to them all, chairman of the board and long-serving Chinese employees alike, for their patience in spending so much time with him, and for searching their memories so thoroughly in aid of the Company's history. It is a pity that many of the anecdotes they told him, for reasons of space (and, in some cases, of diplomacy,) cannot be included.

INTRODUCTION

IN February 1940, at its power station in Hok Un, the China Light & Power Company and its friends celebrated the opening of a new building, housing a new boiler and turbine with a generating capacity of 12.5 megawatts which, at the pressing of a button by the Governor of Hong Kong, was then added to the existing output of the station.

Mr. Lawrence Kadoorie, the Company's chairman, made a speech in which he succinctly traced the main lines of the Company's history, and made also some sagacious predictions about its future.

'Briefly stated,' he said, 'the history of the China Light & Power Company is the history of the development of Kowloon.... There are those who well remember the days when Kowloon went lightless by night. In the course of time its few suburban roads – if narrow pathways could be dignified by the term roads – were lighted by kerosene lamps.' And he proceeded to paint a short but vivid picture of those former times in that part of Hong Kong territory which points like a beak southward into the waters of the harbour from the wider areas of the New Territories. He related how it developed in parallel with the development of the Company's activities in supplying light and power, and how the commercial development of Kowloon and the development of the Company were activities that had gone very much in tandem.

'Today the Company's property at Hok Un comprises an area of no less than eight acres. The selection of the new site speaks well for the vision of those responsible. In a public undertaking of this nature, breadth of vision is a valuable asset; and confidence in the future, backed by the judicious expenditure of required capital ahead of time, is essential....'

'Kowloon, today, has a significance beyond that of a merely suburban, residential area.... It is to be hoped that nothing will prevent Kowloon from developing into a manufacturing centre of some importance. This fine new building [the power station] is frankly designed with an optimistic view of the future and is symbolic of the faith of the China Light & Power Company in the great progress and development of the Colony of Hong Kong in particular. Industries, ranging in size from the manufacture of joss sticks to the building of ocean-going steamers, as different in their nature as the preserving of ginger and the mining of lead ore, are today dependent for their operation on the power supplied by this station....' He wished prosperity to the customers 'with whose success our future is so intimately bound up.'

Thus, in a few paragraphs of his address on that day in 1940, Lawrence Kadoorie aptly summed up not merely the story of the Company's past years, but also predicted with an accuracy that must, as time went by, have surprised even him, the outline of its future. He underscored what must be the essential theme of any history of the Company – the inextricable and by any standard quite extraordinary interaction of the growth of Kowloon's population and industry with the growth and activities of the Company.

Doubtless the story could be repeated in other parts of the world as power from electricity supplanted the power of steam *used directly* in industry to drive the essential machines. But there is perhaps no example so neat, so compact, none so remarkable in many aspects and in many an episode, illustrating the simultaneous development of industry and the source of its energy, as that which can be followed in the symbiotic development of Kowloon's industrialisation and the Company's expansion.

The restricted terrain, the nature of the life of the Colony itself which is in many ways unique, the near-total absence in it of any raw material suitable for manufacturing purposes and, throughout most of the Company's history, the sequence of turbulent events which took place across the border as well as in the world at large, many of them deeply affecting Hong Kong – all these add up to make a fascinating story.

BACKGROUND

I N the world of today when the exploration of outer space, the sight in colour close-up of the faces of the farthest planets are familiar in homes round the globe, and when the harnessing of nuclear energy is a commonplace (if a controversial one), it may seem odd to recall the fever of excitement that swept the Western world when the Age of Steam dawned. The power of steam in all its manifold potential convulsed the popular mind and brought expectations of marvels to come. Indeed, even in sober scientific circles, the same thrill, the same sense of a new age dawning, implicit in the use of capitals at that time when people named it the Age of Steam, was felt. It seemed to most that a hitherto unimagined opportunity for mankind's productivity, and for comfort, leisure, and happiness was about to rise like a new and greater sun over the horizon.

There was an optimism in the nineteenth-century air when the potential of machines driven by steam power was realised. Locomotives drawing trains, at first the wonder of the age, rapidly became the norm, and a whole new industry, the tourist trade, came into being. With cheap fares the lower-paid people of Britain found they could enjoy holidays at little cost and no inconvenience. With the spirit of new adventure, they took to the railways by hundreds of thousands and frolicked at journey's end by the sea – something that only the rich had ever before in the story of mankind been able to afford.

Initially, what was certainly the greatest social change in the nations of the West since the Renaissance, was brought about basically by the harnessing of the power of steam under pressure to drive machines. For the power of the human muscle, or that of some animals, steam was substituted. But the achievement did not, any more than the achievements of the Renaissance, come all at once. It had involved a slow search for the means to utilize the power of steam with reasonable efficiency.

At the same time, in another field of experimentation, a series of what appeared then to be entirely academic experiments with the production in small quantities of electricity in laboratories, came to occupy a place of more promise than mere scholarly interest. The final step came when the still marvellous energies of steam were applied to drive what was theoretically a very simple machine whose product was an electric current. This current constituted the second factor in the Industrial Revolution. For it could be made to produce light at the touch of a finger on a switch, and – equally astonishing in its implications – to drive other machines without the use of directly applied steam power.

The theory of how to produce an electric current had been known for some time, but the application of steam power to produce the necessary motion to make it continuously and in regular and measured amounts, did not come until long after the first practical steam engine.

One of the major stumbling blocks was how to design and build a reliable boiler to make steam at pressure and continuously. Nowadays the problem may seem an easy one to solve. But all great steps forward in technique, like the conjuror's rabbit coming miraculously out of the hat, appear easy once they have been made. The evolution of workable boilers was slow and fraught with hazards, not least among which was the extreme danger of their exploding with disastrous effects. The statistics for the year 1880 in the United States reveal 170 recorded explosions with a loss of 259 lives and 555 persons injured. Seven years later the figures had risen to 198 explosions with 652 persons either killed or seriously injured. Many explosions occurred that were never reported.

In the last two decades of the twentieth century, at a time when we tend to take most technological advances for granted, a basic fact is often forgotten: virtually everything modern technology makes or accomplishes is made or accomplished by means of the energy of electricity.

Apart from small but significant amounts of electricity produced by the power of water pressure in certain favourable sites round the world, apart from some electricity produced by gas turbines which work in the same way as a plane's jet engines, small amounts made by Diesel engines working on oil, and a minute quantity made directly by trapping the rays of the sun – all the world's electricity continues to be made by means of steam pressure turning a generator.

Even electricity from nuclear energy, from those cores of enriched uranium closely guarded and rigorously controlled in the hearts of special power stations, is made in the same way. The energy of the nuclear reaction still has to heat water and raise a head of steam to drive the turbines which turn the generators that churn out the electric current. Nuclear power is simply another alternative to coal or oil as the source of heat. So we are still firmly in that Age of Steam which seems at first sight so old-fashioned. And it would seem likely that for the foreseeable future this will continue to be an inescapable truth. Coal may have been largely replaced by oil for some time, and the advent of nuclear energy as a source appealed greatly, but more recent world events have made oil both costly and of doubtfully regular supply. Nuclear energy production, rather in the manner of the steam boiler's evolution, is going through its growing pains.

The other, later, revolutionary industrial invention in the field of motive power was the internal combustion engine. In practical terms, however, such engines cannot be made to produce electricity as efficiently (and therefore at low cost) as do the now highly sophisticated but still steam-driven machines that were at the heart of the Industrial Revolution, and which were later adapted to make electricity.

It may seem a contradiction in terms to those not directly involved, a paradox, that the super-technical world of today, two hundred years after the dawn of the Age of Steam, still runs on the same old motive power – steam. But the fact is inescapable.

The story of how electricity was first made on a commercial scale and sold to the public is one of great interest in itself. But in relation to the story of the China Light & Power Company there is an added interest in that the Company was surprisingly early in the field. Hong Kong, bold and venturesome as usual, understood the possibilities of the new business very rapidly after its first trial in the West, and plunged in where, as it turned out, more sagacious angels might have feared to tread.

There is no doubt about the date of the first production of light by electricity. In 1808, Sir Humphry Davy demonstrated an arc-light to the Royal Institution in London; and the first mechanical arc-lamp, regulating itself as long as the carbon electrodes burned, was made in 1847. But the dating of the first power station producing commercially available electricity presents a more difficult problem.

Behind the eventual achievement lies the story of the gradual working toward such a possible result by several men of vision and practical talent. In 1857, Professor F.H. Holmes used a machine to make electricity and lit a lighthouse at the South Foreland in England. Another Holmes machine dating from 1871 powered the

beam of another lighthouse until – incredibly – the year 1915. This sturdy generator is now in the Science Museum in London.

Then the famous ring armature of Gramme was demonstrated in 1870 and, together with other technical advances, brought the production of manageable electric current nearer. The first public display of electric lighting in Britain was at the Gaiety Theatre in London in 1878, and some other experimental systems were installed in London in the same year.

The enthusiasm with which electric light was met even brought about the playing of the first floodlit football match in the world – at Sheffield in 1878 – before a crowd of 30,000 fans. And two years later a small hydro-electric plant was installed by Sir William Armstrong at his country house in Northumberland. There exists a curiously lugubrious engraving depicting Sir William and his wife, alone at a dining table, pliant butler in attendance in the background, eating in the light of a strange contraption suspended above them in the vast spaces of the room – a Swan incandescent lamp.

All these early lighting units had their own generators, and most were of a temporary nature. But with the invention of the incandescent lamp the picture began to alter. For here was a means, both safe and requiring no skill or knowledge at all, which could provide light in every home or commercial premises.

There were three power stations which started to produce electricity commercially at about the same time, and it is not possible to give one or other pride of place as the first. But perhaps the most interesting was the Holborn Viaduct station in London which began its supply on 12 January 1882. Its establishment was due to the efforts of Thomas Edison, an American and one of the most prolific inventors of his time. He it was who realised that the individual generating units which were the rule at that time could never be economic. His was the

Left: The dining-room of Sir William Armstrong's house in Northumberland lit by a Swan lamp in 1880. Below: An artist's reconstruction of the Holborn Viaduct station. Note the conduits at the right in which cables could be conveniently run. The boiler is on the lowest level with the turbine above, while the accounts and administrative offices are at the upper street level

idea of supplying electricity in the same manner as water and gas were brought to every door.

Already, in New York at Pearl Street, he had planned for a power station to supply large parts of Lower Manhattan and, as a combi-

The Mansion House, London, lit by Siemens arc lamps in 1870

nation of trial run and advertisement, he sent his assistant to London to build a power station there. The motives for this action are not really clear, but it must be remembered that at the time, the late nineteenth century, Britain was still world leader in industrial invention and modern industrial thinking. It was perhaps natural to try out a new technical process in the country where the Industrial Revolution had begun.

No plans of the Holborn Viaduct station have survived. But from contemporary accounts and an examination of the building, which survives to this day, we can reconstruct the layout of the revolutionary station. The initial permission to build and run such a facility had to be sought from the City of London Corporation, and from them was also won a contract to light the viaduct with electricity for an initial trial period of three months free, and thereafter at the same rate as the Corporation was already paying for gas illumination.

Edison's assistant took a lease on No. 57 Holborn Viaduct, consisting of the ground floor premises which were made into showroom and offices, and the two lower floors, below street level, which communicated with another road at the back on the lowest level. On this lowest level the boiler was installed with ready access for coal from the street below the viaduct. Above it, on the next floor which was specially strengthened with massive steel joists, still there today, the generators were placed. And thus, in a remarkably short time, London's first (perhaps actually the world's first) commercial power station was set up.

The pioneering aspects of this generating station and its operation were many. Virtually all the hardware relating to the conduction of electricity from the generators, its modification so that it was of suitable voltage for the customers, the actual means of transmission to the destinations, the switches, the lampholders, and other gear, had been specially and newly designed. There was no other way, for there was no supply of such material on the market. The original listing of customers exists, together with the number of lamps (slightly under one thousand) supplied with current in the buildings adjacent to the station. This number was soon to be augmented by the Post Office which decided to light its telegraph operating room with four hundred lamps. The apparently extravagant number is explainable because of the low candlepower of lamps at that date.

The surprise caused by this new system of lighting was reflected in the popular press, one newspaper even printing a story about Edison's assistant who was said to 'have passed the whole current for 1,000 lamps through his body without any ill effect.' What – more probably – he had demonstrated was that a 100 volt current was tolerable, whereas the 2,000 or 3,000 volt current commonly used to work the arc-lamps with which some of the public were doubtless familiar could hardly be termed safe.

Holborn Viaduct station was in operation for about four years. And during that time many of the problems inherent in the commercial generation and distribution of electricity were uncovered. One of these, a perennial one that still operates today although now there are adequate means to cope with it, was the vast difference in the amount of electricity demanded by the customers at different times of day. Electricity cannot be stored like gas or water, ready for use when needed. It has to be used as it is made. There is no way (even now, after a century of commercial production and vast technological experience) to keep it in quantity and let it out when someone wants it. When demand occurs, the electricity has to be generated *then*. When there is no demand for it, there is no point in generating it since it has no place to go, and no way of accumulating.

Since, in those days, all the load was used in lighting, daytime demand was very small. But come the evening this demand rose

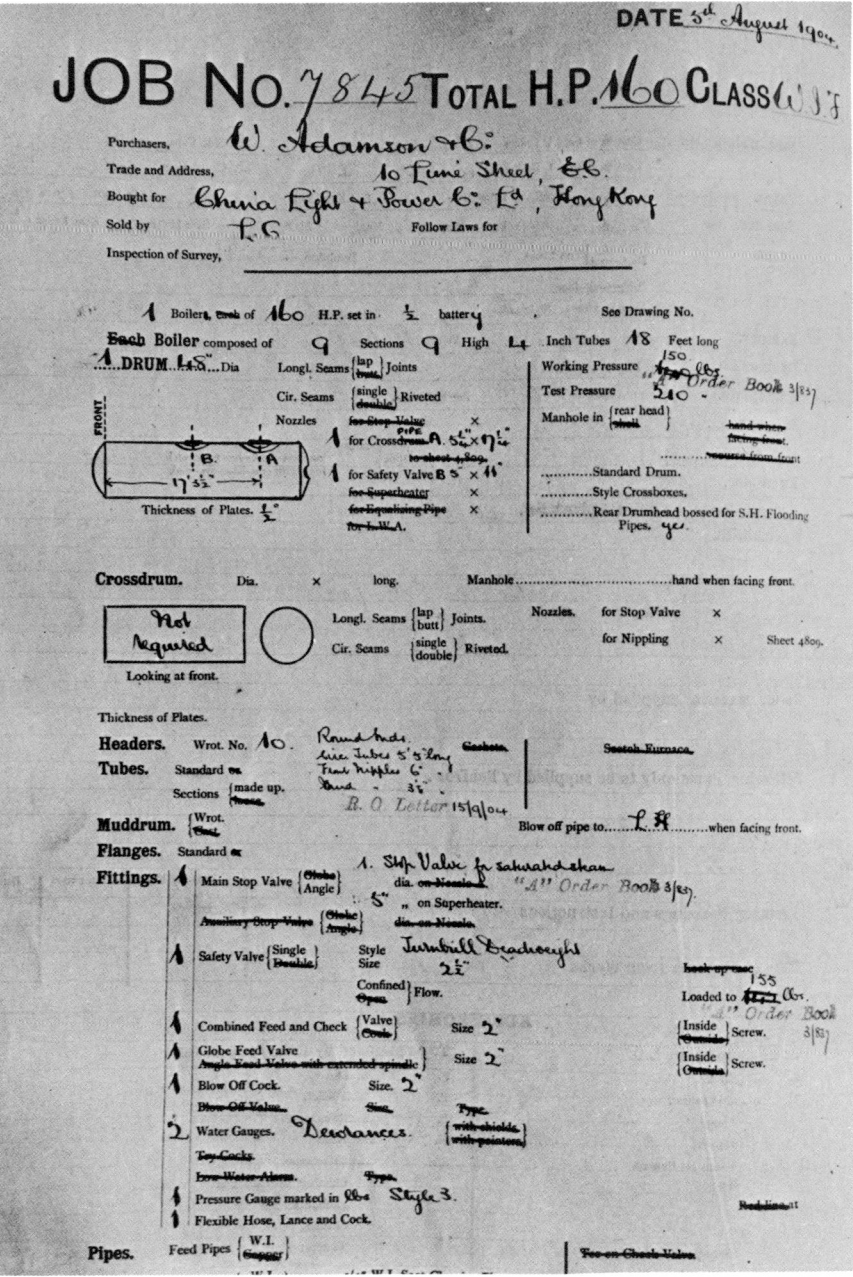

steeply and had to be met rapidly. How to operate machines efficiently, which were virtually idling during the daylight when they could in fact have been working at full output all the time, was a commercial as well as a technical problem. But, had this been the only difficulty, the station might well have gone on from success to success. Alas there was a major impediment to expansion in the form of Joseph Chamberlain's ill-conceived Electric Lighting Act. Under the terms of this Act, Parliamentary permission was needed to lay underground cables, and it was forbidden to string them in the open air. The general fears expressed in the clauses of the Act were of fire (after all, gas went underground and seemed likely to be in danger of being ignited by the electric cables). The life and maximum expansion of the Holborn station depended largely on its situation. For within and under the viaduct itself there was a maze of tunnels and conduits through which the wiring for distribution could be fixed, without any exposure to the open air, and without seeking government permission to put it underground. But where the fortunate conduits ended, so too did the potential for any expansion in distribution to supply customers further away.

Nonetheless, in those first heady days of public lighting, enthusiasm ran high and very large sums of money were invested in generating stations similar in design and scope to the Holborn one. After four years had elapsed it seems that Edison in the United States felt he had done enough by way of advertisement for his planned New York station and since the enterprise in London was not then capable of further expansion, it might as well be closed down. So once more the Holborn Viaduct reverted to gas for its nightly illumination.

The economic possibilities of electricity generation and distribution had, however, been amply demonstrated. And the lessons learned were taken up with surprising rapidity all over Europe and in places as far away as South America, India, and of course in the Treaty Ports of China where Western influence was strong. The order books of those times still preserved in the archives of the principal boiler-makers, Babcock & Wilcox, an Anglo-American company, are replete with specifications of hardware very like that supplied for the Holborn Viaduct station, destined for shipment to the most exotic addresses all over the world.

By the 1880s, the first entries for Canton and Hong Kong appear.

Left: The specification for Job No. 7845, dated 5th August 1904, for a boiler supplied by Babcock & Wilcox in London (See page 11)

In 1883, the Lee Yuen Sugar Refining Co., Hong Kong, got its boiler on 19 October, while a certain Mr. Kretchmar of Canton took delivery of his boiler – for what purpose he required it is not known – a little later. The order specification was signed by the then managing director of the boiler-maker's London office, and he appended in his own hand at the bottom of the sheet of details: 'This job must be carefully got up – nothing short-shipped, & no mistake made. It is

important.' Just how important it was to make sure everything needed to set up the equipment in distant parts was sent together was to be learned the hard way by China Light at a later date.

At some point in the 1880s, Fung Wa-chuen, the compradore of Russell & Company in Hong Kong, headed by Robert Gordon Shewan who was later to reorganize it under the name Shewan & Company, started a small power station in Canton. There is no extant record of the order for its boiler but it can hardly be doubted that Babcock & Wilcox supplied it. In fact a fairly accurate surmise about what type of boiler it was can be made from the drawings and specifications of boilers supplied elsewhere at about the same time. The technical drawings and all details still exist, and a press report of 26 November 1898 confirms the presence of Babcock & Wilcox boilers at the Canton station by that date.

At this point, or just a little after, still in 1898, and only sixteen years since the opening of the first commercial power station in London at Holborn Viaduct, the ancient city of Canton, capital of Guangdong (Kwangtung) Province in southern China, began to receive its first hesitant supply of electric light. The fact is in a way one measure of the confident spirit of those times, and of the confidence in the future as it seemed ensured by the power of new technology.

A. Furnace
B. Ash pit
C. Path of hot gases from burning coal
D. Damper to control draught from chimney
E. Gas exit to chimney
F. Downtake headers
G. Side cleaning doors for soot removal
H. Downtakes
I. Wrought crossbox
J. Main steam stop valve

K. Saturated steam inlet to superheater
L. Dead-weight safety valve
M. Hot gas baffles
N. Single loop superheater
O. Steam space in steam and water drum
P. Water level in drum
Q. Uptake headers
R. Steel suspension
S. Feed water inlet

The pulley wheels over each end of the drum are for a wire from the front of the boiler by means of which the fireman can control the damper (D) to give a suction of the desired amount in the furnace (A)

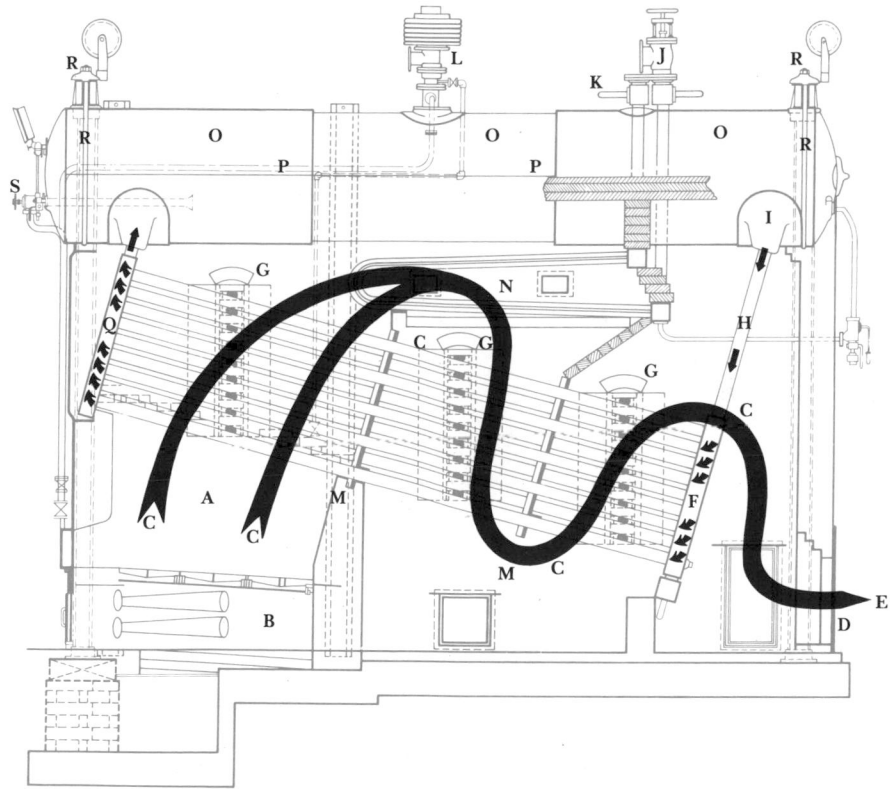

Left: Part of a note written by the general manager of Babcock & Wilcox on the specification for a boiler to be sent to the Far East in 1890. Above: A simplified drawing of the boiler specified in Job No. 7845 (page 8). The flow of heat from the coal-fired grate is indicated, together with the direction of the water circulation

HONG KONG, CANTON, AND THE FOUNDING OF THE COMPANY

ON 25 January 1841, the British flag was hoisted on Hong Kong Island at the orders of Captain Elliot, quite without authority from his home government. He did so under the terms of a settlement reached with the Chinese authorities which was aimed at putting an end to armed conflict between the two peoples over the question of trading rights at the port of Canton. The fact that this settlement was repudiated by the Peking government when they heard of it, and that it led to the First Opium War between the two sides, and that the signatories were both swiftly dismissed from office by their respective governments, did not prevent the enterprising British from establishing a colony. It was not until that war was won and the Treaty of Nanking signed in August 1842, and its ratification achieved in June 1843, that the already burgeoning settlement of Hong Kong became officially a British possession. The tip of the Kowloon Peninsula was not ceded until the end of the Second Opium War and the signing of one more treaty, the Convention of Peking, in 1860.

Kowloon was ceded 'with a view to maintaining law and order in and about the harbour of Hong Kong.' This was an unfortunate phrase since the military authorities on the island interpreted it to mean that Kowloon was their preserve, whereas the civil government wished to develop the small triangle of territory for residence and recreation, together with commercial and port facilities on the southwest shore where there was deep water. This sometimes acrimonious state of affairs was finally settled in 1864 when a compromise was reached, some reclamation having been carried out, and a sea wall started. Plots were then marked out and sold to private interests.

Kowloon developed around several centres, the first at Yaumatei, and then others at Tsim Sha Tsui, Mong Kok, Hung Hom, and up to what became known as Boundary Street. Main roads, hardly those wide and thunderous thoroughfares that we know today, were formed – the ancestors of Salisbury Road, and of Nathan Road which was then called Robinson Road after the governor of that name.

In 1898, the land backing Kowloon as far as a natural geographical

Left: The title page of Steam, *August 1900, showing the world revolving, propelled by means of steam jets*

An old photograph of Kowloon seen from the jetty at about the turn of the century

line was leased from China for ninety-nine years, adding 355 square miles to the British colony under the name of the New Territories. The scattered villages of the area contained a highly conservative and tradition-bound population among whom there arose great indignation and anger at the transfer of their homeland from Chinese to British rule without the slightest consultation.

In a volume about China published in London in 1903, the process is described as being 'very strongly resented' by the inhabitants. 'Owing to their poverty and inaccessibility, they were probably seldom plagued with visits from Chinese officials: and they objected to their sudden transfer to the care of the more energetic "foreign devils." So when the Governor ... arranged a dramatic scene to take place at the hoisting of the British flag on the frontier, and invitations were ... issued to officials and their wives and the society in general of the island to be present at this historic occasion, the evil-minded inhabitants prepared to surprise them. The police and the guard of honour,' who went out the previous day found 'to their consternation ... that the new subjects of the British Empire had dug a trench on the side of a hill ... not 800 yards from the spot on which the flagstaff was to be erected, and were ... armed with jingals, matchlocks,

Brown Besses, and old rifles – antique weapons ... but certainly good enough to kill all the ladies and officials to be present. ...'

Companies of soldiery were sent post-haste and 'chased their fellow-subjects over the hills ... and captured enough ancient weapons to stock an armoury. ... Little resistance was made, but the picnic arrangements for the dramatic hoisting of the flag did not come off.'

This somewhat romanticized account of the hoisting of the British flag appears to be composed of a conglomeration of stories. The flag was in fact hoisted at Taipo on 16 April 1899. The ceremony was repeated in several other places in the New Territories later. But in fact, such was the strength of Chinese dislike of the change of masters from the known Manchu to the unknown British, that it was not until the 'battle of Taipo' had been won by British armed forces that the Chinese were more or less convinced of the unassailable fact of British rule. And skirmishes occurred in many places after that.

Symptomatic of the feeling at the time of the hoisting of the flag was the fact that the governor did not attend, but ordered the ceremony to be conducted by James Stewart Lockhart with a strong military party, the British presence to be underscored by the 'stirring salute' that resounded over the site from the guns of two fully-dressed naval ships.

It was only with difficulty, six years and many a skirmish after the initial hoisting of the flag, that a road was pushed through in 1904 to Taipo, which became the administrative centre of the region.

It was this – at first sight – distinctly unpromising region of Kowloon and in due course the New Territories that a bold man, Robert Gordon Shewan, decided to supply with electric light. Enterprise had indeed characterised the businessmen of Hong Kong from its very inception, but it is tempting, considering the actual circumstances of 1900 in Kowloon and the New Territories, to credit Shewan with clairvoyant powers when he registered The China Light & Power Syndicate Ltd. on April 23rd of that year.

R.G. Shewan was as farsighted and determined a man as any in Hong Kong's history with, at that time, perhaps only one equal in these qualities – Paul Catchick Chater, who was to be drawn into the enterprise. Shewan is remembered as a good speaker, and a man inclined to become deeply and emotionally involved in whatever he did. His activities included chairmanship of the Green Island Cement Company, and directorships of the Hongkong & Shanghai Banking Corporation and the South China Morning Post. He also served for a

Robert G. Shewan. This photograph was taken about 1908 and seems to be the sole extant likeness

time on the Legislative Council as the elected representative of the Hong Kong Chamber of Commerce. But his principal business was as a partner in the firm of Shewan, Tomes & Company.

This company was one of the oldest in Hong Kong and in South China. Its predecessor, Samuel Russell & Company, started in Canton in 1818, an American firm originating in Boston and merging in 1824 with another American firm, Perkins & Company, which had a slightly older history, having been founded in 1803 by Col. T.K. Perkins, a Boston man. The product of this merger, Russell & Company, operated from Canton, at that time the sole Chinese port open to foreign trade. Its other partners included merchants from New York, Connecticut, and Massachusetts, and the business rapidly expanded, so that Russell & Company was soon the most successful and powerful house in the region, having business connections in London with Baring Brothers, and in France with Rothschilds. The

Russell & Company 'factory' (as offices and godowns were called in those days) at Canton stood in the midst of that famous row of foreign 'hongs' – companies and their establishments – at a time in the 1830s when Western trade there was at its peak. After the cession of Hong Kong and its initial development, the company set up a branch in the Colony on Queen's Road with, as resident partners, Warren Delano and George Tyson. The physical link between Canton and Hong Kong was an excellent steamer service operating frequently.

Mr. Shewan, who joined Russell & Company in 1881 when he was twenty-one years old, had been engaged by the London agents Baring Brothers. He was the son of the captain of the *Lammermuir*, a fast tea clipper that in a race to England with a cargo of tea once beat the crack Jardine vessel *Cairngorm*. Shewan could not have guessed when he arrived in Hong Kong on St. Valentine's Day 1881 that he was to spend fifty-two years as a merchant in the city.

In charge of Russell & Company's offices when Shewan came, were William Howell Forbes, and Charles Alexander Tomes, another Bostonian. Ten years after Shewan's arrival the business was re-organized and taken over by him as Shewan & Company, and in 1895 when Tomes joined as partner the name was changed to Shewan, Tomes & Company.

It was this company which registered the China Light & Power Syndicate in 1900 with a capital of $200,000 divided into two hundred shares of $1,000 each. Its sole object was to provide electricity to Kowloon but, not long after, an opportunity presented itself which was related. We do not know whether the first idea of starting an electric power company in Kowloon was in some way the result in Shewan's mind of his knowledge that the compradore of Shewan Tomes – Fung Wa-chuen – was already engaged in producing electricity in Canton. It may have been. The Canton Electric & Fire Extinguishing Company, founded by Fung Wa-chuen and a few Chinese friends in 1898, gained the concession from the Viceroy of Guangdong Province for lighting Canton and its surrounding area. The company later approached Shewan Tomes for help in financial difficulties, with the result that the China Light & Power Syndicate took over the compradore's company. Negotiations produced an agreement, dated 27 June 1900, under which the Syndicate paid $80,000 in cash and $20,000 in twenty of its own shares.

Thus China Light acquired the Canton power station. In the same year the Company also acquired the land on which Kowloon's first power station was to be built a little later.

Little or nothing has to date been brought together in any published source about the life of Mr. Shewan's compradore. But since, indirectly, it was he and his ill-run electricity company at Canton which dominated both the energies and the financial aspects of the Company between the years 1900 and 1909, it may be worth constructing at least an outline biography of a Chinese who was certainly one of the outstanding men of his race in Hong Kong at that time.

Fung Wa-chuen in common with many Chinese used a number of variant names in the course of his life. Fung Wah-chün, Fung Shui-cheung, and Fung Shui are three commonly encountered in various records, the last doubtless because in other characters it resembles the sound of *feng sui* – meaning the auspices or the favourable influences affecting any particular locality – which in Cantonese would be pronounced *fung shui*.

We find him first in early 1874 as the prize-winner for the best spoken English at Queen's College, in Hong Kong. On 14 April of the same year he was appointed a pupil teacher at the college, under the name Fung Shui. Then, on 13 April the following year, he became assistant teacher at the same college. Between the years 1876 and 1878 he was assistant master, and in 1879 became acting first assistant, in which post he remained for the following year. The listing of 1881 does not show his name, so he appears to have left this job by then. The *Yellow Dragon*, Vol. 3, No. V, of November 1903 – the magazine of Queen's College – in listing the careers of former masters affirms he was a Chinese Assistant in 1875 and gives his alias as Ma Chün, adding that he was (then or later?) compradore of Shewan, Tomes & Co.

The Jury Lists from 1882 to 1888 mention him as Fung Shui, assistant to Yan Wo Opium Firm, Cleverly Street; and in the 1883 Opium Commission, Fung Wa Chuen is described as 'compradore, National Bank.' The affairs of the various opium firms in 1880 came to a head with cut-throat rivalry between groups formed in Macau and in Hong Kong. But the detailed complications of the whole matter need not concern us here. Fung obviously had an interest in the Yan Wo company and its activities, and also appears to have assisted in the flotation of the National Bank of China, and was also involved in the Wai Sing lottery at Canton which was the means of placing bets on the candidates for the Imperial Examinations – rather as though they were thoroughbreds in the race of the year.

The National Bank of China was organized in 1891, its principal sponsors being Russell & Co. which itself failed in the same year. Another sponsor was a Chinese who was a principal with the Yan Wo Company, of which Fung was a member too. A Bank announcement of 20 January 1892 averred that the Bank would proceed according to the terms of the original prospectus 'except it is severed from all connection with the late firm of Russell & Co., under which firm it was started, and that the 15 per cent of the net profits ... to be paid to that firm ceases, of course.'

Now, the successors to Russell & Co. were Shewan, Tomes & Co., of which Fung became compradore, as we have already discovered. He was a director of the Tung Wah Hospital in 1892 and in 1901, listed as Fung Wah Chun, alias Shui Cheung; and he was first of all director, and then chairman of Po Leung Kuk in 1894 and 1899 respectively.

St. Stephen's College at Stanley, publishing the Jubilee Issue of its magazine *The Chimes* in its fiftieth year (1952), names Fung as one of the leaders in founding the school who signed a petition to the governor on 2 March 1901 to establish a school where English as well as Chinese would be taught to the children of Chinese. The fees were to be sufficient to support the school without charge to the Colony. And indeed the College opened on 23 February 1903 with seven pupils, one of whom was Fung Man-siu (probably a son of Fung Wa-chuen).

So the worthy compradore had had a very varied career in Hong Kong. He seems to have achieved many exalted offices, from chairman of the Chinese Chamber of Commerce in 1900 to Deputy of Foreign Affairs to the Viceroy of Canton in 1909 – just before the sale of the Canton station by China Light to its new Chinese owners was completed in July of the same year. In the same month of that year, the *Hongkong Telegraph* reported that 'Mr. Fung Wa Chuen of Hong Kong has been largely instrumental in bringing to a head the successful negotiations. He has been working continuously for the past three months.' And since on 9 July the same newspaper reported the new general manager at Canton was Pun Pui Yu, that chapter of Fung's life then seems to have closed. But there was still a compradore of Shewan Tomes in 1930, on the fiftieth anniversary of the company, by the name of Fung. We last hear of Fung Wa-chuen as he gave his power of attorney on 27 July 1914 to Fung Shiu-wa, who was probably one of his sons. Fung was then in Tientsin and his son in

Hong Kong. Fung the elder provides in his life an early example of what was to become a fairly classical pattern for Chinese tycoon-philanthropists, of whom the Colony has been fortunate in breeding very many since then.

In the year 1901, at a meeting held on 9 January, the Consulting Committee which had been set up to guide the Syndicate decided that the existing available capital of the Company was insufficient, and that a company should be formed to which the business could be handed over. This decision resulted in the incorporation of the China Light & Power Company Ltd. on 25 January 1901. On the following day this new company signed an agreement with the Syndicate acquiring all its assets, promising to pay expenses incurred on voluntary liquidation, and to allot the Syndicate's members 10,000 fully paid $20 shares in the Company.

At this point Mr. Shewan formed another Consulting Committee whose function was to direct Company affairs, a body that continued to operate until 1927 when it was replaced by a Board of Directors. Paul Catchick Chater, Hong Kong's second great business leader of the times, was asked by Shewan to join the committee, and he remained a member until his death in 1926. Among other members was Henry Percy White, a prominent businessman who had come to Hong Kong and joined the shipping firm of Douglas Lapraik Ltd., becoming its manager in Hong Kong. White later became a director of the Company and died in 1929.

Paul (later Sir Paul) Chater had arrived in Hong Kong in 1864 at the age of eighteen, employed as an assistant in the Bank of Hindoostan, China and Japan, a post from which he resigned two years later. He was born in Calcutta of Armenian Christian parents, his mother being the granddaughter of the famous Armenian merchant Agak Catchick Arnkiel who was honoured by George III in 1790. By reason of ancestry, and on account of his immediate family, Chater grew and matured in surroundings which were intimately connected with the world of oriental trading.

As an exchange and bullion broker, Paul Chater became an influential member of the business community, and was to set his indelible mark on Hong Kong as the originator of some of the most ambitious reclamation schemes on the island's shores, notably the Praya Reclamation extending from Pedder Street west to Western Market, and later the much more ambitious reclamation which formed vast stretches of new land seaward of Des Voeux Road and to

20

Paul (later Sir Paul) Catchick Chater in about 1908

the east. With James J. Keswick, Chater started The Hongkong Land Company in 1889. And this company built many of the principal new edifices of the now fast maturing city of Victoria – Prince's Building, Alexandra House and Queen's Building where The Mandarin Hotel now stands.

Chater had been in the godown business on the Hong Kong side before he succeeded in getting authority for the great reclamation eastward, and so it was natural for him to be interested in wharf and godown facilities on the other side of the harbour as well. From studies he had instigated, he realised that the most feasible site for berthing ocean-going vessels would be at Kowloon, and he therefore set up the Hongkong & Kowloon Wharf & Godown Company in 1884. Within two years of its start the company was handling 70,000 tons of cargo per annum.

These were not the only matters which occupied the interest of Paul Chater. He it was who had advocated the acquisition of the New

21

Territories area for many a year before it came about. It was therefore natural on this account too that he would become a member of the Consulting Committee of China Light. During a long and distinguished career he was a member of the Legislative and Executive Councils and was knighted in 1902. A director of many companies, his

The ornate façade of Marble Hall at the head of Glenealy, home of Sir Paul Chater. The site is now occupied by an apartment block named Chater Hall

interests lay also in horticulture and in art. His collection of paintings and other antiques was housed in an imposing residence called Marble Hall that he built at the head of Glenealy on the island. It seems not to be known whether, in the matter of the choice of a name for his residence, Chater was influenced by the resounding lines from the second act of that famous operetta *The Bohemian Girl*:

> *I dreamt I dwelt in marble halls,*
> *With vassals and serfs at my side....*

but it is possible, considering the immense popularity of the songs from what is now a somewhat risible piece (whose companion from the same time and pen was another, called *Alice, Where Art Thou?*). Chater belonged very much to the slightly raffish world of his early years as did many another young man who would carve out for himself a powerful career in business – West or East.

One further aspect of his business activities that was central to his membership of the Consulting Committee was the fact that he was a director of the Hongkong Electric Company which had been formed in 1889 and had been producing electricity for Hong Kong Island since 1890. In order to ensure an independent electric company for Kowloon and the New Territories, his support was vital. The best way to neutralise a rival is to ask him to join.

It so happened that Paul Chater was also a director of the Wharf & Godown Company, and that Robert Shewan was chairman of the Green Island Cement Company – both companies neighbours to left and right of the new electric company at its first site, in Kowloon.

It is no exaggeration to say that without the foresight of Robert G. Shewan in his vision of Kowloon as a potential city, and his provision of its light and power, and without the energetic and equally far-sighted mind of Paul Chater both in Hong Kong Island and in Kowloon, Hong Kong as we know it today would probably have a quite different look, and would not have developed so astonishingly in the fields of shipping and industry as it did during their lifetime and afterward.

Fortunately, when both were dead, others of perhaps equal talent and determination, and equal business foresight and competence, were ready to continue the work that had already shown how well founded it had been by these pioneers.

PROGRESS IN CANTON, FIRST LIGHT IN KOWLOON

I N the last decade of the nineteenth century, Canton was still a traditional walled Chinese city. Its circumference was about six miles and its massive gates were closed at night. One of China's major trading cities, it lay at the apex of the sprawling Pearl River delta whose sinuous channels were then, and still are, used by a large variety of craft, but whose main channel accommodated the passage of larger vessels to and from Hong Kong about ninety miles distant – and indeed from other parts of the Asian world, as had been the case for many many centuries before the arrival of the Portuguese in South China in the latter part of the fifteenth century.

When China Light acquired the Canton Electric & Fire Extinguishing Company in June 1900, the whole aspect of Canton was radically different from that of Hong Kong. The Canton streets were seldom more than eight feet wide, whereas in Hong Kong in the city centre and also in the Western residential areas broad avenues were the rule, even if in the Chinese quarter the alleys were dark, dirty, and narrow. At Canton the lanes were 'so constructed as to get the breeze, at the same time shutting out the direct rays of the sun. In the hottest season there is always a cool air after midday in the narrow streets....' A guidebook of 1903 lists the architectural attractions of the city, and continues: 'among the most interesting features ... before all, the Great Curio Street, Tai-sing-kai. The immediate approach is somewhat forbidding, but directly one gets into a real native business quarter the fascination becomes intense. Such gorgeous decorations in wonderfully carved and richly gilded wood-work, such antique designs in the bold hieroglyphic characters of the language....' And the writer goes on to enthuse at the porcelains, silks, ivories, 'fantastic Knick-knacks (*sic*)'. '... this is Canton – a huge bazaar from one end to the other, with throngs of contented-looking people always on the move from morning to night.'

'The European quarter, Shameen (Sand-bank), is located on the

Left: Physic Street in Canton at about the end of the nineteenth century was typical of many another in the city. The signs that are legible advertise medicine shops, mattress makers, money changers, among others

Seen from the Pearl River, the Canton power station sedate in its elegant building. Only the smoking chimney gave it away for what it was

river to the south of the Western suburb, an ideal settlement though somewhat confined. There are many handsome buildings ... and a beautiful avenue of lofty banyan trees extends for a thousand yards through the centre.'

Some of those trees and some of the buildings are still in existence today, and although the former gardens have largely been turned into fields for Chinese youngsters to play games, the place still has a solid and distinctly non-Chinese look about it.

Down-river from the shady walks of Shameen, the original building that housed the first power station in Canton also still stands. By now, of course, it is unremarkable in appearance, being surrounded by later buildings also not in the Chinese style: whereas, when it was first erected, it ranked with those foreign structures long a bone of political and fiscal contention not far away on the ghetto strip of Shameen.

In its early days during the last years of the nineteenth century, it was doubtless a source of wonder what strange matters might be going forward inside its walls. And when complete, there was further wonder at the magical substance, invisible but apparently coursing powerfully along the wires emerging from the internally

26

humming structure – a substance incorporeal but capable of passing through the foreign metal strings to terminate in equally foreign objects of spherical shape made of glass, which lighted up at night with a constant and windproof flame.

China Light not only took over this house of wonder, but the obligation inherited from the predecessor company to operate a pump to supply the mains with water for fire extinguishing in various parts of metropolitan Canton – and fires in this still fairly medieval city were of frequent occurrence.

In fact the power station at Canton taken over by the Company was not the first venture into electricity production in that city. On 27 January 1890, the *Hong Kong Daily Press* reported that a Chinese merchant from San Francisco had applied for permission to set up an electric light company at Canton and Fatshan. Permission was granted. Three days later the same source noted that the San Francisco Company for Electricity in China had elected Wong Chee-san as its president. The stock was $200,000.

On 10 February of the same year the *Hong Kong Telegraph* reported: 'Canton to have electric lights. ... A merchant from San Francisco has floated a company and has brought all the necessary plant to Canton. ...' The project had the support of the Viceroy. But this seems to have been another company as its merchant head was not Wong Chee-san but Huang P'ing-chang.

By 8 April of that year, the *Hong Kong Telegraph* announced that an American Syndicate to produce electric light in Canton – we do not know which – had sent out a large '200 horse power boiler (*sic*)'. But it was then discovered the boiler was far too big to pass through the narrow Canton streets without the demolition of several *li* of houses in its path. Just where it was to be sited is not known, but it would appear odd that the location should have entailed the boiler's passing through the streets at all, since what a boiler needs is water (in this case from the river) and fuel (which would be most easily brought by river also).

However, it was then decided to wait until a new boiler specially adapted to pass through the city streets could be constructed in Hong Kong.

Just what became of these two ventures, both apparently unconnected with the company formed in 1898 by Fung Wa-chuen, would require more research, and might even then not come to light. But the correctly sited power station taken over by the Company would appear to be the first venture that succeeded in any measure at all in producing electricity in the venerable city of Canton.

Back in 1898, the opening of the 'Canton Electric Light Works,' as the *Hong Kong Weekly Press* termed it in an inaccurate report published on 26 November, was described thus: 'Passengers to Canton may see, about a mile below the Dutch Folly Fort, a building in foreign style with a smoke stack, now in the course of erection and approaching completion.' The shareholders were stated to be 'mostly Canton officials and Hong Kong merchants. The current is to be generated by three large dynamos and engines supplied by Messrs. Johnson & Phillips of London, the makers of the Hongkong Electric Company's machinery, the engines being supplied with steam by one multi-tubular boiler and three large Babcock & Wilcox boilers. The wires are to be carried through the city on brackets attached to the walls, and one wire is to be carried on to Shameen.... The light is to be used for street illumination of the city, and applications for private installations have been so numerous that already the duplication of the plant is under consideration. The whole of the work is being carried out from the designs and under the supervision of Mr. W. Danby, Mr. W.H. Wickham being the consulting engineer. It is expected that the concern will be in operation in about four month's time.'

Danby was partner in the old-established Hong Kong firm of architects, Leigh & Orange, at that time named Danby & Leigh and, after 1890, called Danby, Leigh & Orange. Mr. Wickham was the manager of the Hongkong Electric Company which had been in operation on the island of Hong Kong since 1890. Wickham had been sent out initially by his company, Johnson & Phillips of Charlton in Kent, with their equipment for that station.

There is some confusion of statements about the equipment that was first installed in the new Canton station. According to Lawrence Kadoorie it was thought that two (not three as stated in the newspaper report) sets of generating equipment were installed before the Company took over, each of 125 kW capacity, the first in 1898 (which must have been during the course of construction of the building), and the other when it was completed in 1899. But a mention of 'two engines' in the second annual general meeting of China Light on 30

May 1903, confirms the fact that only one was present at the take-over and that a second engine was installed by China Light before 1903. In 1902, the first Annual General Meeting was told by Mr. Shewan: 'The old company had only one generating set, and in the event of this breaking down, the customers had simply to go without light until it was repaired.' He also mentioned: 'Our next care was to add another engine and generator to be in reserve in case of accident, and also another new boiler.' The steam was provided by coal-fired boilers, and the problems encountered in working them efficiently because of their 'extravagant coal consumption' were continual and worrying.

The transfer of the Chinese company at Canton to China Light did not go smoothly. At the first statutory meeting of China Light on 13 April 1901, at which Mr. Shewan took the chair, and at which Fung Wa-chuen, the instigator of the Canton company, was present among other directors of the new China Light, optimism reigned. 'Electric light companies require as a rule rather a long time to grow to fruition, so much time being necessarily consumed in making the installation, but as regards Canton, we are fortunate in that respect, as we took over a going concern there. It is true that it was not going very well then, but I am pleased to say that things are different now.'

Mr. Shewan, doubtless in consideration of the feelings of Fung Wa-chuen, skated lightly over the fact that the former owners had made practically no provision for spare parts or the replacement of any other item that might be required. 'These,' he said reassuringly, 'have now arrived and we shall be kept busy for some time to come in fitting up further installations for the new orders we have on hand.' These orders, presumably, were for the new generators and other accessories.

The chairman was optimistic about Chinese acceptance of electricity. 'In consequence of the fear of fire which very naturally haunts the minds of the shopkeepers, etc., in that crowded town, the electric light is growing in popularity every day. To such people as the proprietors of theatres, restaurants, flower-boats, etc., and to all those in trades which require late hours, the advantage of our light over kerosene is obvious.' Flower-boats were floating brothels, a very ancient institution in China, and it was perhaps natural that they were to be found among the first enterprising customers whose 'late hours' of business required the service of the convenient new light.

But, Mr. Shewan complained, 'Chinese-like' the customers 'waste time in the endeavour to drive a bargain and beat down the prices.'

One of the Canton 'flower boats'. These and their land-based equivalents were among the Company's first customers in the city

In those far-off days of confident empire-builders and self-assured Western entrepreneurs, such Chinese tactics were regarded as reprehensible, and obstructive of their wishes, although the same behaviour was thought a natural part of the Western businessman's means of maximizing his profits.

The following year, 1902, the first annual general meeting of China Light was held on 24 May. This year the picture of the Canton affair was not so enthusiastic. Over a year had elapsed since the 1901 meeting, a year of struggle and uphill work in Canton. Reporting a loss of over $7,000, Mr. Shewan remarked: 'Those who are familiar with the management of industrial concerns like this can alone form some idea of the state of utter neglect and confusion that we found the place in when we took over, and much time and money had to be spent before we could get things into anything like working order.' He apparently felt at this meeting, despite the presence of Fung Wa-chuen, that he could now speak out on the chaos the Company found on take-over, and the Chinese director is not recorded as having said anything in reply.

The original single generating set frequently broke down. 'We are very cramped at the Factory' (as he called the generating station – a hangover from the old usage when offices, godowns, and other premises of companies in the east were so called) 'but . . . we have kept room for one more engine and the generator. . . .'

'But, in spite of all, business was steadily pushed in the direction of new customers and, to give you some idea of our progress, I may tell you that as against 225 Chinese and 460 foreign lamps on the 28th February last year we had 1,240 Chinese and 1,150 foreign lamps on the 28th February this year.' Chinese acceptance of electricity for lighting was gaining ground. The measuring of the output of electricity by the number of lamps it lit may strike a somewhat quaint note nowadays, but this remained for long the basis of calculation of how much electricity was being supplied. Those were the days of the carbon filament lamp which used rather a lot of electricity and for the most part appeared to produce almost as much heat as light.

The rather slight demand for light in daylight hours, the inadequate nature of the coal storage, and the consequent thefts of coal from the Company's stocks, a single boiler that could not be adequately cleaned since to do so would take it out of service for too long, were the burden of the chairman's tale of woe. He gave much credit to Mr. Belden – about whom we know almost nothing but the name – who was the intrepid manager of the Canton station. The adjective is hardly too striking for what this persevering and patient man must have gone through there, with a largely untrained staff whose comprehension of the mechanical and electrical problems involved in the day-to-day running of the undertaking must have been small indeed, all of whom he must have had to train from scratch.

Mr. Shewan is almost the only person involved who is on record as commending Belden 'for the patience and determination with which he faced these obstacles and set himself to teach and train the raw native workmen.'

At the meeting, however, the picture painted by the chairman was nevertheless summed up by him in the thought that 'we have seen the worst of our troubles there.' Alas, that proved not to be so. And at the next year's (the second) annual meeting, he admitted he had been mistaken, and declared a loss of $17,000. He attributed this almost entirely to the 'faulty engines with which we are working there.' Both the original one installed by the Chinese company and the one added by China Light proved unsuitable. And he commented once more on

Generating plant in the Company's Canton station in 1908. The 125 kW Belliss & Morecombe engine is identifiable by its number – 1835

'their extravagant coal consumption,' which made it 'impossible for us to work at a profit.' He proposed therefore to replace them by 'a new set of the most modern and most economical design.' And for about $80,000 he estimated that three engines 'two of which would give us one hundred per cent better results than the present two,' should be installed, 'while we should have an extra one in reserve in case of accident.' This is one of the first instances of a policy whereby China Light consistently attempted to anticipate future demand and to make provision to meet it by taking prudent steps in advance.

The management and the directors of the Company were slowly learning the complicated business – as full of problems then as it still is in some respects today – of manufacturing and commercially marketing electricity in the most efficient manner. The general picture that may be gathered from reports of those early meetings of the young Company is one of intelligent direction and also of keen application to the problems at hand, albeit under considerable and diverse stresses and, sometimes, with a somewhat naïve optimism about the chances of the equipment then available and in use in the climatic and labour conditions of South China.

Problems with boilers, coal thefts and faulty engines at Canton were hardly the only ones. Electricity was conveyed to the customers by means of wires strung either on brackets attached to the buildings on the way, or attached to Chinese fir poles. And this, involving bare wires running through certain parts of the city, proved to have dire inherent problems. First was the likelihood of sabotage by the populace for this or that reason; second was the ease with which the Chinese, ever quick in the uptake, could syphon off the current by means of bamboo poles through which a wire was run and hooked at the far end over the Company's supply wires; and third, the incidence of high wind and typhoons in the area in the summer season which meant that this portion at least of the Company's property was subject to considerable damage or outright loss at frequent intervals. Great expense had to be incurred if the damage were to be repaired quickly, and the peculiar circumstances required heavy stocks of spares to be stored. The penalty was loss of revenue from the customers who had lost their supply. One final torment was the incidence of fire, and even of great conflagrations such as that of 1904 in which the Company's distribution system was very badly damaged and revenue was 'severely curtailed for some months.'

The rather primitive means by which the current was brought to the customers in those days strikes a comic note now, but anyone who remembers the Orient in the days just after the Second World War will easily recall in countries such as Korea, and elsewhere – not to say in Hong Kong itself – the forest of suspended hooked bamboo poles in every district where the populace was crammed into makeshift accommodation, and by means of which it obtained electric supply for lighting and even for fans and old battered refrigerators. Likewise, in Canton at the turn of the century, the overload on the Company's wires was often such that they became almost red hot, and when it rained gave off an appealingly Chinese mist – but at grave expense to the generating equipment and the Company's profits.

The theme of the Canton enterprise took up much of the Company's time and energies, and this is reflected in the volume of space devoted to it in the minutes of the various meetings. But at those same meetings the progress of the Company's projects in Hong Kong can also be followed – a story that is in several ways, not least financially, much entangled and intertwined with the tale of Canton. It was a tale of two cities, with Hong Kong much the lesser metropolis.

At the Company's statutory meeting on 13 April 1901, Mr. Shewan, having dealt with progress at Canton in quite optimistic terms, turned to affairs in Hong Kong. 'At Kowloon, or rather at Hung Hom, we are not in such a good position, as our station is only in the course of erection there, and at the rate of progress common to most builders and contractors just now, it is impossible to say when the period of production over there will be reached.' He hoped, however, that another six to eight months would see the Company in a position to supply electric light, 'and when that time arrives we have every reason to believe that we shall find a good demand for the light.'

Just over a year later, in May 1902, at the first annual meeting of the Company, Mr. Shewan dealt at length with the situation in Canton, and then turned nearer home.

'As for Kowloon,' he said, 'we have been in the hands of the contractor, and work has dragged along and not been done as only the Chinese contractor knows how not to do it. Every kind of threat and entreaty has been used to urge on the work, but to little purpose, and it is still a case of hope deferred.... However ... we have some hopes that in three months' time we shall have all the machinery installed and the works running.'

He described the 'valuable piece of ground of about 60,000 sq. ft. on the Des Voeux Road' – the name was later changed to Chatham Road – adding that although the plant was on a modest scale at present 'provision has been made for any future additions and extensions.' He felt, although no contracts had yet been entered into, that the government, the Dock Company, and 'other factories and private consumers' would soon force the Company into thinking about 'extending the works.'

The statement of accounts laid before the shareholders at that 1902 meeting showed a balance of nearly $21,000 to be carried over to the debit of the next year's account. But 'since no revenue whatever has been derived from the works at Kowloon' and although at Canton 'the record has been one of steady progress,' the accounts should be viewed as reflecting more the state of 'preliminary expenses than as an actual loss on working.'

Accounts for the year ending 28th February 1902.

PROFIT AND LOSS ACCOUNT.

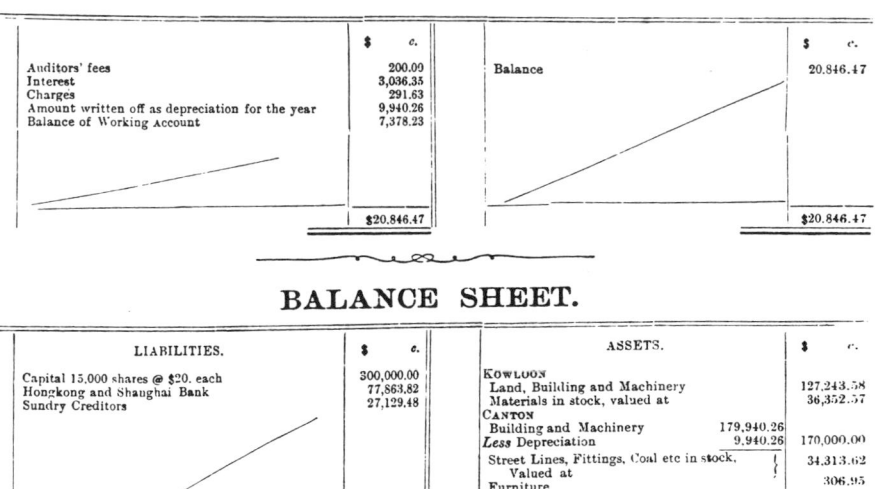

	$	c.		$	c.
Auditors' fees	200.00		Balance	20,846.47	
Interest	3,036.35				
Charges	291.63				
Amount written off as depreciation for the year	9,940.26				
Balance of Working Account	7,378.23				
	$20,846.47			$20,846.47	

BALANCE SHEET.

LIABILITIES.	$	c.	ASSETS.		$	c.
Capital 15,000 shares @ $20. each	300,000.00		KOWLOON			
Hongkong and Shanghai Bank	77,863.82		Land, Building and Machinery		127,243.58	
Sundry Creditors	27,129.48		Materials in stock, valued at		36,352.57	
			CANTON			
			Building and Machinery	179,940.26		
			Less Depreciation	9,940.26	170,000.00	
			Street Lines, Fittings, Coal etc in stock, Valued at		34,313.62	
			Furniture		306.95	
			Value of Fire Insurance premia on unexpired policies		475.03	
			Sundry Debtors		12,554.96	
			Cash in hand at Canton		2,900.12	
			Balance of Profit and Loss Account		20,846.47	
	$404,993.30				$404,993.30	

By the time of the second annual meeting in 1903, after dealing at length with the disappointments in Canton, the chairman recorded 'continual struggles with the contractor over the extraordinary delay which took place in completing the building' (the station at Kowloon) before it began production of electricity in February of that year.

The Company's power station at Chatham Road, Kowloon, about 1908

In fact, the Company's problems with Chinese contractors were not at all unusual in those times. There exist numerous laments from officers of the government on the same question. In part, the problems were caused by the lack of experience of the Chinese contractors in constructing Western-style buildings, in part by their eagerness to obtain contracts which led to their underestimating hopelessly the costs of both the material and labour involved; and, last but not least, the general feeling among Chinese that Westerners had the big money and they might as well squeeze some of it out of them.

Orders were coming in, but it appears that insufficient thought had been given to the time it took 'to make the necessary communications and put in installations. We have now installed over 500 lights, bringing in about $1,900 per month. . . . We have three sets of engines and generators, two for use and one for reserve. At present we can do all we require with one set. . . .' The foresight of the management in these early and financially restricted days was remarkable, and was to prove at least one excellent constant in the future management of the Company down the years.

The new power station in Kowloon had begun to produce electricity on 2 April 1903, and a somewhat tardy description of it appeared in the *Hong Kong Weekly Press* toward the end of the month.

'The station is situated on the sea front of the main road leading to Hung Hom, and covers an area which leaves room for a considerable extension of the works should increasing business necessitate it.' The 'power house,' is described somewhat euphemistically as a 'large airy building,' which is hardly the impression given by the admittedly poor extant photographs of it which show a rather lonely structure with a modified classical façade topped by a pediment with a circular window, and one modestly diminutive chimney rising behind. The station, at least as it appeared in a photograph of 1908, stands isolated on what appears to be a dirt road with some scrubby grass in the foreground, while at the end of what was probably the wall of its compound in which doubtless the coal was stored, there rises a somewhat more graceful building of two stories in the colonial domestic style: There seems to be no record of the fact, but it may well be that this was the quarters of the station's senior staff. A few other distant buildings appear beyond it, and only the presence of a telegraph pole indicates that even in 1908 there was much need for communication in the area.

This power-house, the newspaper account continues, 'holds the generators known as two-phase high tension dynamoes [*sic*]. These were made by the famous Westinghouse Company of America, and each has a capacity of 75 kilowatts; they are driven by patent compound surface-condensing engines, capable of developing over 100 h.p. each, and manufactured by Ball & Wood Co. of New York. Downstairs from the power-house is the boiler room, where the plant is of an equally up-to-date type. There are three boilers built on the water tube principle, each of them with a capacity of 100 h.p. Technically known as sectional boilers, they are of the latest American pattern – efficient, safe, easy of access for cleaning purposes and presenting every facility for quick and inexpensive repairs. In the store and godown attached to the station [it does not appear on the 1908 photograph] is to be found a large stock of electrical fittings of every description.'

It must be remembered that in the early days of electricity generation and distribution there were no handy supplies, or suppliers, of the components necessary to convey the current to the customers. Almost all of these – wire, insulators, all manner of fittings – had to be ordered from the West and stocked. Some items were locally made in quite considerable quantity.

'The station ... at present under the management of Mr. Johnstone, an electrical engineer of experience who supervised its erection, has been designed for supplying light and power over a radius of two miles, and in the latter direction possesses special adaptability, its two-phase system doing away with expensive switch arrangements for the starting of motors necessary in the case of other systems. The main lines have been completed to the Green Island Cement Co.'s works at Hok Un in one direction, and to the Kowloon Hotel in another. . . .'

The initial generating capacity of this primitive little station was 255 kW – adequate for anything that seemed likely to turn up by way of business at that time.

That same optimism which had prepared three generating sets when only one was immediately required, is reflected in the Company's attitude to its, at that time and for long enough to come, somewhat tenuous finances. The first year's losses were small enough, but those in the second were larger. At the 1903 annual meeting Mr. Shewan outlined how the Company's indebtedness to the extent of about $220,000 arose from the fact that the capital had not been increased when the Canton power station was taken over. The Canton works were now worth over $200,000. He then made a remark which can only have referred to some plan, doubtless involving Paul Chater, to amalgamate with the Hongkong Electric Company. 'The reason why we did not ask for more capital' at the time 'was that, as most of you are aware, we had great hopes ... of merging the two concerns [Canton and Kowloon] in another much larger electrical undertaking. The negotiations as to this have, however, been protracted ... and meantime we have had to find the necessary funds for continuing the business in the best way we could.'

Some sort of corroboration of that awareness by the general managers present at this second annual meeting of what Mr. Shewan was talking about, comes from the history of the Hongkong Electric Company, *A Mountain of Light*, by Austin Coates. On page 51 we find:

'It will be remembered that the Company [Hongkong Electric] had originally proposed to light Kowloon. With the formation of the China Light & Power Company in 1901, under the very determined and somewhat emotional Robert Shewan, this became a live issue. Shewan, like Chater, saw Kowloon as a city of the future. And being a man who became personally involved in everything he did, he saw this personally. He had the wit to realize that if his company was to "take" Kowloon, as armies "take" cities in war, he must have Chater on his side, and successfully persuaded him to be a member of China Light's two-man consulting committee. . . .'

'With the advent of Shewan, a committed man, on the Kowloon scene, Chater changed his mind about Hongkong Electric's aims . . . in respect of Kowloon. Chater saw Kowloon almost as Shewan did. He felt a kind of loyalty to it. . . .'

It cannot be doubted that this was the attempted merger which Shewan referred to in his account to the meeting of 1903. And from this decision taken by two of the most dynamic personalities of the times, stems the fact that not one single, but two separate electricity producers supply the Colony of Hong Kong to this day.

Shewan reckoned that in order to pay for 'new engines' for Canton, and to cover the present indebtedness, the Company needed about $350,000. He proposed to raise this sum by an issue of 'say 15,000 shares of $10 each, and debentures for $200,000 in 8 per cent bonds of $1,000 each at $975, or of $100 at $97.50.'

He continued: 'As an inducement to new shareholders we propose to put them on equal terms with the old shareholders by writing down the old shares to $10 each, and as a further inducement, and also to show their own faith in the future of the Company, the general managers will guarantee a dividend of 6 per cent on the new shares for three years.'

This manoeuvre, however reasonable it may have seemed at the time, was to be the cause of much trouble in the future.

'I fully sympathise,' the adroit Shewan went on, 'with shareholders in their very natural disappointment with the result now laid before you, but you will gather . . . that things are by no means so bad as you might have thought. The general managers are among the largest shareholders and have suffered accordingly, but still have every confidence in the future of this Company, and willingly take up their full share of any new issue.'

Odd though it may seem, there were no questions – a situation that continued for some years at Company meetings. Sir Paul Chater (he had been knighted in 1902), Dr. J.W. Noble, and Mr. J.H. Lewis were elected to the Consulting Committee.

Thus ended the first assessment of the position of the Company after the commencement of generation at the Kowloon station. Basically, the only hanging question was how the new issue of shares

*Mr. L. Marston was manager of the Canton station
from about 1905 to 1908*

would be taken up. But, reading the reports of those far-off meetings in the early days of the Company, it is hard not to be impressed by the confidence that seems to exude from the participants, even in the most difficult times.

As to those who made the electricity, very little beyond some names of the staff of the Company in its formative years seems to have survived. Here and there in the minutes of board meetings one or other is commented on as having done wonders in difficult circumstances, or as having been replaced by another man. Not by any means are even all the *names* of the staff recorded in surviving documents.

Among managers, Mr. Belden (circa 1901–1903) and Mr. Johnstone (circa 1903–1905), do not even have an initial recorded. Mr. L. Marston (circa 1905–1908) appears to have followed

Johnstone. Mr. S.F. Ricketts managed the Canton station for some time, and also served briefly in 1909 as secretary of the Company. An assistant engineer for the Kowloon station was engaged in 1912 because 'the supervision of the new rather complicated engines was deemed too much for one engineer alone.' But we do not know his name.

It would seem that after the Canton fiasco of 1909, the European staff was cut down.

By 1913, the manager was Mr. C.N.N. Hamilton who was an associate member of the Institution of Electrical Engineers, and he was assisted by Mr. R.C. Long, whose qualifications were similar. By 1913, the staff numbered fifty-eight. These two European engineers were in charge of fifty-two Chinese and four Indians.

The First World War resulted in frequent staff changes from the United Kingdom as men left to join the armed forces, and eventually the whole foreign staff was renewed. This inevitable process entailed much expenditure on passages outward from the United Kingdom and also homeward, together with other special allowances. A new superintendent named Ireland proved to be a very energetic man and succeeded in greatly improving the load and in generally furthering the interests of the Company.

Shameen at Canton as it looked in the first decade of this century

DIFFICULT YEARS: 1904–1918

THE problems of running a viable power company in a foreign land – however colonial Hong Kong was in those days – must have caused many a chairman, director, and shareholder, not to mention engineer and station manager, to scratch their heads and wonder if it was really worth the candle after all. It had seemed such a good idea when Mr. Shewan started it off – this making of electricity with the still exciting power of the steam boiler driving the turbine that drove the generator, and carrying the current to every home, every shop, every factory, to each place of business or pleasure, and thereby making a profit.

The inexperience of the Company was certainly as profound as was the optimism that its board and (on the whole) its shareholders displayed with such surprising consistency. Both attributes were probably natural at the time. Experience in running companies generating electricity was confined during the early years very largely to Western nations whose economies and industrialization were much more highly developed than the economy of Hong Kong which, in the early period of the Company's story, had little industrialization in the strict or large sense of the word. The other vital difference between the situation facing the Company in Kowloon and that of companies in the West was that the population was not particularly numerous, and the overwhelming majority were Chinese. Estimates of the number of Kowloon inhabitants are largely guesswork during the early years of the twentieth century but, even by 1911 when a somewhat firmer figure was arrived at, the number did not exceed 68,000 souls.

And the Chinese soul – apart from the Chinese pocket – did not take readily to the expense of electricity for throwing light on daily and nightly activities. Not, at least, in any great numbers. In 1911 the total number of the Company's customers among those 68,000 was just under 500, and quite a number of these were certainly non-Chinese who, on the whole, could afford more than their counterparts in the Chinese segment of that entirely lopsided society.

The underlying factors in the Company's difficult years between its first lights in Kowloon and the year 1918, were in large measure these. But there were others. We have already seen how an insistent problem with all power companies (even those in metropolitan centres such as London) was the fluctuation of the demand for electricity in those formative years when its use was confined to lighting. Even the introduction of the electric ceiling fan in the mid-nineties on Hong Kong Island, where the Hongkong Electric Company had been in operation since the end of 1890 (at first with street lighting only) did not make an appreciable difference. The simple reason was that not enough fans were installed. By and large, even those Chinese who had been extravagant enough to install lighting – one light or two in many cases, an act regarded with a mixture of amazement and surprise at the extravagance of such a procedure – did not take to electric fans which consumed very much more current than carbon filament lamps, the source of light at this period. Westerners were the users of cooling fans, and there were then few enough of both in Kowloon.

By the end of September in Hong Kong the humidity normally

A breath of
the open road!

The Electric Fan

BUY A FAN AND
ENJOY YOUR SUMMER

THE CHINA LIGHT & POWER CO., (1918) LTD.
Showroom; 62, Nathan Road, Kowloon.
Phone K. 677.

drops quite sharply and, as the temperature somewhat more slug-
gishly falls, fans were naturally little in use. The design of both living
and commercial accommodation – that graceful mingling of Western
classical with, often, the equally graceful Chinese roof – was well
suited to a hot climate, but desperately uncomfortable in the colder
months before the end of March. Westerners seem on the whole to
have become more active and ebullient as the thermometer fell, while
their shivering Chinese servants and employees sat in windswept
domestic quarters and offices, numbed with cold. Chinese houses were
certainly much warmer in the winter months than Western ones, but
were thought to be unbearably hot in summer.

There were yet other matters inhibiting the Chinese from more
widespread use of the Company's electricity. While Westerners tended
until long after the turn of the century to make few alterations to the
clothing they would normally wear in their occidental habitat (before
the days of dry cleaning this must have made summer gatherings
odoriferous, although it is not commented on), the Chinese had been
used for centuries not only to different weights of clothing for the
extremes of seasons, but to the long gown, a garment almost infinitely
adaptable to hot or cold conditions. Any Chinese who is old enough
to have experienced the normal use of the *cheong sam* (the term applies
equally to male and female varieties) will affirm its coolness in
summer and the pleasing warmth of the padded variant in winter.
Hence, to some extent at least, the Chinese were immune to the
blandishments of the electric fan. For choice they would certainly not
have worked in winter in those airy offices of the Western *hongs* (even
wearing their winter robes) had they been given the choice of working
in Chinese-designed buildings.

In the West, electricity was very rapidly harnessed to replace
energy formerly supplied by manual, animal, and water power, or
directly used steam power. But the small 'pimple on the backside of
China,' as the Colony was termed inelegantly if accurately enough,
was, in the first many years after the introduction of electricity, what
we would now term an underdeveloped country. It had almost no
industry except cottage industry. It had a population adapted to and
suitably clothed for the extremes of its climate (apart from the tiny
minority of foreigners who pursued their own perverse sartorial ways),
people who were in general impecunious except for a small upper
stratum of well-to-do families.

It is hard to gauge the extent of innate distrust in the new form

44

of lighting by the Chinese. There was certainly much evidence of superstitious dislike of the idea in Canton where the Company was struggling to convert an ever-increasing number of the almost completely Chinese population (ruled moreover by traditional Chinese in the traditional Chinese manner) to using electricity.

To understand the nature of Chinese popular distrust of things foreign in general is not hard. The very distrust of the British themselves even of things French and, at the turn of the century, their estimation of China and the Chinese as belonging to an entirely inferior civilization, provides a ready-made example of national chauvinism. It should not be supposed that the Chinese were free from the same attitude. When it came to electric light – the illumination that could be called forth in a glass sphere dangling on the end of two wires at the mere touch of a toggle – it seemed the immutable laws, that say no smoke without fire and no light without flame, must have been altered by some devilry or other. The reaction among Chinese – somewhere between amazement and fear – which only a decade ago was normal among many peoples in the world when photographed by a polaroid camera and shown the result in a minute or two, partook of the same character of human distrust of the unknown.

Such intangibles and imponderables had much to do with the day-to-day business of the Company, whose *apparent* potential in customers was in fact not a potential that could in any way be calculated in simple terms of the numbers of Chinese.

The other recurrent and equally imponderable problem which dogged the production of electricity was the inefficiency of the machines that produced it. It was to be quite a long time before the consumption of coal or other combustible material could be controlled in such a way that the maximum possible energy was extracted from that process; and even longer until the energy, once obtained, could be applied with maximum efficiency to turbines and generators, thus manufacturing electricity economically.

The record of early boilers improved, as we have seen, with the invention of the Babcock & Wilcox type, but maintenance was still a frequent problem. And the same may be said for the machinery driven by steam, or gas as the case might be.

It might be thought that now, in the last twenty years of the twentieth century, after a hundred years of commercial production of electricity, such problems as the thermal efficiency of the conversion of raw materials to electricity, and the design of the newest plant, would have virtually eliminated all these old-fashioned problems. But such is not the case. Occasionally, even today, a boiler blows a tube; and all boilers have to be cleaned at definite intervals when their running efficiency is falling. All boilers must have their burners replaced. The sad sight of one of the most modern burners injecting atomised oil to that Dantesque cauldron of hell-fire which can be seen through a peephole in the boiler's side, buckled and corroded, all but melted in the intense heat and malignant gaseous atmosphere of the interior – at once underlines the point. Nothing is infallible in the process of making electricity.

These facts make it all the more apparent that the optimism of the Company and the doggedness of its staff in the power station were absolute necessities if business were to be continued.

By the time of the third annual meeting of the Company on 9 June 1904, presided over by Mr. C.A. Tomes (taking the place of his partner in business, the usual chairman Robert Shewan) the Chinese resistance to electric lighting was slowly breaking down. 'The Company has made considerable advances since the last meeting, and we hope for steady progress now towards a dividend basis. The Chinese demand for light in Canton is as active as we could wish, and we have all the new installment [installation] work in hand to which we can conveniently attend. The number of skilled wiremen is limited, and all we have are fully occupied, and others are taken on as fast as they become educated.' Mr. Tomes presumably meant 'trained in the job.' The point is of passing interest, since it appears that many of the original electricians or 'wiremen' in both Hong Kong and Canton were recruited from the Chinese population of San Francisco where, unlike the citizens of Hong Kong, there was a pool of 'educated' (as Mr. Tomes would have said) labour.

In 1904, the chairman continued: 'The large fire in the Canton native city in February was unfortunate for us, as besides the destruction of poles, wires, transformers, etc., our revenue was curtailed for some months.' It sounds a fairly unexciting affair, perhaps because his audience were well acquainted with what happened from reading the local newspapers. These give full and dramatic accounts. In fact there had been several fires in Canton in the first week of February. But in its issue of the 24th, the *Hong Kong Daily Press* reported the major one. Fire broke out at 5 a.m. in West Canton about ten minutes' walk from Shameen, where 'several restaurants and other places of resort are situated. When the fire broke out a great number of singing-girls and ... residents fled, and took refuge on the boats moored in the Shameen Canal.' And doubtless the Company lost a number of its customers, owners of the flower-boats from which the sing-song girls fled. 'The fire was the work of incendiaries as an order had been passed lately by the Viceroy of Wong Sha that all flower-boats at Kup-Yap should move ... a considerable distance away, thus taking away the business of the singing-girls in that district.... Many girls were forcibly carried away to be sold or held for ransom. Over one hundred houses ... were burned down....'

Two days later the same newspaper enlarged on its first account: 'Owners [of brothels] were seen dragging hand-tied women along the streets by ropes, fearing they might be stolen and re-sold to other keepers.' And the total of houses gutted was now said to be about 350.

For the time being the Company's revenues, as Mr. Tomes said, must indeed have diminished sharply from that particular red-light district.

Curiously enough, nothing was mentioned by Mr. Tomes or by the newspapers of any firefighting during the blaze – and yet the Company was contracted to supply water via electrically driven pumps for just such an emergency.

But there was moderately good news too from Canton: 'Of the three main engines lately ordered, one is in position, and was started in April and is doing very well, and the second is nearly ready; the smaller one for the day load is now running, and relieves the strain previously borne by the main engine, and will give a more satisfactory and economical supply of current. Almost all the foreign residents in Shameen are customers of the Company, and in the native city the wiremen are entering the official district and the houses of the well-to-do gentry.'

The Company's new engines being installed were by Belliss, the small one catering for the light daytime load being a 30 kW set consisting of alternator and engine. 'In spite of all these difficulties and disappointments there is ... no reason we should lose heart. The business is there, and will,' Mr. Tomes thought, 'prove a very profitable one if we persevere with it.... The Shameen community have only lately insisted upon our running a day load in order to supply them with power for electric fans, etc., and we do not anticipate any difficulty whatever in obtaining fresh customers for all the extra supply from the new engines. . . .'

By 1904, then, it seemed that the diligence of the Canton staff, the foresight of the directors, and the patience of the shareholders, together with the increasing realisation on the part of the Chinese of the convenience of an electric supply, had set the course toward commercial success. The shambles, financial and material, of the former company's operation at Canton had been put to rights. Demand was stepping up regularly, new and more efficient generating equipment was installed, and there was a progressively better understanding of the problems involved in the business, not least of the special problems posed by a large variation in demand between day and night and the accompanying difficulties in regard to the efficient operation of the generating equipment. The Company was justified in looking forward, barring accidents and unforeseen events, to a profitable future.

Then, striking a further optimistic note nearer home: 'The revenue from the Kowloon plant increases slowly, but profitable business is bound to come in time as there can be no doubt about the future importance of the peninsula.'

Spoken in 1904, one can see how the confidence of Mr. Shewan (reflected in Mr. Tomes' words) in Kowloon and its potential had made itself felt among his contemporaries. The sight of Kowloon as it then was – hardly more than a huddle of houses here and there, rice and vegetables growing between them, tattered patches of banana trees interspersed – could hardly have aroused such assurance of the terrain's future in any but the most enthusiastic mind. Robert Shewan was nothing if not the possessor of just such a mind. It is his outlook that was voiced by his partner.

The remainder of Mr. Tomes' speech mentions another point which runs through the history of the Company, and through that of all other early electricity undertakings. 'All important capital expenditure we trust has come to a stop for some time to come.' Building a successful electricity company, it was beginning to dawn on even the most optimistic, was a capital-intensive affair. And it is to the Company's credit that at almost all times capital was procured in one way and another so that plant not then required could be ordered and installed against the time (which inevitably came) when more capacity was needed. Mr. Tomes was prudent as well as optimistic.

Mr. Tomes noted that the new shares, arrangements for which were in progress, had already attracted applications for some 10 per cent of the authorized issue. 'If any shareholder should want a portion,' he suggested, rather as if addressing children at a birthday party, and for once urging them to eat as much as possible, 'he has only to apply.'

In that same year Mr. Shewan was writing to the papers on the poor quality of government officers, 'the more able and energetic among whom quickly pass out of the Colonial service into the law and other professions where the rewards are much greater. In proof of this, may I point out that almost all the principal firms of architects and civil engineers ... have been founded by gentlemen who were sent out by the Colonial Office at the Colony's expense.' While it seems he is lamenting the expenditure of public money on their passages, he appears also to be applauding the enterprise of the resigning civil servants as they purposefully strode into the private sector. Mr. Shewan was a man of quite complex mental processes.

By May 1905, the issue of new shares had been completely taken up, and at the meeting of June that year the chairman announced a profit at Kowloon of over $6,000, and at Canton of almost $48,000, for the past twelve months. 'We have there [in Canton] a large and wealthy city and our resources have been strained to the utmost to keep pace with the demand. Our manager, Mr. Marston, and his assistants have had to overcome many unforeseen obstacles ... not to mention the tax on their strength in having only raw untrained native labour. They have been constantly engaged in laying new lines in various directions through the city.' Negotiations were concluded for the extension of the area at Canton so as to enlarge the property the plant needed. The latest addition, the third Babcock & Wilcox boiler, was now in operation, and 'another engine alternator set was ordered from home.' It had in fact just arrived and was being set up.

But the Chinese authorities had modified the original concession given to the Company in such a way that it was more in their own favour, at the same time allowing the extension of lines to light the *yamens* (offices and other premises) of the Viceroy, 'the Tartar General, the Governor of Canton, and other official residences.' There was 'every indication' of steady increase in business, and profits were increasing every month.

Yet 'the Company has had to borrow right and left and has had to pay dearly for its loans. You have only to look at the Profit and Loss

Account to see what a hole in our profits interest to the Bank and other creditors makes. So, to put the Company on its feet, we propose to raise $200,000 more capital.' An extraordinary meeting was held immediately, at which the capital of the Company was increased by that sum to $500,000. The new shares, 20,000 of them at $10 each, were offered. These were taken up in their entirety by the China Provident Loan & Mortgage Co., of which Shewan Tomes were the general managers.

The following year financial results were better, and on 7 April 1906, the chairman announced that profits at Canton had risen to $50,000, and at Kowloon to $10,000. And, for the first time, the Company paid a dividend amounting to 6 per cent on the capital of $500,000. If the shareholders' hearts were uplifted by this event, their hopes were to be dashed in the following years. The Company did not manage to pay another dividend until 1919. Granted that in 1909 there was a return of capital due to events that were not foreseeable in 1906 when that initial dividend was paid, as ever the basic hard facts of intensive capital expenditure associated with the business of the Company took its toll on profits, leaving nothing to spare in all the intervening years.

In fact, the profits in 1906 would have been much better had there not been a Chinese boycott of American goods. This came about as a retaliation for American restrictions then being placed on the entry to and residence of Chinese in the United States. The Cantonese did not for some time understand that the Company was not an American firm – perhaps the presence of Mr. Tomes (who *was* American) as a partner of Mr. Shewan in a separate business, which did indeed derive great profit from China Light, confused the issue in their minds. But it was some time before the misunderstanding was straightened out. Moreover, the price of coal had risen 30 per cent in the year under consideration.

It was decided to order a 200 h.p. diesel engine-alternator set to 'work side by side with our present steam sets' so as to cope with the increasing load and that expected to materialise in the wake of the Chinese concession for street lighting in Canton city and 'areas beyond. Our weak point is still our finances,' said Mr. Shewan. And the meeting ended on that sobering note.

Reading the minutes of most of these annual meetings, it is surprising that almost no comment came from the shareholders. Perhaps the reason lay in the fact that the majority of the Company's shares were in the hands of its consulting committee and a few others.

The following year, 1907, the profits were a little up and would have been higher 'if we had not had rather bad luck.' Last year it was the boycott at Canton, and 'this year our earnings have been curtailed by two severe outbreaks of fire there.' Interest on borrowed money reduced the profits further but, said the ever optimistic Shewan, 'I cannot complain for this money was badly wanted.' Yet 'I do feel it is hard that we should lose over $7,700 in discount on the small coins which we receive in payment of our bills, and which we cannot well refuse to take from our customers. Many of these ... are British coins which the Government who issues them should never allow to fall below their par value.' The government had made a very unwise over-issue of coins, and the interior of China was 'flooded with them. The provincial Governments in China retaliated with a still baser coinage, and industries like ours have to suffer' from the lack of forethought of the Hong Kong government which now seemed 'helpless to remedy the situation' it had brought about. 'British coins are at a heavy discount in a British Colony....'

The governor of Hong Kong was in fact attempting the difficult operation of saving the situation by withdrawing such coins from circulation, but the problem was to take about a decade to solve.

The cost of coal was not quite so high as in the previous year, but its quality, and therefore its capability of supplying energy, was poor. 'So we have decided to abandon Japanese in favour of Australian coal.'

Mr. Shewan's business-like, laconic statements that 'losses from the typhoon in September were about $2,500 in capital and a small loss in revenue from Kowloon, and from fires in Canton about $1,600 in capital and a heavy reduction in revenue ...' give no conception, to one reading the minutes of the meeting long after that date, of the nature of the typhoon he mentioned so cursorily.

The *Hong Kong Daily Press* of 19 September 1906, referring to the previous day, supplies the information in its editorial. 'Although the terror of the typhoon is always with us in Hong Kong, it is fortunately not often that we suffer such calamitous ones as that which inflicted hundreds of thousands of dollars worth of damage yesterday, sacrificed a number of lives which at present we can only guess, rendered most of the poor Chinese boating [*sic*] population homeless....'

It was the worst typhoon since 1874 and came with no warning from the Royal Observatory. Lawrence Kadoorie, then a small boy of seven, was living with his family on the Peak in a house called

Modrina at Jardine's Corner. 'In those days,' he recalls, 'there was no electricity, and lamplighters went round each night lighting the street gaslights. We suffered severe damage to our home. The wind blew the end of the verandah on to a greenhouse in a garden below, and such was its force that it tore a gas bracket from the wall.' In those days houses on the Peak were lit by gas. 'The house next door was built on 4-foot columns, and suffered badly. The whole house was moved off its foundations and deposited five feet away!' This house belonged to a Mr. Sharp who presented Matilda Hospital to Hong Kong in memory of his wife.

In an article in the *Daily Press* the scene over the harbour is described: 'The Kowloon foreshore and buildings present a heart-rending scene. Workers were employed for two hours picking up corpses. Kowloon was harder hit ... than any other part of the Colony. The devastation ... was simply appalling.' Yet the sea wall of the docks held firm. There is no direct mention of China Light's power station adjacent – perhaps the Company's operations were too small and too new in the business of the Colony to attract such newspaper notice.

It appears from reading the newspapers of the following period that a disgraceful state of affairs obtained in the Observatory, which was scarcely in touch with any other weather station in the general area. The Observatory, accused of this, attempted to rebut the statements made and attributed the lack of warning by them to the typhoon's being of local and sudden origin. This was later shown to be totally untrue when reports from Manila arrived telling of the typhoon's passage there. The Observatory lost about as much face as an institution could.

A typhoon relief fund was set up, with Sir Paul Chater as its chairman, which collected and later paid out well over $200,000 – a very large sum for those days – to owners of lost Chinese boats, to widows and orphans, and to others in distress from the storm. The reports of their plight make harrowing reading, but they fill out the picture of life in Hong Kong in the days before radio and other sophisticated means permitted the Observatory to predict virtually to the minute the arrival of typhoons and their strength as well.

Although the Company's profits had again risen in 1907, it was indebted to the extent of $350,000 because of further expenditure on new plant for Canton. And, further extensions there being planned, it was thought prudent to raise half a million dollars in the form of 6 per cent debentures. But Mr. Shewan, indomitable gentleman that he was, remained optimistic. 'I certainly think we have good reason to look forward to a better and more profitable business in future, for we have in Canton a large field which it takes all our resources to cope with, while in Kowloon, although it is only the day of small things with us there' – a felicitous phrase, one of many recorded from his addresses – 'our business grows steadily.'

Once more, no questions were asked. Once more the chairman's optimism was to prove, if not unfounded, to be at least on hazardous ground. For a depression which had already begun in the West was starting to affect Hong Kong, and money which he intended to borrow was hard to come by. The £70,000 which the Company attempted to borrow in London (it was worth then about $600,000) was offered only on terms so severe that the idea was abandoned. But something had to be done, and quickly, for the Bank was pressing for repayment.

Finally, the method adopted at extraordinary meetings held on 14 and 30 March 1907 was to offer shareholders 5,000 debentures, each with a nominal value of $100, but issued at $80, these to be accompanied by ten 'special' shares of $1 each. Each special share for which at the time $1 was paid, was in future to be equivalent to an ordinary $10 share as far as rights to dividends and divisions of assets were concerned – in accordance with a resolution which made the following provisions:

> a The holders of these shares shall be entitled rateably in proportion to the numbers held by them respectively to one half of the net profits of the Company which it shall from time to time be determined to divide and to one half of the assets which in a winding up shall be available for distribution among the members.
>
> b No dividend shall be paid before the year one thousand nine hundred and eight and all shares will rank equally for dividend without respect to their face value.

Apparently the guarantee of a last dividend on part of the subscribed capital was quietly allowed to lapse. A further $25,000 had to be defrayed for 'underwriting new capital' in which doubtless China Provident Loan & Mortgage Co. were once more involved. The necessary money was thereby obtained.

The special shares were quoted on the Hong Kong stock exchange on 10 June. Their price was, appropriately, from then on, the same as that of the ordinary shares which declined from $10 at the beginning of 1907 to half that value in mid-June.

The saga of the special shares was only begun. In 1909, Mr. Shewan advised: 'we must not grumble ... at the special shareholders, for they came forward at a critical period when, had it not been for their assistance and the money they advanced, the Company would have had to ... wind up for want of funds. So if we have any money to divide today, we have to thank them for it.'

These somewhat curious proceedings must seem to have been prejudicial to the interests of the shareholders. It would appear with hindsight that the Company could have borrowed on more favourable terms. The creation of the special shares with their automatic special privilege equal to those of ordinary shares, is little short of astonishing. But no one raised a voice in question, far less in protest.

Then comes a mystery which, so many years afterward, and with no one who attended the meeting which took place on 31 October 1908 still living, will probably remain forever unsolved. It had been, and still is, the ordinary policy of the Company to submit for publication in the press details of what went on at annual general meetings. Yet in 1908 none were published in any newspaper, and no minutes appear to be extant – although minutes of each and every other annual meeting of the Company since its inception have survived. All that seems to be known about the meeting is that it was held later in the year than normal, with accounts presented for 18 months instead of twelve, and that it was divulged at the meeting that negotiations for the sale of the Canton facilities were in progress.

It is probably idle to speculate on the reason for the absence of information – but the historian must suspect that it had something to do with those special shares, and perhaps also with the need for some secrecy about the Canton talks – although this latter aspect is less likely because nothing done in Canton was ever secret for long.

The problem that had arisen in Canton had, indirectly, to do with (just for a change) the *success* of the operations there. Business was expanding rapidly and the fact that the profits were going to a non-

Chinese company outside the borders of China, began to raise doubts in the official Chinese mind about the propriety (to use no stronger a word) of continuing the franchise which they had granted to the Company. Despite the fact that it seems the viceroy of Guangdong (Kwangtung) province was receiving 4 per cent of the Company's revenue, he and other high officials such as the police chief began refusing to pay their lighting bills. Their argument was that mandarins don't pay bills to foreign companies existing at their pleasure in China. There was a boycott threat against the Company in Canton – which, had it been put into effect, would certainly have completely destroyed the hard-won profitability. Feelings against the foreign *hong* ran high, and in the circumstances it was obviously in the eventual interest of the Company to negotiate.

In those days of foreign dominance round the coasts of China which had resulted from a series of treaties extracted from the Chinese by armed force, little love was lost between those who attempted at the end of a weak and even trembling dynasty to keep the foreigners in check, and the leading foreign interests in the Treaty Ports, as they were called. In Guangdong province anti-foreign feeling generally was more inflammable than elsewhere – in proportion to the sorry record of the British there in the past. It was remembered that the British had consistently been the aggressors from the time of the 1830s onward. Cantonese were not likely to forget the sack of Canton, nor how it was held to ransom until a vast sum of money and some sort of treaty were extracted. And no Chinese could ignore the further bleeding away of territory and trade from his country as the nineteenth century progressed.

So there was obviously not much the Company could do but try to make the best terms it could. After many months of talks, the Canton enterprise was sold to the Ta Ching Kwangtung Electricity Supply Co. for $1.3 million,and payment was completed on 31 July 1909 – some months before the eighth annual meeting of the Company that year.

At that meeting Mr. Shewan made what appears to have been an attempt to pacify what were doubtless dissenting voices among the shareholders regarding the sale of the Canton business. 'Into our reason for parting with the Canton factory, I need not go very deeply. When we said in the Report that it was obvious we were losing ground in Canton, we thought it would be obvious to everyone.' Apparently it had not been quite so. And he went on to demonstrate that 'our monthly earnings had fallen from $8,760 to $8,060; if that is not losing ground, then I don't know the meaning of plain English.'

In fact the Company had lost much more 'ground' than that at various periods in its financially uncertain history, so Mr. Shewan's words were not very convincing. He then made the attempt, perhaps sensing this, to convince the meeting that the Chinese had every right to take over the Company in Canton – 'a very natural and proper desire,' he called it. What he seemed to want to play down was that the Company was driven out of Canton. It seems likely his pride was wounded by the affair.

The accounts had been made up to 31 July instead of February, so as to include the final payment from the Chinese authorities. Having 'made a virtue of necessity' and driven 'the best bargain we could,' the capital sum received had been used to pay off debentures of $450,000 and the required premium of $50,000, together with other deductions in paying debts and sundry creditors. Cash in the bank was currently about $670,000. 'As of course we have now no use for such a large sum ... we propose to repay $500,000 to shareholders as a return of capital, say $5 per share on 100,000 shares.' Over $100,000 would remain in the bank for use in development at Kowloon.

The shareholders, showing signs of restlessness at this affair, seemed also confused about how the chairman could pay out half a million dollars from the $446,000 profit. But it was pointed out by Mr. Shewan that he was repaying capital, and not profit. 'Then comes the question of how the money is to be returned. I regret ... that it is not so simple as it looks, for it raises some knotty legal points. The difficulty' he continued (and doubtless everyone present saw it coming) 'is ... with the special one dollar shares. We cannot "return" a shareholder five dollars when he has only lent us one.' The saga of those ill-conceived shares continued. Indeed it took the advice of a Mr. Palmer, said to be the greatest living authority on Company Law in England, to sort the matter out. Eventually, all formalities having been completed according to his advice, $250,000 was returned as capital to the 50,000 holders of regular shares, each share thus reduced to $5 in place of $10. Then another $250,000 was paid to special shareholders 'out of ... undivided profits,' in the form of a 'dividend or bonus of $5 on each $1 share.' And thereafter each special share was to be equivalent to a regular $5 share in regard to all future dividends and distribution of assets.

Thus, with what might be termed dextrous sleight of the financial hand, Mr. Shewan eliminated the problem child he had himself originally fathered. Clever man.

He was more comprehensible and straightforward on the subject of how the Canton sale was conducted. 'At last I was summoned to Canton and met Fung Wa-chuen and a rabble of Chinese who filled the whole *hong* and who he said were the new shareholders to be. The only man I was interested in was the Shansi banker who was to provide the funds for the purchase and I finally discovered him, very dirty and looking more like a rickshaw coolie than a banker. However, he was willing to guarantee the payment of ¥1,000,000 for the Canton business [equal to $1.3 million] and handed me an order for $100,000 as bargain money.

'We then all went over with a mob of Chinese and chairs and chair bearers to the British Consulate (Mr. H.H. Fox was then Consul) who had been waiting for us from three o'clock – it was then about seven – and signed the sale agreement before the Consul, but not before he had nearly wrecked the whole business by suddenly demanding that Shameen should be supplied with current free. He was finally persuaded to give up this idea and we all returned to the *hong* to a huge banquet which the new shareholders thoroughly enjoyed.

'It was very late when I returned from the scene to the Canton boat, and the first thing I did when I awoke in the morning was to see if the $100,000 was still in my pocket. On arrival in Hong Kong, I took the money to the bank and the sight of it relieved the mind of Mr. S.H.H. Smith, who had been getting very anxious.'

Sometime before the factory was finally handed over, 'the Chinese purchasers asked if they might come in and count the stores as they feared that on the last day they might all be removed by us. On the day they took possession they were given an old iron safe which stood in the *hong*, and remarked what honourable people the Keechong Hong [the Chinese name for Shewan Tomes] were as no one would have known that the safe did not belong to Keechong.'

At the end of that 1909 meeting, Mr. Shewan, still apparently smarting under attacks from both the public and his own shareholders, addressed the assembled company. He was obviously rattled by letters and articles in the Hong Kong press on the secrecy that seems to have shrouded the negotiations for the sale of the Canton 'factory,' and by the abuse of shareholders and others who found the whole question of the special shares a dubious manoeuvre.

The meeting declared over, Mr. Shewan thanked all for attending.

But, said he, 'I will just take this opportunity to make a remark.' He was always glad when shareholders asked for information and always pleased to give it. 'But information that may be used to the prejudice or detriment of the Company's interests we cannot give.... Some shareholders are not always its best friends.... We are not to be coerced or intimidated by the blustering and vapouring of outsiders with no real interest in the Company, nor am I the least perturbed by the foolish letters of disappointed speculators to the newspapers dealing with figures they do not understand.... One muddlehead – I am sorry I cannot find a better word – writes plaintively asking where are the other nine lacs [$900,000]. I cannot tell him. We received thirteen from the sale, five of which have already been paid back, leaving nearly seven lacs in cash in the bank, out of which we are trying hard to pay you back another five lacs. That makes ten out of thirteen, but where I am to find another nine on top of that and pay nineteen out of thirteen, I do not know, unless the gentleman expects me to repeat the miracle of the loaves and fishes or the widow's cruse of oil. Another anonymous scribbler,' complained he, sold out at the bottom of the market, 'and invokes the aid of the Registrar of Companies, for what I do not know, unless to have us all locked up for the consequences of his own miscalculations. The Registrar of Companies is not the official he requires; it is a Commissioner in Lunacy....'

Despite his protestations, the lingering suspicion that some fire actually underlay all this smoke persists in the mind after reading the evidence.

Not more than a few weeks before this outburst, Mr. Shewan was in full spate in a letter to the editor of a newspaper on the subject of the debate on whether to impose a liquor tax or not. He is eloquent, even passionate, on this subject too, reminiscent of many a present-day writer to the daily press on the injustices of Hong Kong society and how instantly to remedy them.

But there it was – the end of the Canton affair. A paragraph in the *China Mail* of 2 August 1909, gives pause for thought about how the new owners of the Canton power company managed to run it.

'An electric light box at the Viceroy's *yamen* in Canton was found to be leaky [*sic*] a few days ago. No one knew what to do but all were in great fear. An engineer in charge of Admiral Li's Bureau was sent for and the main wire was checked so that all the lights in the *yamen* went out. It became rumoured abroad that the *yamen* was on fire and ...

The old station at Canton had, by 1981, been enlarged and embellished with a new façade (compare the picture on page 26)

soon a fire brigade was on the scene ... but found its services were not required. The Electric Light Company then sent some engineers who remained at work until the following day.' These 'engineers' were soon to lose their Western bosses, and we may wonder how the infinitely more difficult problem of running the station was dealt with, without the presence of fully trained personnel.

The old Canton power station still stands by the Pearl River, not far from Shameen. The dowdy, Victorian look of its two-storey façade apparently lasted unchanged until the early 1930s when a radical alteration took place. Three further stories were added to the building and its façade took an architectural leap backward in time. Now it presents to the yellowish waters of the river a red brick face and windows of pleasing classical proportions, the whole appearance somewhat reminiscent of Wren's façades at Hampton Court Palace in London. In fact, if the trees lining the river in front of it were trimmed to cone shapes as they are at Hampton Court, the illusion would be very convincing.

Inside, the scene is a strange mixture of the mechanically obsolete

and a set by Gordon Craig for a 1920s movie dealing with a kind of Wagnerian 'dark satanic mill'. Two of the old boilers were still in use until 1974, and their murky Heath-Robinson exteriors confront piles of worn-out machinery and burnt-out transformers. Of three turbine sets, one is dismantled, its vanes split and gap-toothed; another is idle, while the third still spins, going on load now and then when demand rises in Canton's other power stations. Some of the old control panel is on the wall and an ancient wind-up telephone still in use. The pre-plastic days of bakelite still hold sway and, although the earliest machine dates (according to its still legible plate) only to 1927, it is not hard to imagine that time has stopped in 1908 and the Company has not long given over control.

This old building is to be demolished as soon as new generating equipment has been added elsewhere. And then the long and chequered story of the old station will reach its honorable conclusion.

Meanwhile, the operation in Kowloon was doing little more than cover expenses. Before his outburst after the end of the 1909 meeting, Mr. Shewan had indicated the confidence he had in the future there. '... it would be folly to abandon the place and throw away the benefits of all our past work there....' But, he went on, 'we must be better fitted to cope with it than at present.'

Coming hard on the loss of the Company's sole profitable venture, Canton, his steadfast optimism, while in itself an encouraging attitude, must have sent shivers down the spine of many a shareholder. The prospect might indeed be good in regard to the distant future, but meanwhile: 'Our present ... steam engines are of an obsolete type, and very wasteful and costly to run. We must have ... engines of the latest and ... most economical description.' And, further blow to the shareholders, 'we must also make provision ... to lay all our lines underground.' This would use up all the surplus cash, but the shareholders would then have the satisfaction of having an up-to-date factory, and power more than sufficient for all demands for some time to come. Cold comfort, it must have seemed, even on a warm September day. Perhaps with a feeling that their backs were to the wall, the shareholders in truly British style seem to have gritted their teeth and taken it all without even the flinch of a question – and Mr. Shewan had once more carried the day.

A year later, at the next meeting, the assembled shareholders were

Left: The boiler-house of the Guangdong Power Company's station at Canton in 1981. The coal-fired boilers were no longer in use, but the scene gives some idea of an old-fashioned boiler-house

told of delays in despatch of the machines ordered from Britain but that, emphatically, it was modern gas engines like those on order that would produce electricity, and therefore money, more efficiently than the old steam ones. Three British Westinghouse vertical gas engines of 150 kW each were on order, the old steam plant would later be scrapped, leaving only the old 70 kW gas engine; and a completely up-to-date switchboard would replace the existing archaic one. The first gas engine had arrived and was being installed. The other two would soon come. Thereafter, two would be in use while the third would be kept as standby.

It is an interesting comment on the uneven development of generating equipment and its accompanying motivating power from various sources that Mr. Shewan was scrapping steam-driven equipment in 1910 in favour of gas engines, while today the Company's new power station at Castle Peak (an undertaking that would have staggered even the forward-looking mind of Mr. Shewan) is designed to run on coal, producing steam, although there is provision for oil firing also; and that gas engines (gas turbines) – infinitely more efficient than those primitive engines of 1910 – are not intended to play a major generating role.

In 1910 the chairman noted that there was an encouraging growth in the number of lamps in use by customers, but that the demand for electricity did not show a corresponding increase. This was due to the introduction of the 'more economical metallic filament' lamps which gave much more light than the old carbon filament type, without a corresponding increase in current consumption. In phraseology characteristic of him, Mr. Shewan said: 'On the other hand, what is our loss is our customers' gain. We must content ourselves with the hope that the lower cost will increase the demand all round, and thus in time more than offset the present reduction in our bills.'

He also announced a contract to supply the Kowloon-Canton Railway. This major engineering undertaking had been actively encouraged by the governor, Sir Matthew Nathan. The project had its origins back in 1898 when The Hongkong & Shanghai Banking Corporation and Jardine, Matheson & Co. formed the British and Chinese Corporation, whose aims were to provide capital that might be required for future developments within China. After its formation, the Boxer Rebellion broke out, and soon after that was suppressed came the Russo-Japanese War. Railway-building in China became the subject of cut-throat competition among various Western powers and consortia formed among them. British interests in these projects were to some large extent represented by the British and Chinese Corporation. In 1899 the Corporation came to an agreement with the Americans who had a concession to build a railway from Hankou (Hankow) to Guangzhou (Canton), but the concession was later taken from them. In 1905 the Hong Kong government redeemed the concession by lending the viceroy of Hebei (Hopei) and Henan (Honan) provinces £1,100,000 at $4\frac{1}{2}$ per cent interest. The Crown Agents in Britain advanced the government the money at 4 per cent interest, and in 1905 converted it to a loan, simultaneously increasing the sum to £2,000,000 sterling. This formed part of the funds for building the Kowloon-Canton Railway – except that part of it in Hong Kong territory, which was taken over by the government. This sector was completed in 1910, and the sector from the border to Canton two years later.

The contract to supply lighting and power to the new railway was expected to increase the Company's revenue from output, and thus yield a moderate profit. In fact it emerged in the years immediately ahead that the profits were meagre and that the chairman's optimism had been largely unfounded – the more so as the Company was required to deposit as an act of its good faith the sum of $5,000 with the Colonial Treasurer.

The Company made a disastrous foray into the retail business in electrical fittings. Having established considerable stocks of these, it was discovered that fashions changed rapidly 'and a fixture that is in good demand one day is unsaleable the next. We have ... had to send some of our stock to the auction rooms as the only means of getting rid of it.' The docile shareholders asked no questions, something that comes as a surprise when they had just heard news of what amounted to the loss of moneys by an act of commercial miscalculation derived from ignorance of the retail trade on the part of those who directed the Company's destinies.

Yet another setback proved to be the delay in receipt of the new equipment, the first set not being installed until 1911 and the other pair until 1912. At first the new gas engines were found to be erratic in operation and less efficient than hoped. At the 1911 meeting, the chairman told of how the British company had failed to send all the parts at one time, and of the problems of removing an old concrete bed and forming a suitable new one for the new equipment. The engineer who came out from England to erect the new engines was required to stay at his post much longer than anticipated, and he eventually managed to make the recalcitrant machinery work more to the Company's satisfaction.

The population of Kowloon, a mere 68,000, had not yet shown much enthusiasm for electric light in their homes, shops, or places of entertainment. The price of a kilowatt hour for lighting at the time was possibly higher in Kowloon than the 30 cents charged by the Hongkong Electric Company on the island. The chairman was undoubtedly correct in stating: 'Kowloon does not seem to have reached a sufficient degree of affluence yet to induce a demand for electricity.' He considered that the Company's charges were 'as low as they need be,' but the matter was being looked into in case some alteration could be made.

In fact Kowloon developed only rather timidly over the following

Dr. J.W. Noble, a well-known American dentist,
for long closely involved with the affairs of the Company

several years. The number of consumers kept rising – in July 1912 they numbered about 560, a year later about 680, while in July 1914 there were nearly 900. Hardly a spectacular showing, but one that was probably achieved only by quite considerable efforts on the Company's part.

Among those present at the 1911 meeting, chaired in the absence of Mr. Shewan by his partner Mr. Tomes, were Mr. H.P. White and Dr. J.W. Noble who formed the Consulting Committee, together with four Western shareholders and a secretary. But there was also one shareholder named Fung Shiu Wa (who had also been present at the 1910 meeting, and was to attend the 1912 one, thereafter to drop out of the Company records).

The meeting was otherwise memorable (if that be the correct word) for a series of questions put to Mr. Tomes on 'the real capital of the Company' by Mr. G.J.B. Sayer, to which he received somewhat dusty answers. The surprise resided in the asking of questions at all. It had never happened before in the history of the Company.

By 1912, at the meeting held on 28 September, Mr. Tomes again presided, reporting that the Kowloon plant was now working efficiently, that the old steam plant had been scrapped quite recently, and that the number of consumers had increased by 15.6 per cent (in real terms, the Company had attracted eighty-six new consumers!) The increase in 'lamps and motors connected to the mains, expressed in kilowatts' had risen by 36.8 per cent, while total receipts from current sold were up by 18 per cent.

The following year, 1913, Mr. Tomes again stood in for Mr. Shewan as chairman (it was not until the following year that the latter again presided. There appears to be no explanation available for this but Mr. Shewan suffered ill-health from time to time, returning to Britain or taking vacations in Japan). The full extent of the new business predicted had not been reached, but the number of consumers had risen by 21 per cent. Despite this, the output in terms of kilowatts was lower than the previous year due to widespread use of the new metal filament lamps. But receipts from sale of current showed a small improvement of $5\frac{1}{2}$ per cent. There was a suggestion that some of the spare day-time load be used for charging the accumulators of electric motor buses, and the idea was being looked into. But the notion, although it came up in tentative form for a couple of years after this, was eventually dropped. The staff and the board were nothing if not persistent in their efforts to get things moving but the times were unpropitious.

There had been no hints of the ominous clouds forming in the political skies of Europe in previous years' meetings. But in 1914 the October meeting took place against the fact of the First World War, which was then a few months old. Mr. Shewan was 'glad to say that so far, since these accounts were closed last July, our earnings do not seem to have been materially affected by the outbreak of war.' The net profit available for distribution was somewhat over $25,000. Tenders for new plant had just been received from England and America, and Mr. Shewan reminded his hearers that the necessity for its purchase had been made clear at the extraordinary general meeting the previous June. He thought he would be able to obtain the funds needed at 8 per cent per annum. Consumers had increased by 29 per cent, and current supplied by 24 per cent. It was a short, uneventful meeting.

The new generating equipment for which tenders had been received consisted of two 750 kW steam-driven turbo-alternators along with the boilers required to provide the steam. But with the war intensifying and communications by ship suffering disruption and delay, and with the take-over of all supplies of engineering exports from Britain by the Ministry of Munitions, the Company's agents had their work cut out to secure anything for Hong Kong. The two new boilers were made by Babcock & Wilcox, as usual, and had a capacity of 9,000 lbs. of steam per hour each. They were delivered in 1915, while the corresponding pair of 750 kW turbines, made by British Thomson-Houston arrived in 1916. The work of setting up all this plant was done more or less on schedule, the first unit being in operation by March, 1916, and the second soon after. The old gas engine installation was retained for standby purposes, but later sold when it was no longer needed.

Electricity could now be generated with fair efficiency, yet the financial returns were still less than had been hoped. The price of coal had risen in response to the war situation, and by 1917 it was around three times more expensive than in 1914. A one hundred per cent rise in fuel bills per annum took a big bite out of revenue. So, too, did the necessary and continual extension of China Light's network distributing the current to the consumers. After 1914 the process accelerated rapidly, and the financial burden indicates this fact. In the five years, 1910 to 1914, the outlay was about $38,000 while in the next four years to 1918 it stood at $176,000 – nearly five times greater.

The 1915 meeting was postponed a while because Mr. Shewan was serving on a jury. The Company's balance sheet showed no improvement on the previous year – 'disappointing' as the chairman said. But, optimist that he resolutely was, he went on: 'The improvement is there, nevertheless, as in spite of the reduction in the number of residents in Kowloon which took place at the outbreak of hostilities, we have slightly increased the number of our consumers and our gross revenue was higher by about $8,000.' The whole European staff had changed during the year owing to men joining up, and the cost of extra passages paid for them offset the rise.

In the middle of the Great War, as the Europeans came to call it, Mr. Shewan chaired the 1916 meeting in a mood of moderate – perhaps moderated – optimism. 'Financially our position is quite sound and we have ... paid for all the new plant and can easily pay the interest on our debentures out of income. ...' But he foresaw the need for more new plant soon and, while not proposing to pay a dividend at present he thought it would not be long before the Company could pay a 'modest' one. The sum of $260,000 was raised in debentures, once more from the China Provident Loan & Mortgage Co.

A preview of things to come appeared in the following year, 1917. The net profits, in spite of everything (and Mr. Shewan listed the adverse factors) were more than $67,000 against those of the previous year of $26,388. 'I do not think you will be disappointed at our not recommending a dividend,' he said with an equanimity that appears – in retrospect – armour-plated. His reasons were, among others, that 'this Company is really in its infancy and will require a good deal more capital before it is able to cope with all the business which we feel lies before it in the future.'

The first mention is made of the now unsatisfactory nature of the Kowloon power station site, the harbour having receded somewhat due to reclamations, which made it more difficult to obtain the flow of sea water for cooling and entailed handling the coal for the station over a greater distance. 'Changing from one site to another and rebuilding will of course be expensive.' But it would have to be done one day. To re-install would cost an estimated $250,000 with the additional acquisition of another 1,500 kW set.

The old bogey – blunder, as it had proved – of the special shares had once again to be explained by the chairman. He must by now have rued the day the company created them. 'It is clear that we must give the one dollar shares whatever we give the five dollar shares.'

But in order to pay for a move to a new site and for even more new generating equipment, the sum of $250,000 would be needed, and also it would be a good idea to pay off the debentures of the same amount. It was therefore the opinion of the Consulting Committee that the shareholders should receive one new $5 share for each of their existing shares – 100,000 shares would be offered to them at par in proportion to their existing share holdings. 'But we shall not want all this money at once.' The Company would need money to pay for the site and the filling in, for erection of new buildings, for moving existing plant, and for 'the new turbine set from home.' This would be covered by a first call of $2.50 per share.

'The necessary resolutions for winding up the present Company and registering the new one' would be laid before the shareholders at a meeting quite soon. The new company would have a capital of $1,000,000, and this would involve winding up the old one and registering the new one while at the same time eliminating the whole idea of those tedious special shares.

Negotiations between the Company and the government, which had been taking place, resulted in the acquisition of a new site for a new power station on Marine Lot 93, which was situated at Hok Un between the Cement Works and Kowloon Docks, right on the edge of the reclamation in Kowloon Bay. The new lot was about the same size as the old one, but since it was once again on the waterfront, access to sea water for cooling and to boats bringing coal was direct and economical. The government gave an allowance of $40,000 to cover the value of the old power station buildings and the cost of filling in the new site; and the Company could remove from the old anything useful to them in the new station.

There were the usual chilling suggestions that the new construction would in turn entail all lines being laid underground, with the large expense that this would necessitate, and the expectable problems connected with delayed deliveries of new equipment owing to continuing hostilities in the West.

Finally, at an extraordinary general meeting convened on 11 December 1918, it was decided that the Company should be voluntarily wound up and at once reconstituted under the name: The China Light & Power Company (1918) Ltd. Shewan, Tomes & Co. or their successors would continue as the new Company's General

Managers 'so long as the General Managers for the time being (if a corporation) or (if an unincorporated firm) any one or more partner or partners in the firm of General Managers individually or collectively shall hold not less than one thousand shares of the Company.'

In this process of forming the new company, each share in the old company was replaced by a fully paid $5 share in the new Company. The $50,000 credited for the special shares therefore gave way to a capital of $250,000 for the corresponding new shares, and the difference of $200,000 was to be carried as 'goodwill.' In addition, 100,000 new and partly paid ($5 nominal) shares were issued to existing shareholders on a one-for-one basis – the first call on each share being $1.

China Light & Power (1918) Ltd. was thereby set up, and on 28 December 1918 it was incorporated, and deemed to have taken over operations from the old firm on 1 August 1918.

On the whole, the Company had weathered the difficult war years tolerably well. While the First World War did not hit the Colony or the Company with anything like the impact it had had elsewhere, there was considerable difficulty now and then with erratic supplies and other problems resulting from the internal situation in Great Britain and from the hazards of shipping lanes where prowling U-boats lurked and took their toll.

Life in Hong Kong had suffered from the loss of many volunteers to the armed forces fighting in France, and from the total uncertainty that lasted a very long time about who was actually going to win the war – the Germans or the Allies. Not least, it was those war years which began an internal, partly intellectual and partly emotional process in the minds of Westerners and Chinese in the strange Colony of Hong Kong.

A great moment of change had arrived, in the way such moments can be seen reaching their climaxes throughout history in general. The process is subtle, its ingredients often wholly unrecognized. Yet the momentum of change surges and strengthens as the time comes round; and at some point there comes a general recognition that, in the words of the old saying, 'things will never be quite the same again.' This is one of the truest of all sayings. The fact that it is self-evident hardly matters. The phrase represents a communal knowledge that history progresses (or at least continues, if we do not wish to see its motion as progress) in distinct steps. History seems not to like the gradual curve of change that the more reasonable of the human species might envisage as best. It prefers the lurches and pendulum swings of drama. And these come on unsuspecting mankind – which, unsuspecting, has generated their impetus – for the most part without the lead-up that a good dramatist would use to introduce them.

The world was inexplicably altered by the Great War – not simply by its ferocity and by the loss of a generation of Western youth, but by factors much less definable. It probably had something to do with the crumbling of classes, both in the East and West, not very obvious then (with the process often thought contemporaneously to be insidious) but later visible in social change of a profound nature.

The repercussions of this kind of social phenomenon in a colonial circumstance are often more stark, more apparent, than in the *detail* of the societies contained within the colonial situation – in the case of Hong Kong the Chinese and British social frameworks, which did not individually change much then.

Almost unnoticed in any important way, the system of government in China that had persisted for more than two thousand years had crumbled in 1911 to an aromatic dust, like those artifacts from ancient tombs suddenly opened to the contemporary air. Civil disintegration was soon all but complete there. History put its boot in the next Chinese foothold, and China began fundamentally to change. A new world outlook began to formulate all over the continents.

Even in colonial backwaters, among which Hong Kong and Kowloon at the time must be firmly included, those winds of change that were to be aptly identified by a statesman more than forty years later, were blowing like some out-of-season gusts – by no means of typhoon force, but tangible all the same. From the end of the Great War the British Empire began to lack the lustre of a monopoly, to seem, in all but the most blimpish minds, liable to change for the worse – or at least for the smaller and more puny. The automatic superiority of the British past wilted a little, never to recover, except in frenzied bouts of patriotism aroused by later barbarous events.

Kowloon was still a backwater, its population increasing slowly, its requirements for electric light and power – now that that latter word was coming into regular use – gradually growing. The more immediate forces affecting the territory were those which stemmed from the break-up of ancient China, from the incipient civil war which was not to become a real one for long enough, from the forces of republicanism and nationalism focussed on Dr. Sun Yat-sen. This product of a Hong Kong education, around whose name clustered the hopes of many progressive Chinese in China, was to prove only a step toward a new beginning in ancient China, not radical enough to weld the fragments of the old together. The process of reunification of China – one that it had undergone several times in its long history – was as usual long and bloody, shattering, as well as eventually revivifying.

It is against the events in China, quite as much as those in the West, that the future of Hong Kong – of Kowloon and the Company – have to be seen.

PROGRESS IN A NEW ERA

EVENTS in China and the changing outlook and increasing tempo of life in the world in general form the background to the decade after the First World War in Hong Kong, and the Company's story cannot be seen in isolation from them. The dominant problems, however, were domestic ones, at home in Kowloon.

The newly reconstituted Company, in tune it seemed with the spurt in the growth of the population and industry of Kowloon just after the War was over, did extremely well in the first full year of operation in its new form. The gross profit – profit before deductions for interest, depreciation, and certain fees – was $186,000, a sum representing a 50 per cent increase on the corresponding figure for 1918. The shareholders were paid a dividend – at last – at the rate of $8\frac{1}{2}$ per cent from the date of the incorporation – and regular annual dividends were paid in the following years, with the exception of the period, then far in the future, of the Second World War and the year of rehabilitation which followed on its end (1941–1946).

In the expanding commercial situation of the immediate post-war years, it seemed that the fortunes of the Company had at last turned. The population of Kowloon which had been only 68,000 in 1911, stood at 123,000 by 1921, and went on practically doubling itself each decade. In 1931 it was to reach 265,000 and by 1941 was 581,000. In normal demographic terms the increase is staggering – but in many ways other than numbers of people Hong Kong tends to defy normal expectations. In later years, after another world war, the explosion of people in the territory was to prove all but catastrophic.

The reflection of this rise in population can be seen in the Company's electricity sales figures. In the first year after the war sales were 2.7 million kWh, and two decades later on the eve of the Japanese invasion of 1941 they amounted to 57.7 million kWh – representing a more than twenty-fold increase or, in other terms, an annual growth rate of just under 15 per cent.

The accounts presented to the annual general meeting in December 1919 were made up for the fourteen-month period ending 30 September of that year, along with the statement that it was first the intention 'to make the new date the 31st December but it was found that the accounts could not have been presented within the statutory period without certain legal formalities, so the 30th September was substituted.' And ever since that time the Company's financial year has been reckoned as the year ending 30 September.

The 'goodwill' – that relic of the contentious old special shares – had been reduced from $200,000 by writing off $67,000. There was a curious, interesting comment appended about this figure. '$50,000 of this sum represents the profit earned by the Company between 30th July 1918, when the old Company in a legal sense came to an end, and 1st January, 1919, when the new Company [had been] incorporated.... Such profits cannot be distributed but must be used to write down the goodwill or some fixed asset.... The dividend therefore is out of the earnings of nine months.' And the remainder of the so-called goodwill was subsequently reduced by annual amounts until finally it was eradicated in 1924. The ghost of the special shares was thus finally laid.

It could not be said that the Company's skies were entirely free from clouds – for by now everyone knew that increasing demands would in due course have to be made for more capital – but in 1919 the outlook was sunny enough. Only one threatening shape loomed up for a time. It became known that the Hongkong Electric Company on the island had asked Preece, Cardew & Rider, well-known London consultants, to give their opinion about a possible extension of their supply from the North Point power station across the harbour to Kowloon. The London consultants advised that 'it does not seem necessary in Hong Kong to have more than one generating station.' Looking back on that statement from 'authoritative' opinion it would seem to be the experience of later years in other fields of Hong Kong endeavour that consultants from Britain very often come up with wrong answers. At that quite euphoric period of electricity generation and rising consumption, Mr. Shewan's constant optimism was beginning to seem justified. Yet the consultants from London were convinced that the Colony required only *one* power station. They were to be proved deeply wrong.

In fact their advice was not taken by Hongkong Electric – perhaps because that company sensed the determination of Mr. Shewan in his activities in Kowloon, and perhaps too because of the increasing viability of China Light at this point. The matter was dropped. But the fact that it had been raised at all remained as a small hanging query over the future.

The second meeting of the new Company, in 1920, heard of further satisfactory progress. For the twelve-month period (as opposed to the fourteen-month period accounted for in the financial statement of 1919) the profitability of the Company had increased, and a 10 per cent dividend (amounting to $80,000) was paid out. $3 had been paid up on the 100,000 new shares more than a year before, and the remaining $2 was being called up, payable in two instalments in 1921.

Mr. Shewan countered the tentative moves of Hongkong Electric and the question of that company's sending cheap electricity across the harbour with an announcement. 'With modern plant and increased production our costs should be reduced, and in view of this we have decided to meet the wishes of our friends in Kowloon and reduce at once our charge for private lighting. From 1st January [1921], therefore, the rate for private consumers will be 20 cents per unit which, for a modest installation like ours will, we think, compare favourably with what is charged elsewhere. In the good times to come,' and we can almost hear Mr. Shewan's voice as he made this ringing statement, 'when Kowloon has developed as it is bound to do and our turnover has correspondingly increased, we should be able to put our customers on a still better footing, but we cannot afford to do so now, for the present reduction will make a substantial difference to our earnings.' He went on to say that although putting 'our main lines underground' had involved heavy initial cost, upkeep would thereby be reduced. The chairman also noted the establishment of provident accounts for 'the benefit of our staff who have served us very faithfully.' The amount for this in the accounts for the year was $3,500.

Mr. Shewan was right about the immediate future, for in the ensuing year the shortfall due to the lowering of the unit rate for lighting was made up by increased consumption. With the capital expenditure at almost $1 million – a very large sum of money in those days – the Company was again having to borrow heavily, which pushed up the interest charges against its gains.

In the same year, 1921, the new Hok Un power station was acknowledged to be behind schedule. Work begun in 1919 after the site was acquired from the government had at first progressed well enough, and the foundations were laid in the area of reclamation where the station was to be located. In that year the Company had ordered the equipment from the United States – two Westinghouse 1,000 kW turbo-alternators, and two Babcock & Wilcox boilers, each

Above: The 'old' station at Hok Un about 1925. Overleaf: Part of the turbine hall of the 'old' station in the same era

with an output of 10,500 lbs. per hour. Some of this was ready for shipment within a few months, but the Company requested the makers to delay sending it in order that nothing would arrive before the structures to house it were complete. The intention was to complete the new installation and have it in commission by September 1920.

These hopes proved sanguine, to say the least. Manufacturing delays hit the remainder of the ordered machinery, and owing to labour disputes it was a year late. The first new boiler and the first 1,000 kW turbine were not finally put into service until September 1921, while the second set went on load shortly after that.

Then came the move from Chatham Road, from the old station, to Hok Un (as the Company has resolutely kept calling the site which would more normally be spelled Hok Yuen – the Garden of Cranes being the improbable Chinese name of the area). The move entailed shifting the two 750 kW turbo-alternators from the old station, together with three accompanying boilers, and re-installing this plant at Hok Un. A further boiler was also added, and at the same time the old gas engines and generators were sold off. Thus, now empty, the former 'factory' could be returned to the government as agreed.

The area of the new site on which the Hok Un station had been built amounted to 90,000 sq. ft. It was assessed by a Mr. Mowbray Northcote 'at the conservative figure of $2 per square foot.' The adjustments made to the value of various assets on the books at this time, so as to reflect more realistically their worth, showed this as a sizeable gain. But, on the other hand, buildings and fixtures, and overhead mains transmission were now written down considerably because 'these items suffer more severely from wear and tear than the others.'

On the morning of 9 November 1922, some few hours before the fourth general meeting took place at 11 a.m. in St. George's Building, the newspapers carried an advertisement proposing that the Company's authorised capital be increased. Mr. Shewan, upset by this mistake – presumably on the part of some member of his staff who sent it to the papers a day too soon – began with an apology. 'It was not the intention to publish the advertisement until after the share-holders had received a full report of the proposals,' he assured them. But he had good news; and after that, bad. The good was that earnings had again increased and units of electricity sold had risen by 20 per cent. Mr. Shewan attempted to answer a query from Mr. C.A. da

Roza. Debentures, he said, had been considered as a means of raising capital but it was felt that they would not be raised in sufficient quantity. He pointed out to Mr. da Roza that the shares now stood at $14, and that an adequate dividend could only be paid on this figure if shareholders agreed to take the new shares at a premium.

Further discussion ensued before the unruly shareholder's amendment on debentures was put to the meeting and declared carried. Then, later, the *original* resolutions were put to the meeting, and they too were declared carried! Mr. da Roza pointed out that *both* could not possibly be carried; and Mr. Shewan rose to say he had meant to say the amendment was lost. A poll was then demanded by Mr. da Roza. But the point was made that there had to be a demand by at least one fifth of the capital represented at the meeting before a poll could properly be taken. As a result of this the Articles of Association had to be consulted, and also the share register: this last showed that among those who agreed to a poll, Mr. da Roza held 4,000 shares, Mr. Lee Hysan 9,620, Mr. A.V. Apcar 8,000, Mr. A.A. Guterres 1,000, and Mr. A.S. Ellis 1,700, a total of more than the required one-fifth.

Mr. Shewan therefore had to accept the demand for the poll, and a date for it was fixed for 9 December.

As it turned out the poll was never held. A further extraordinary general meeting, held on 14 December, revealed, in the words of the chairman, that 'since [the previous meeting] an understanding has been come to with the dissentient shareholders,' and the demand for a poll had been withdrawn. Now, 200,000 shares were to be offered at par. But he registered his annoyance by adding: 'We still think that the original scheme was the best in the interests of the Company, but we appreciate the arguments against it and, in any case, must bow to the wishes of the Company.'

The new proposal was adopted unanimously. 'Before you go,' said Mr. Shewan, 'I have very much pleasure in inviting Mr. da Roza to join the Consulting Committee....' Both he and Mr. Alves recorded their opinion that Mr. da Roza was a 'very worthy man in every way.' And Mr. Shewan added that the step had been taken to show that 'we have only the best welfare of the Company at heart.... We have invited Mr. da Roza to show that we are not antagonistic at all ... [and that] the shareholders ... are sometimes the best judges of what is best in their own interests.'

With that little sting to remind them, perhaps, that the chairman

Mr. H.P. White

hadn't changed his mind in spite of everything, Mr. Shewan ended his remarks.

Mr. da Roza joined the Consulting Committee, remaining a member, and later a director of the Company, for many years.

These events must have given Mr. Shewan pause for reflection on a note which the General Managers (Shewan Tomes) had written not long ago requesting information from the Works Manager. It contained the casual words: '... should much appreciate your assistance in the way of a memo as to present position to cover any questions that may perhaps be asked, though Committees are like lambs as a rule.' The advent of Mr. da Roza evidently meant there had been a change – the lambs had begun to grow into rams.

When China Light was founded in 1901 the Consulting Committee had consisted of only two men, apart from the ex-officio chairman. Mr. (later Sir) Paul Chater and Mr. H.P. White were the original members. From 1903 to 1912, Dr. J.W. Noble, a well known Hong Kong dentist who was American by birth and is said to have owned the first car in the Colony, served on the Committee. Joseph Whittesley Noble was a man of considerable substance. He appears

78

first on 5 April 1890, returning to Hong Kong to 'resume practice.' The following year he is listed as one of four dental surgeons in practice together in Bank Building, and in 1893 we find him heading his own group, with a branch in Singapore and another in Mayfair, London. Noble & Co. continued until 1914, after which Dr. Noble appears to have left dental practice, although the firm was still listed until 1941. Dr. Noble was an active director of Dairy Farm, joined the board of the South China Morning Post in December 1906, and had considerable property on the Peak.

When the Company was reorganized, two new members joined it – Mr. A.H. Compton of David Sassoon & Company, and Mr. T.F. Hough, another prominent businessman. In 1922, Dr. Noble replaced

Sir Robert Hotung

Mr. Hough, but left within a few months and was succeeded in 1923 by Mr. Lee Hysan. Following the death of Sir Paul Chater in 1926, Sir Robert Hotung joined the Committee, which then comprised five members in addition to the chairman.

The decade of the 1920s was really the point at which the Western world of Europe and North America finally turned away from the nineteenth century and much that the rich and passionately assured society which it nurtured had meant. It was the age of disillusionment, in part the result of the carnage and high-level blunders of the Great War, of the ruthless expenditure of a whole generation in an orgy of unparallelled blood-letting. Formulations of what had happened and what ought now to happen in this new world when the bloodshed had stopped were not hard to find. They were as various as Communism, women's liberation, and the general, diffuse, but heady feeling that somehow a new age was dawning, powered by new technology and offering near-future benefits of a material kind only known before by the very rich. This was quite true. What was also true and not realised then was that each new benefit brings with it the price tag. And that is generally paid by the many for the few.

The 'scene' of the twenties, in the Western world where the action was, filtered through to the colonies, to Hong Kong. Hard as it may now be to imagine the *quiet* of a great city in business hours in those times, it is easily within living memory to do so. To be sure, the trams in Hong Kong clattered on their way, clanging a bell or two at importunate jaywalkers in Central; there were a few one-decker buses which mostly did not attempt the hills, and some cars; even a few taxis which boiled on the way up Garden Road and occasionally, in their chronic state of non-maintenance, caught fire in the summer heat. These and former taxis were mostly Citroens. The importing company was formed by Charles Ellis who had started life working in Sir Elly Kadoorie's office and eventually became a rich man. The old Peak Tram, however, was as reliable as the trams themselves – ever since 1888 when it opened.

But the world of Hong Kong was changing in response to changes in the parent country, Britain. The electric refrigerator began very slowly to replace the old ice-box supplied daily with blocks of ice of doubtful hygienic quality; the cocktail arrived with early jazz and liberated fashions for women; as did the 'bob' haircut and abbreviated skirts, cigarette-smoking in public, and the blatant use of make-up, which was formerly confined to the stage and the more raunchy scenes of life that people still connected with Parisian depravity. All these were signs of a new era.

Yet streets were still quiet places, the sound of the human voice as audible as anything else. And, everywhere, ceiling fans twirled silently and papers blew out of windows when not firmly held down by weights – which, in offices, were often simple pebbles from the beach. It was still the era of 'white duck' for men's wear, of cloche hats and strings of long beads for women, and only a little later in the decade did 'sharkskin' come in for men's suits, regarded as the height of fashion at the time.

In some ways Hong Kong was well up with the times, in others still deeply embedded in the aura of Victoriana. While for long after the twenties haughty hostesses on or about the Peak could be heard asking new arrivals (male) in the Colony: 'Are you married, or do you live in Kowloon?' – the latter then supposed to contain the looser-living part of European society – in complete contrast the main streets both of Hong Kong Island and of Kowloon were lit by electric light. At this time in the majority of English and European city streets the lamplighter was still making his rounds as evening came, lighting the gas lamps which were *de rigueur*.

The year 1919 saw the Company involved in Kowloon street lighting, supplying and maintaining the 'lanterns' of a suitably high candle-power – 55 of them in that year, 205 in 1920, 246 in 1923, and 346 in 1924. Reading such small numbers it is always necessary to adjust ideas about what was a profitable action in those days more than half a century ago. Every aspect of living cost little, and a couple of hundred street lamps were worth supplying with current, even if the Company had also the chore of their upkeep.

The actual consumption of electricity grew remarkably in the early 1920s. Maximum demand in 1920 was 1,060 kW, but by 1923 had risen to 2,500 kW. The annual increase in the three years 1921, 1922, and 1923 was approximately 33 per cent. This required further generating units. A 3,000 kW turbo-alternator was ordered from British Thomson-Houston and commissioned in 1924. Babcock & Wilcox was asked for four boilers with a capacity of 20,000 lb. steam per hour each – these, being equipped with economizers and induced draught fans, boasted relatively high efficiency and were in service in 1925.

Shortly after the 3,000 kW set went on load, the Company contracted with Metropolitan-Vickers for another 5,000 kW generator, and that arrived in 1925 and was commissioned the following year. The generating capacity at Hok Un station now stood at 11,500 kW.

At this point a change was made from the previous 60 cycles per second frequency of the current, to the British standard 50 cycles, and new units were suitably designed for that. Other equipment installed included two 50 kW direct current house-sets made by Greenwood

& Batley, together with a 50 kW Brush motor generator – both of which were put to use to supply emergency lighting, and to operate the solenoids by which remote control of switching could be effected.

Now, of course, the station was running out of space, and in 1925 the Company applied to the authorities for more room on the east side of the existing site. The purchase was in due course made and the necessary reclamation carried out. The area was later extended further until, in 1939, it comprised about 350,000 sq. ft. with an uninterrupted sea frontage of about 1,300 feet in length.

1926 saw another fundamental change. The low distribution voltage of 100 was raised with the consent of government to 200 volts and the three-phase voltage went up to 346, the reasons being that the low voltage entailed the laying of heavy and costly cables, unnecessary at the higher voltage. The Company then went ahead with a conversion programme that was to take five to six years to complete, and which cost in the region of $300,000.

With these numerous and expensive projects either in hand or in view, a further call had to be made early in 1924 on the shareholders for more funds. Authorized capital was increased from $2 to $3 million by the issue of 200,000 new $5 shares, for which initially $1 was paid up. These shares were fully paid up by 1928, at which time the authorized capital went up to $3.6 million. By now the process whereby the Company continued to install machinery and other equipment to meet actual and projected future demand and transmission and distribution, was doubtless remorselessly familiar to the shareholders. The process did not and has not ceased. By 1929 the authorized capital stood at $5 million, at double that in 1931, and at $15 million in 1938.

Much expenditure was entailed not only in buying the equipment to generate more electricity but also in the means to transmit it to new substations and thence distribute it to the customers. The early beginning in 1919 in laying all important lines underground and dispensing with overhead lines was continued in a more intensive manner in the following years. When the demand increased drastically in 1924, in the Yau Ma Tei and Mong Kok districts, the existing underground feeder system was extended substantially. Simultaneously the Company developed new substations, new sites being bought for these in Kau Pui Shek and Kowloon Tong for building in 1925, while additions were made to the existing substation at Yau Ma Tei and another was in the process of erection at Sham Shui Po. By

1926, work was in hand on the first two consumer substations to serve Kowloon Docks and the Peninsula Hotel.

The middle years of the 'twenties were times of labour unrest in the West, of strikes and marches and demonstrations which disrupted production. A new era in society in general was reflected by a new image of trade unionism in Britain in which militancy began to be a serious factor. But it was much more the events in a disintegrating China over the border than any reflection of events in Britain that affected labour relations in Hong Kong.

The seamen's strike of 1922 started in mid-January and at once immobilized several scores of ships in the harbour or at the wharves. In the normal course of maritime trade several more vessels arrived in port each day, so the confusion was considerable. Sea voyagers were stuck in vastly overcrowded hotels. The strike was in part a protest about the rising cost of Chinese living – of rice in particular – and also against what the Chinese seamen saw as the low wages paid in the circumstances. That it was in some degree an anti-foreigner strike is also certain, and it spread to Shanghai and elsewhere.

Food began to run short, sympathy strikes were called and employers of labour, from hotels to butchers, found their staff had left them. The exodus of Chinese to Canton was a daily and crowded event until on 1 March a Governor's Decree suspended the train service to Taipo. The strike continued until a settlement was reached on 6 March.

The seamen's strike did not greatly affect the fortunes of China Light. It was not until 1925 and the general strike that the Company felt the pinch. The general strike followed on events in Shanghai where a group of young Chinese students took to the streets of the International Concession and marched, shouting and handing out anti-foreign pamphlets. At one point they were confronted by armed European and Eurasian police and ordered to break up and leave. This had no effect and the police fired over their heads. The marchers did not stop, and finally the police, fearing their weapons might be seized, fired into the demonstrators, killing seven of them.

The horror of life in Shanghai for all those (and there were millions of them) who did not have, and could not make, a living wage is well documented by observers of many nationalities. The decision on the day following the shooting, made by well over a thousand students who resolved on a general strike, reflected that aspect of Chinese life in the city. That the strike had a political basis and was actively encouraged by the Russians in order to undermine British, Japanese, and other foreign dominance in China in the manufacturing and in the Maritime Customs fields, cannot be doubted. But political motivation tends to come on the heels of human anger at conditions. The general strike was no exception.

The British took action and sent reinforcements from Hong Kong. The strike spread to other places and closed schools, made idle many factories, seriously affected food supplies, and generally made chaos of what was previously (for foreigners anyway) a semblance of order. We are now far enough away to see this incident in Shanghai with its repercussions in its historical perspective. It formed part of the long struggle, begun back in the nineteenth century, in which the Chinese increasingly resented their exploitation by foreigners, and struggled in many a campaign to achieve freedom from it. But the whole situation in China, made more acute by the fall of the last dynasty in 1911, eventually interwove the anti-foreign struggle into the violent tapestry of what became civil war.

The detailed story of the general strike and the turbulent incidents at Canton, followed by the increasing exodus of Chinese from Hong Kong, need not be followed here. What probably saved the situation for the Company were the valiant efforts of the European and 'local' staff (that is, non-Chinese staff engaged locally), together with Chinese volunteers. The volunteers were in fact raised by a leading Chinese, Dr. S.W. Ts'o, who opened an office in Hong Kong's City Hall which, within three days, was inundated with Chinese volunteers. He had succeeded where the authorities had not even attempted.

The station was kept running and electricity supplies continued without interruption, due entirely to the loyalty and immense amount of time and work put in by all non-striking employees. The Company recognized this later by awarding bonus payments to those concerned.

But the troubled situation in the Colony sent demand for electricity tumbling, and income fell correspondingly. Mr. Shewan, addressing the annual meeting of shareholders in December of 1925, remarked: 'During the last three months of our financial year [ended 30 September], our revenue, owing to the exodus of customers to Canton, fell off to the extent of about 55 per cent, and although the lighting load is gradually coming back to normal, we cannot as yet say the same of the power load supplied to Chinese factories and workshops.' But in spite of the events of the year the number of customers rose from 7805 to 8924, and the 10,878,241 units generated the previous year rose to all but thirteen million.

In fact, the sale of 'power' dropped again the following year and did not exceed the 1925 level until four years later. Dividends, naturally enough, had to be cut, and it was not until 1929 that they reached a sum larger than that paid in 1924.

Since its inception, at this time well over twenty years before, the Company had been advised by its Consulting Committee, whose decisions were executed by the General Managers, Shewan Tomes. At the annual meeting of 1926, the chairman put forward the suggestion that the Consulting Committee should be replaced by a board of directors. Mr. J.M. Alves, a leading shareholder, voiced what seems to have been the general view when he said: 'I think the days of such an anomaly as the Consulting Committee should be over in this Colony, as members of such a Committee should know that according to the local Companies Ordinances, "Director" means any person occupying the position of director by whatever name called and includes general manager, manager, and any person on a consulting or advisory committee.... Members of the Consulting Committee are perhaps inclined to transfer responsibility to Directors when trouble arises, whereas, if they are known as Directors, they must accept full responsibility for anything connected with the Company; of course, this is as it should be.'

The following year, 1927, the change was made. The Company's Articles of Association were revised and the new articles approved in March, coming into force one month later. They provided that the powers of control previously vested in the General Managers should now devolve on the board of directors which itself took the place of the old Consulting Committee. Shewan, Tomes & Co. would continue as the Company's General Managers indefinitely and, acting in that capacity, their senior partner or his deputy would be an *ex-officio* director of China Light and also, subject to approval by the directors, would be the Company chairman. Some slight adjustment was made to the terms of remuneration for Shewan Tomes and included in a new agreement between them and the Company dated 21 April 1927.

The changes did not involve any new faces – the members of the former Consulting Committee becoming directors, with Mr. Shewan as chairman. But, a year later, in April 1928, there occurred a highly significant event in the history of the Company. One of the directors, Mr. Lee Hysan, died suddenly. It was realised that as a consequence the family would have to pay a very considerable sum in death duties. They therefore disposed of a large parcel of China Light shares which, so it is believed, was principally taken up by Sir Elly Kadoorie. Sir Elly joined the board of China Light shortly afterwards.

The real significance of these events was that the Kadoorie family for the first time began to take a direct interest in the affairs of China Light – with consequences that certainly could not even have been imagined in the late 1920s. The firm establishment of the Company as the sole supplier of electricity to Kowloon, consolidated over the years of troubles and problems and in the face of considerable difficulties both financial and other, was now to come under the scrutiny and be given the assistance of the first member of a family of immense commercial acumen and vision.

THE KADOORIE FAMILY AND
LAWRENCE KADOORIE

To find the origins of the worldwide dissemination of the Jewish people we must look back to the year 70 AD when the Romans under Titus captured Jerusalem and, in fierce reprisals for the resistance of the Jews then and in years before, destroyed the Temple and conducted a bloody massacre. An unknown number of Jews – perhaps hundreds of thousands – were banished, scattered all over the neighbouring countries, and later all over the world.

In the ensuing centuries a large community formed in Baghdad, among whom were the Kadoories who in the course of time became one of the leading Jewish families in that city. Among others whose names are well known were the Somechs, the Sophers, the Gubbays, and the Sassoon family. To both of the latter the Kadoories are related by marriage. 'The two families, Sassoon and Kadoorie, were merchant farmers,' according to Lawrence Kadoorie. 'Currency for trade in those days,' a hundred and more years ago, 'was in the form of flocks of sheep often left in the care of nomads who, as it were, acted as bankers for the owners.'

Lawrence tells the family story with great clarity. 'My father, Eleazar Silas Kadoorie, later to become Sir Elly Kadoorie, was one of seven children. He arrived in Hong Kong, via Bombay, on 20 May 1880, to join the firm of E.D. Sassoon and Company. His position was that of a clerk, at the princely salary of 37 rupees a month. His elder brother, Moshi, who had preceded him, was also employed in Sassoon's and later, in 1883, he was joined by a younger brother, Ellis (later Sir Ellis Kadoorie).

'In due course, my father was transferred to North China where he spent some time in the Treaty Ports of Shanghai, Weihaiwei, Tientsin, Wuhu, and Ningpo. Many are the stories he had to tell of those early days. But one, a minor event which took place while he was at Ningpo, had a major effect upon the future of the family and, as it turned out, of Hong Kong.

'Due to the absence of the manager, my father was left in temporary charge of E.D. Sassoon's office in Ningpo. An outbreak of plague in that city caused him to withdraw a barrel of disinfectant from the stores without the permission of his senior manager. For this

he was severely reprimanded. Feeling this was most unjust, he protested to such an extent that he was sent back to Shanghai to report to the Head Office. There, he was told not to argue but to obey. His further protests resulted in his being fired, and ... he returned to Hong Kong where his brother Moshi gave him HK$500 and told him that was all he could expect! No doubt this happy occurrence upon which the family fortunes are founded should be depicted by a barrel of disinfectant, rampant, on the Kadoorie coat of arms!

'My father then set up as a broker. He was generally liked, and with native intelligence, hard work, and good luck managed to build up his fortune.' Sir Elly, with Mr. Sassoon Benjamin and Mr. George Potts, set up the brokerage firm of Benjamin, Kelly and Potts which became the leading brokerage firm in Hong Kong and played a large part in promoting China Light & Power as a local company. This connection played an important part in the strong friendship which developed between Sir Elly and Robert Shewan. Toward the end of the 1890s, the young "Kelly," as his friends now dubbed him (and it was the name he used in the brokerage firm), visited England. There he met the Sephardi philanthropist Frederick Mocatta whose niece Laura Mocatta he married in 1897. He brought her out to Hong Kong – a place and a type of life which she found at first very hard to become accustomed to. The Mocatta family, who were of Spanish origin, left Spain for Holland at the time of the Inquisition. Later they settled in England where, in the year 1684, they established the firm of Mocatta and Goldsmid. This company has been bullion broker to the Bank of England since 1696.

Lawrence Kadoorie recalls the restrictive atmosphere of those times. 'Hong Kong was always snobbish. It still is, a little bit, but nothing like its former type of snobbery – which literally ran in layers. Government House [Mountain Lodge, the governor's summer residence] was on the Peak, the very top. And as you went down, the social strata descended accordingly. So anybody living in Kowloon was very far away from anybody living above May Road. It was a big status symbol to live *above* May Road. The whole atmosphere from the point of view of anyone coming out from England who had any situation at all was surprising. They couldn't at first understand what was going on. When my mother came out in 1898, she also suffered

Left: Sir Elly Kadoorie, a photograph taken about 1939

from this somewhat unfriendly reception. There were all sorts of things you had to conform to – like leaving the right number of cards and bending the corners to show you actually left the card yourself. Until an old resident put a card in your box, thus recognizing your existence, protocol forbade the newcomer to call.

'Kowloon had definitely a small-town atmosphere compared to the big city. It was a place where people went for picnics. In those days there were no motor cars. So people had launches and went over to Gin Drinker's Bay. Gin came from Holland in square stone bottles. You took a case with you, I was told, and went to Gin Drinker's Bay, and by the time the orgy was over, you had somehow to manage to get back again!'

Such was the kind of life that Westerners found themselves partaking of, in the Hong Kong of those former times. In this general context – or outside it, in the case of the Kadoorie family, and many others too – the events of the inter-war years took place, and the story of China Light must be viewed.

Lawrence Kadoorie, aged forty in 1939

90

Lawrence Kadoorie was born in Hong Kong in 1899, and his brother Horace in London in 1902. During the next ten years their father, with his partners George Potts and Sassoon Benjamin, succeeded in building up their firm Benjamin, Kelly and Potts to become the premier brokerage house in Hong Kong.

In 1910 Sir Elly and his wife decided to retire to England where their children were at school. But business requirements unfortunately obliged them to return to the East in the following year. Sir Elly then re-established a head office in Shanghai in 1911. A few years later, in 1914, the family foregathered in Canada for the summer holidays. During that vacation the First World War broke out, making it impossible for the boys to return to England. The large party, augmented by friends, ran out of cash but finally managed to return to Shanghai where they spent the remainder of the war years.

'There never was and never will be another city like Shanghai between the two wars – a city of extreme contrasts, combining the attributes of East and West. The Paris of the Orient ... a paradise for adventurers. Here my brother and I continued our education – the international outlook of Shanghai broadening ours and giving us an understanding of what it was to become a citizen of the world.'

In the early 1920s Sir Elly bought a house in London at 6, Princes Gate, and it was there that they entertained King Faisal of Arabia and Emperor Haile Selassie of Ethiopia, enlarging their circle of friends in France and England.

Lawrence Kadoorie recalls how 'one Saturday afternoon in London, it was pouring with rain, a horrible day. The front door bell rang and who should be outside in a very wet raincoat but Robert Shewan. He said, "Oh, Kadoorie, I was passing and came in. Can you help me out? Can you let me have some cash. It's Saturday, and I can't cash a cheque and I'm stuck."'

Mr. Shewan stayed for tea. During the course of this he remarked he had just had a cable offering him St. George's Building in Hong Kong, of which he already rented the first floor. He asked whether he ought to buy the building, to which Sir Elly replied: 'By all means you should take it. Why don't we make a little company? I have a piece of land in Kowloon, and there's the rope company in which I have

Sir Elly Kadoorie (right) in Paris in the 1920s with, it is thought, King Faisal of Arabia

interests. Let's make it a company and call it Territorial Estates.'

In due course this came about. But then the bottom dropped out of the Hong Kong property market forcing Sir Elly, eventually, to take over the company and thus to acquire St. George's Building.

Lawrence was a pupil in the chambers of the well-known barrister, J.E. Salmon, and later became a student at Lincoln's Inn, eating several dinners there but never having time to complete his legal studies and be called to the Bar. Horace wished to become a farmer, but again pressure of family affairs made this impossible. Early in his career he took over the running of Marble Hall (the Kadoorie home in Shanghai), an experience which stood him in good stead when he became chairman of the Hongkong & Shanghai Hotels Limited.

The family interests in this company extend back to last century, and are particularly evident in the Peninsula (owned by Hongkong & Shanghai Hotels Ltd.). Horace Kadoorie is less well known to the man in the street than his elder brother Lawrence, perhaps because of his quiet and self-effacing disposition. His preference has always been to make his contribution to worthwhile projects from the background, whether these were business or social in nature. His contributions in many fields of life have nonetheless been recognised, and he has been honoured by many governments and institutions. In 1976 he became Commander of the Most Excellent Order of the British Empire, and in 1981 received the Honorary Degree of Doctor of Social Sciences from the University of Hong Kong. Prior to these honours, Horace had been made Chevalier de la Légion d'Honneur in 1939, and received the Solomon Schechter Award from the World Council of Synagogues in 1959: the Ramon Magsaysay Award for Public Service was awarded him in 1962, while in 1966 he was made an Officier de l'Ordre de Léopold.

Continuing, Lawrence Kadoorie said, 'Marble Hall was the house my father had commissioned to be built during his absence from Shanghai. Unfortunately the architect, a certain Mr. Graham Brown, a stepson of the famous actress Marie Tempest, took to drink, with the result that this residence became a palace. To put it mildly, it was something of a surprise to us, upon our return to Shanghai, to find the architect in hospital with the D.T.'s, and a house with a ballroom 65 feet high, 80 feet long, and 50 feet wide, and a verandah 225 feet long. However, the real shock came when the contractors produced orders showing that the architect had in fact commissioned these splendours which we were now called upon to pay for.

'Happily, my father was fond of entertaining friends, and Marble Hall became well known to visitors from all parts of the world. Today, under the People's Republic of China, it has become a Children's Palace.... It is pleasing to know that this house, of which my father became particularly fond, is now used by thousands of happy children benefitting from the courses provided.

'It has been a long tradition in the Kadoorie family to share their good fortune with others. My uncle, Sir Ellis, built a number of schools in Hong Kong, Canton, and Shanghai. Basically these ... were intended to provide Chinese students with a background in English ... to assist them in obtaining work with the foreign firms.... In those early days these non-denominational institutions were par-

The ballroom of Marble Hall in Shanghai

ticularly appreciated by Chinese families since the only alternative Western education available for their children was in Mission schools.

'My father concentrated on building schools and hospitals, particularly in the Middle East. His choice of schools for girls and their location was inspired by the fact that at that time women received no education other than at home. These institutions were administered by the Alliance Israelite of Paris, and the Anglo-Jewish Association of London. My father ... made it a condition that all children, irrespective of religion, were welcome. The impact was that girls, now benefitting from a good education, demanded equality of intelligence from would-be husbands rather than just submitting to their parents' choice. Perhaps we can claim to have started a "Women's Lib" movement!

'My uncle, father, brother Horace and I took a personal interest in and contributed to Jewish Community affairs in Hong Kong, Shanghai, and elsewhere. In 1937–38 ... Horace played a most important part in caring for the several thousand Jewish refugees from Russia, Germany, and Austria.... Horace founded the Shanghai Jewish Youth Association and had a lot to do with the Shanghai

Jewish School. These ... created the foundation upon which many of the children of the refugee families later became successful citizens in other areas of the world, particularly in the United States. It is largely due to him that the Jewish youth in Shanghai were given the spirit and incentive to look forward to the future with hope and confidence...'.

Apart from business contacts and his considerable influence in financial circles Sir Elly donated, in Shanghai, a Tuberculosis Sanitorium, a dermatological section in the Sun Yat Sen Hospital, and also other medical facilities. For his benefactions throughout the world he was made a Knight Commander of the British Empire (KBE) in 1926. Among other honours which Sir Elly received were both French and Chinese. He was made Commandeur de la Légion d'Honneur, received the Grande Médaille d'Or de l'Académie Française, the Médaille de la Reconnaissance de France, and the Médaille d'Honneur du Mérite Syrien, Première Classe Or, in 1933. The First Class Gold Medal was awarded him by the National Government of China, and the Order of Brilliant Jade, 1923–24.

Horace remained with his father in Shanghai while Lawrence returned to Hong Kong to re-open the office there. And in 1938 he married Muriel Gubbay, the grand-daughter of Mrs. Gubbay who had befriended his mother upon her arrival in Hong Kong.

Lawrence Kadoorie first joined the board of China Light in 1930 at the age of thirty-one. But his connection with the company went much further back than that date. 'I used to accompany my father to meetings with Robert Shewan, and became virtually his ADC from the age of eighteen onwards, being with him all the time. I remember going to some of the meetings in the former St. George's Building, where Shewan Tomes had the whole of the first floor.'

Mr. G.A. Noronha, later to become chief accountant of China Light, was at that time working at Shewan Tomes. He recalls Lawrence and his brother Horace as young men in the 1920s 'with pink cheeks, down from Shanghai.' Later, when Lawrence had become a director of China Light, Noronha characterises his approach to staffing as 'a strong belief in localization (as it is now called),' that is, of employing local people when suitably qualified ones were available. And this was perhaps the influence of Robert Shewan directly, but also indirectly through Sir Elly who was Shewan's close friend. Noronha recalls the two of them pacing the long wide corridors of the old St. George's Building, deep in discussion. In those days and until well after the Second World War, the accounts departments of both Shewan Tomes and China Light – and the great halls of the Hongkong & Shanghai Bank – were very definitely the province of Hong Kong Portuguese with a thick scattering of Chinese. Since that time, however, the Portuguese element has diminished as Portuguese increasingly tend to find jobs in the West, in preference to their native Hong Kong.

Sir Elly's first connection with China Light was in fact at the very inception of the Company. He was one of the original seven subscribers to the Company's Memorandum and Articles of Association, and his firm provided the sole capital not contributed by partners or employees of Shewan, Tomes & Company.

There are numerous accounts of Sir Elly, but perhaps that of Mr. C.F. Wood, formerly general manager of China Light, may stand for all as typical. 'He was a bouncing ball of energy and kindness. I got married in the late thirties before the war and moved into a Company house [Strafford House] at Tai Po Kau. The construction was so bad that whenever it rained the place leaked like a sieve. One day Sir Elly arrived in the rain and saw the basins in each room catching the streams of water. He noted this, said nothing, and in a matter of days had the roof fixed up for me.

'He was a man who didn't like red tape, a law unto himself, and expected all the jobs he asked for to be done immediately. A *real* gentleman. In the late twenties and the thirties it was the start of a new era. He used to say – to hell with permits. He was a tough taskmaster, fond of a good-looking finished job (and a good-looking woman too). He was a very human person, mostly lived in Shanghai and came down in September for the end of the financial year, and to see all he had wanted done had been accomplished. He loved gardens, and when I was making one in Tai Po Kau he gave me a lot of advice. The following year he remembered, and congratulated me on my success in having followed his ideas.

'One thing that perhaps above all characterised him was his acceptance of total responsibility for any job he asked to be carried out.'

Shanghai was a fascinating place in those days, Lawrence recalls, international, sophisticated, and quite unique. Many famous and important people visited the city providing opportunities for entertainment to be given – all of it in homes. In the 1920s, life everywhere was far easier and more gracious than it is today. People weren't in such a hurry. The climate of Shanghai was delightful – about two months of very hot weather, and then cold brisk winters. It was a place where you could dance all night, go riding at 6 a.m., then work all day and not feel tired.

But life for the Kadoories was far from being a round of pleasure. The impression survives strongly, in all the reports of their activities, of men dedicated to whatever task they encountered or which they set for themselves. Whether it was founding and guiding the activities of this or that hospital or other charitable institution, or taking an active and detailed interest in their investments in a vast array of quite diverse companies, the quality that stands out first and foremost is that of application, diligent attention to detail combined with breadth of vision and an eye always moving ahead to the future and what it might bring.

Allied to these qualities is an unostentatious generosity, a recognition that their own good fortune must be shared with others. Perhaps the largest single benefactors in the Far East over the last decades have been and still are the Kadoories.

Much will be said in later pages of this volume about Lawrence Kadoorie and his connection with China Light; but here, in a brief chronicle of the Kadoorie family, some of the honours and distinctions which he has been given must find their place.

In 1970 he was made a Commander of the Most Excellent Order of the British Empire, and a Knight Bachelor in 1974. Other honours previously awarded include: the Solomon Schechter Award from the World Council of Synagogues in 1959; the Honorary Degree of Doctor of Laws, University of Hong Kong, in 1961; the Raymon Magsaysay Award for Public Service in 1962; Officier de l'Ordre de Léopold in 1966; Knight (Associate) of the Most Venerable Order of the Hospital of St. John of Jerusalem in 1972; and Officier de la Légion d'Honneur in 1975; and Commandeur de la Légion d'Honneur in 1982.

These honours awarded to Sir Elly and his two sons are by no means unrelated to the history of the Company. At the period when this volume ends, in 1982, China Light and the Kadoorie family have become all but synonymous. Honours coming to them naturally reflect honour on the Company also – the two having been intimately connected for more than six decades.

As the present volume comes to its conclusion, Lawrence Kadoorie was to be the recipient of a unique honour which brought not only fitting reward for him, and by association also to the Company, but in a broader sense to Hong Kong itself.

With this historical overview of the Kadoorie family most writers of newspaper and magazine articles are content to lay down their pens. Not perhaps unnaturally – for the charisma of the past and its embodiment in the present in the person of the dynamic and entirely winsome personality of Lawrence Kadoorie inevitably make a very strong mark.

But in fact, as later portions of the Company's story amply demonstrate, the profound Kadoorie interest in China Light seems assured of a proper continuity in the younger generation of the family. Michael Kadoorie, thirty-nine in 1981, like his father and uncle before him, was educated in the West, in Switzerland in his case, and has, from his earliest childhood when he was a regular visitor with his father to the Hok Un power station, been closely connected with the business of the Company. R.J. McAulay, through his marriage to Michael's sister Rita, also has a basic stake with his wife, and has been a director since 1968.

Michael Kadoorie, became a director in the previous year, 1967. While the substantial business wisdom of his father, gained over a long life and in a directorial capacity of so many important and very diverse companies has proved and still proves of daily advantage to China Light, this mantle will undoubtedly fall largely, as the years pass, on the shoulders of Michael. In many ways the responsibility is one he has been brought up, and later trained by close involvement in the daily affairs of the Company, to assume with a certain personal as well as hereditary rightness.

Thus the story, starting with Sir Elly and his often cavalier style of management, modulated by his son Lawrence, whose style has been different from that of his wayward but brilliant father, looks like continuing. And continuing, unlike those wearisome serials to which the latter part of the century has accustomed us on television, with a definite *éclat*. Doubtless the sequel will demonstrate yet another style of management as the environmental factors impinging on the Company and on those who direct it alter with changing times.

Not by chance, is the company Sir Elly Kadoorie Continuation Ltd. so called. The intention is clear. The contemporary facts are equally clear in terms of that continuation.

THE LAST OF THE MANAGERS

In late 1930, Lawrence Kadoorie was invited to join the board of China Light. Sir Elly, his father, lived in Shanghai, and Lawrence moved to Hong Kong to look after the family business interests in the colony. While he held directorships in numerous companies with either a base or considerable interests in Hong Kong, from the beginning his keenest interest was to be centred on the development of electrical supply in Kowloon and the New Territories. The whole of his subsequent career stands as proof of this. In 1935, at the age of thirty-six, he became chairman of the board – the youngest director in the Company's history to hold the office. He was chairman again in 1939–1940, and during that year presided over the opening of the 'new station' at Hok Un. From 1956 to the present he has been continuously chairman.

In the year when he first became a director, the Company seemed to be on a very sound footing, and in fact at the annual meeting of the previous year, 1929, one of the shareholders, Mr. B.W. Bradbury, rose to his feet at the end of it and pronounced what must be characterized as an encomium. 'We have all listened,' he said, 'with the greatest pleasure to the chairman's speech on the working of the Company for the past financial year. It is a review on which we may all heartily congratulate ourselves.... After many years of patient waiting we may now fairly hope that the Company is at last beginning to reap the benefits of its enterprise. That [it] has been through very difficult and anxious times, we must all agree. That the difficulties ... inseparable from a pioneer venture have at last been successfully met and overcome, we can entertain no reasonable doubt.'

He went on to endorse the payment of a bonus to the entire staff of the Company, equivalent to a month's salary, in recognition of their good services. He could not refrain from awarding the 'full meed of praise to the Gentlemen of the Board. Most of us are aware that the Board [was] faced with unusual and complex problems during the past year....'

And certain it was that they were. For, once more, the attempt at amalgamation between the two electricity companies on either side of Hong Kong's harbour had been made. The factors involved were on the surface connected with the difference in tariffs for current exemplified by Hongkong Electric's charges of 14 cents for lighting and 5 cents for power, compared to the Company's 20 cents per kilowatt hour ever since 1921, 20 per cent higher. This charge was reduced on 1 October 1929, to a lighting rate of 18 cents and power rates at 7 cents per kilowatt hour. In both categories discounts were given to large consumers who paid up promptly. The explanation of the alteration in tariffs was given as being a special endeavour by the Company to assist users of power, and that lowering the lighting rate was simply in accordance with promises made at the start of the operation to raise the voltage and thus save on costs.

In fact, there had been murmurings for some time about the difference between tariffs on different sides of the harbour. In March 1929, the chairman of Hongkong Electric, Mr. C.G.S. Mackie, had been approached by shareholders (most of whom were shareholders of China Light) to consider amalgamation of the two companies. The first attempt to do this had been a decade before, and in 1922 the government considered for a time that such a step might be of benefit to consumers, but in the end the question was not followed up because of the problems that would have ensued in joining two companies with entirely different operating structures. These two episodes never came to public notice. But the present attempt attracted much publicity and had to be dealt with accordingly.

Yet other factors entered into the attempt by the Company's shareholders to amalgamate their own with another company. First was the standing of China Light shares on the stock exchange, which, at $13, compared unfavourably with those of Hongkong Electric at $58. The Hongkong Electric shares had been pushed up the previous year by one of what must be regarded as Hong Kong's typical rumour-booms. It had been put about that a bonus issue was on the cards, and in the ensuing rush to buy shares some of the stockbroking fraternity got their fingers badly burned. One, it is said, retired to Shanghai to escape the heat.

Thus, the shareholders of China Light, and the chairman of Hongkong Electric were in a comparatively strong position. This was perhaps boosted in the public and shareholding mind by knowledge of the intended electrification of the New Territories, the franchise for which was not in fact granted to China Light until later in the year 1929, but which was obviously known to be impending or at least in negotiation. The finances involved in such a venture were seen by many as being beyond the means of the Company at that time.

The story of the amalgamation attempt can itself be succinctly told. Mr. Mackie wrote to Mr. Shewan in very direct terms, putting forward several pithy points, all of which were valid in terms of finance and business sense. He pointed out that Hongkong Electric had spent eight and a half million dollars in the last eight years and that only $600,000 of this sum constituted 'new money' – the remainder, almost eight million, had come from surplus profit. In pursuance of the idea, he made the point that China Light would require to spend about $10 million in the next decade in order to develop their impending franchise for electrification of the New Territories; and that China Light's profit was only $530,000 while that of Hongkong Electric was $2,250,000. The amalgamation of the two companies would surely benefit both, and he proposed it be effected on the basis of one Hongkong Electric share for six of China Light.

Mr. Shewan, confronted by arguments that were in sober fact cogent and reasonable, boiled with anger. He saw, with understandable chagrin, all his long and persistent efforts to make China Light into a really viable company and to push it into the future in the New Territories, on the point of possible frustration. But, apart from being an optimist, he was also a man of emotional nature, an 'unhappy man' as one who knew him has described him; and the letter from Mackie got him on the raw. He replied to it, after consultation with the Company's directors, a month later. The directors, he wrote, could only agree to amalgamation 'on terms no less favourable to the shareholders of this Company than to shareholders of the Hongkong Electric Co.' He proposed an exchange of one Hongkong Electric share for two of China Light. He also wanted the inclusion of the Company's directors on Hongkong Electric's board, as well as compensation for redundant staff.

On capital expenditure in Kowloon in the ensuing decade, 1929 to 1939, he averred that this was unlikely to exceed $5 million – not the $10 million assessed by Mr. Mackie. Further: 'Our directors do not regard as equitable the offer for an exchange of shares in proportion to the respective gross profits for the past financial year of the two companies.... Our directors concede that the present day profits of your company are beyond comparison in volume with this Company, but they wish to emphasize the fact that those profits have grown largely as an outcome of the remarkable development, especially during recent years, of the Island of Hong Kong. It is, however, the opinion of our directors that, due to the peculiar configuration of the Island, further expansion on any large scale on this side of the harbour has its limitations.... On the other hand, Kowloon, the proper sphere of the Company's operations and with which it has grown, is relatively speaking only partially developed, and until comparatively recent times modern means of transport on any large scale were unknown there. But, as must be apparent to the members of your board, Kowloon is now rapidly assuming the aspect of a modern and up-to-date centre, its amazing growth at the present day being reflected in the substantial rise during the past half-year of the Company's earnings, and indications are not wanting that Kowloon bids fair to become in course of time a city that will outrival Hong Kong both in size and population.'

Once more, Mr. Shewan, in his indefatigable optimism, was to prove more right than even he could possibly have guessed. 'Therefore,' he continued, 'the future prospects of this young Company, intimately bound up as they are with the growth and development of Kowloon, are, so far as our directors can judge, exceedingly great.' The only point on which the chairman can be faulted in this reply – with its emphasis on the future as equally valuable with the present, is the fact that his anger (apparently) prevented him from signing the letter personally, and instead allowed, in rather poor taste, a clerk to sign for Shewan Tomes.

In return, Hongkong Electric offered an exchange of one share to five of the Company's, which, after a hush lasting all of five months, was turned down.

The affair was then complicated by the intervention of a group of over thirty well known Kowloon businessmen who sent a petition to Hongkong Electric requesting them to supply Kowloon with power at the prevailing (cheaper) Hong Kong rate, via a cross-harbour cable.

Hongkong Electric, realising that this entailed not amalgamation but direct intervention in the China Light field of operation, wisely consulted the government. In the corridors of power the matter apparently received what civil servants are wont to call 'due consideration,' (this process taking a ponderous four months). The reply to Hongkong Electric stated that 'Government does not as at present advised consider it desirable to grant facilities for this scheme.'

'The invasion plans,' as the historian of the Hongkong Electric Company (succinctly as its former chairman, Mr. Mackie) states the matter, 'were put away.' In fact there was, between the original reply by Mr. Shewan and the cancellation of invasion plans, a lengthy correspondence with many a subtle argument on both sides. The crisis eventually passed when the government's reply was made known.

There can be no doubt at all that, tardy and dilatory as government was, opportunist and ill-advised as were the Company's renegade shareholders, the amalgamation would not have been a good idea. The whole style of the two companies was quite distinct, one from the other. The Hongkong Electric Company was run much more in the manner of a normal large undertaking, business-like and bureaucratic. China Light was very largely the child of Mr. Shewan, and had been moulded by his unusual share of optimism and future-gazing so that it had become very much a reflection of his personal vision and style of management. The melding of two such diversely run concerns would have been at least traumatic, possibly worse than that.

With this crisis out of the way, and the disaffected shareholders who precipitated it doubtless suitably chastened, and having returned to the Company's fold, the immediate future must have looked bright enough. To Mr. Shewan, it certainly did. He was, by 1930, a man of seventy years and had been with the Company for almost thirty of them. Had he but known it, his long service was nearing its end. But not quite immediately.

When Sir Elly Kadoorie joined the board of China Light, it was in Hongkong a time of changes in governmental outlook under one of the finest governors the Colony ever had – Sir Cecil Clementi. Perhaps in some sort of response to the social and political alternations in life after the First World War, the Colonial Office in London made, for a change, a better choice than usual. Certainly in Hong Kong his governorship from 1925 to February 1930, was one in which a lot of antique and outworn red tape and bureaucracy in general was swept away.

Sir Cecil was a fluent Chinese speaker and also, an accomplishment almost unique in the ranks of the administration, a good calligrapher. He was more than a good administrator, and he was a diplomat too.

Mr. J.P. Braga, about 1939

These talents were precisely what were required, at this time especially. His efforts in the normalization of Sino-British relations culminated in the recognition of the Kuomintang as the government of China.

Under his rule Kowloon progressed rapidly, with new reclamations at Sham Shui Po, Lai Chi Kok, and at Kai Tak where the Colony's first airport was opened in 1928. Sir Cecil was the promoter of the Shing Mun Valley reservoir scheme which, in addition to alleviating the chronic shortage of water which Hong Kong had suffered since its inception (and was indeed to continue to suffer until the 1970s), also had the effect of bringing the New Territories into more prominence than had been the case formerly. The circular road round the area had long been completed (in 1920), yet it could hardly be said that the New Territories was more than a backwater until the latter part of the decade. Under Sir Cecil, the government received suggestions from China Light on how a supply of electricity could best be brought to the countryside in order to encourage progress in the small towns of the area.

Sir Elly Kadoorie, ably assisted by another board member who had joined the Company shortly after he did, Mr. J.P. Braga, a man who was also interested in opening the New Territories, saw to it that a suitable scheme was drawn up. This was eventually submitted to a specially convened meeting of senior government officials under Sir Cecil.

The meeting was not achieved without difficulty, according to Lawrence Kadoorie. Opinion in business circles at the time ran against the idea of China Light electrifying the New Territories. It was deemed too big a job for them. 'My father, Sir Elly,' Lawrence Kadoorie recalls, 'with J.P. Braga, simply said: "We can certainly do it." But every time they tried to get a meeting with someone in the PWD they were stuck. There seemed no way to get their opinion over, until Mr. Braga, who was the first Portuguese to be on the Legislative Council, spoke to the Governor. Sir Cecil Clementi, apparently, replied that a meeting was essential. "I want to clear the whole thing up," he said. Braga replied confidently, "We've not been allowed to talk, but we can do it."' The Governor was about to depart for Singapore on business, but he arranged a meeting at nine in the morning in the dining-room of Government House. 'All the government officials were there, and the Governor asked my father: "Can you really do it – they say you can't." And Sir Elly replied: "Of course we can, we are willing, and we have the money."'

'After various discussions and explanations the Governor was convinced that China Light was capable of doing the job. He asked, looking round the officials: "Why has it been held up like this?" There was a shamefaced silence. The proposals put by the Company were beside him, and he wrote in red on the papers: "This is eminently reasonable." Those speculators who had been buying Hongkong Electric shares were stuck with them as the price fell. And that was a turning point in China Light's history.'

Thus, in the face of formidable opposition and after great delay, approval was obtained. This resulted in the signing of an agreement for the supply of the New Territories on 30 November 1929, between the Director of Public Works and China Light. Everyone realised at the time that this did not signify the immediate expansion of the Company's business but that, rather, it set the scene for ultimate expansion and growth of the Company – in step with Hong Kong as a Colony. The Island of Hong Kong was recognised by all (except the die-hards of the Hongkong Electric Company who continued to argue to the contrary) to have both geographical and size limitations. The fortunate coincidence of a forward-looking and powerful governor with ideas for the New Territories, and the presence of at least two men – three, if we include Mr. Shewan – on the Company's board and management with similar opinions and aims, effected the new look that came over both official and private views on the subject at that time.

Within the Company itself it was felt that before embarking on the physical expansion of its supplies, sound technical advice should be sought on how best to achieve the desired results. Accordingly, the senior partner of Preece, Cardew & Rider, consulting engineers in London, came out to Hong Kong. Mr. (later Sir) A.H. Preece, before his arrival, doubtless had the benefit of general knowledge of Hong Kong electricity matters from the firm's previous involvement in advising Hongkong Electric in 1914. After investigations on the spot, Preece made his first report to the Company in 1929, and followed it by a second in 1931. His view was that what the Company needed was a new power station. The suggested ultimate capacity of such a station was set at 120,000 kW.

The London firm acted as consultants not only on the design and equipping of the new station but also in matters concerning transmission, most importantly in the New Territories. A contract for the main sections was awarded to Calendar's Cable and Construction Co. in July 1930.

The story of the construction is told by Mr. C.F. Wood, later general manager, who had not long joined the Company at this juncture. His father was in South America, and Wood himself was born in Chile. 'I was young and enthusiastic about an overseas job, and in England life after the General Strike of 1926 didn't look too bright. The post of district engineer for China Light was advertised in England at the equivalent of £40 a month. So I applied, was accepted, and came out. I stayed at the YMCA for the first six months. The charges, all-in, including food, were $110 monthly!'

He was assigned to Yau Ma Tei area as his district. 'You had no office, just a chair and a table in some substation. Walking from the Peninsula Hotel [next to the YMCA] to Hok Un station in those days, about 1930, there were just a few scattered villas. In fact when my ship docked at Kowloon on arrival from England I took one horrified look at the place and wondered what the hell I'd come to. The buildings more or less stopped at Austin Road. Kowloon Tong had a small group of villas. The road to Hok Un was narrow and lined with trees, and there was street lighting of a kind. "Twinkle, twinkle, little star!" It was all 100 watt (or even smaller) lamps, more token than

106

'Erecting overhead electric transmission lines' is the caption on this hand-coloured photograph from the 1920s

lighting. The government was mean about paying for any better. Chatham Road came to an end at Wu Hu Street because there was a hill, and then you went right and then left to reach Hok Un.

'It was an odd place in those days. Some of the cinemas used large blocks of ice inside to keep the customers cool in summer. Hok Un had a load then which is less than that of any big commercial building today. I had my salary of $400 a month and $100 housing allowance.

'In six years I was promoted to resident engineer, New Territories –

the youngest contract engineer from Britain – quartered at Ping Shan Land Office near Yuen Long. There was no electricity there, no one could afford it and the price of kerosene was very low. Naturally enough an electricity supply to the quarters was installed in record time!'

The transmission went underground from the Hok Un station to Kowloon Tong and thence via the Lion Rock railway tunnel to Beacon Hill substation. There, the 6,600 volts were transformed to 22,000 volts and carried by the New Territories line 'over the hills to Shing Mun Reservoir Valley, over every bloody mountain you could see.'

The districts of Sha Tin, Tai Po, Au Tau, and Fanling were supplied, and the line continued to Kwan Tei – 'the position marked for the glorious dream of supplying light to China!' Then it struck onward at 6.6 kV to Sha Tau Kok. Meanwhile, 6.6 kV lines were erected in the Tsuen Wan area to supply the Texas Oil Company and the new brewery. The oil company was the first large consumer in the New Territories.

'It was a bad line to maintain,' as Mr. Wood remembers it, 'passing through several areas prone to repeated and heavy lightning which chipped or shattered the insulators of the transmission towers. Between Yuen Long and Tai Po groups of engineers and workmen used to run a competition on how long it took to get the power on again. There was no telephone, so communications were bad. The line was poorly surveyed in some places, and one tower had been built rising from the dry bed of a stream. Come the rains, it collapsed. Another tower was demolished by the tin roof of the contractor's shed which was blown at it in a high wind.'

The work on the line began in 1930 and was completed the following year. Then another 22 kV branch line was built from Tai Po Market to Au Tau, and from there a 6.6 kV extension went on to Castle Peak via Yuen Long and Ping Shan, being brought into use before the end of 1932. The further line from Kwan Tei to Sha Tau Kok was built later. Thus the Company's undertaking to government to supply electricity to practically every important centre in the New Territories was fulfilled.

Meanwhile, substantial improvements had been made in the urban distribution network. A system of ring feeders was formed as early as 1927 to accommodate increasing demand in Sham Shui Po, Kowloon Tong, and Kowloon City. An overhead line went out to Diamond

Hill in 1930, and the following year saw the completion of the tedious voltage change operation which had involved, among other details, the rewiring of hundreds of fans all over the area and alterations to a number of domestic appliances.

Business was beginning to be more lively. In 1929 the Company secured the contract to supply the Green Island Cement Co. at their Hok Un plant which, when it commenced operations in 1931, added 11 million kWh per annum to the demand from the power station. And in the next year, 1932, electricity sales rose by an astonishing 68.3 per cent – a record never since equalled by the Company.

This new contract provided for bulk supply of power at extremely low rates. And from this time onward China Light actively promoted a policy of assisting and promoting industrial development by the use of electricity, something which has been central to the development of Kowloon, and much later the New Territories, as a major manufacturing and industrial conglomerate. With expansion into the New Territories, other bulk supply agreements were concluded with new customers in 1932 – the South China Brickworks at Castle Peak, the brewery at Sham Tseng, and the Castle Peak Ceramic Co.

But the number of ordinary consumers in the New Territories remained a mere handful for quite a long time to come. As the first year of supply there ended in 1932, there were only slightly over 600 of them; and five years later a few more had joined the ranks to make a miserable total of 872.

Inevitably – such is the inescapable fact of an electricity company's life – with an average growth rate of about 20 per cent in output between 1926, and 1932, the time now came around for ordering yet more generating plant. But there was no space to put it. So, to make the necessary space, two of the oldest boilers at Hok Un, each with a capacity of 10,500 lbs. steam per hour, were sold in 1928. They were replaced by a John Thompson boiler, rated at 40,000 lbs. per hour, which was received and erected in 1932. Two more British Thomson-Houston turbo-alternators of 5,000 kW each came on stream in 1931 and 1932. And there were equipment problems related to the change of frequency, requiring in 1931 the installation of two Brush frequency-changers to serve part of the last remaining 60 cycle area.

Then, in 1932, a Babcock & Wilcox boiler of 60,000 lbs. per hour capacity was ordered. Two years later this unit was in operation, completing the generating capacities of what was to be known later as the 'old station' – which at that point had a capacity of 19,500 kW.

At this point in the early 1930s Horace Kadoorie, the younger son of Sir Elly, joined the board of China Light for a time. He rejoined the board in March 1946, and has been a director ever since. His business interests are widely spread, but he has always devoted much of his time to social and charitable work in many parts of the world. 'A charming host and the acme of kindness,' as one director characterises him.

'My brother and I have always worked very closely together,' Lawrence Kadoorie once said in a radio interview. 'We're very proud that in this family we have only one bank account and one cheque book, and have never kept accounts between ourselves.'

It was shortly after the Second World War that Horace Kadoorie had the idea of helping the people of the New Territories. 'They had suffered a lot and there was no organized charity or government help for them at that time. So Horace suggested an agricultural scheme. He had always been interested in farming and, with my father, in growing things.... As a result the Kadoorie Agricultural Aid Association was born. It was a three-part scheme. First, knowledge and expertise had to be supplied by the government. Second, we would supply the necessary finances. And third, the man receiving assistance had to join in and do the work.

'Our theory has always been to help someone to help himself.... That provides a basis for self-respect ... and has proved to be the scheme's success in that all three have been partners.... Since the ... inception in 1951, more than 300,000 people have been helped.'

In the first year of the 1930s, much greater continuity prevailed among the senior staff of the Company than formerly. Mr. J.H. Donnithorne who had been works manager until his retirement in 1928 was replaced by Mr. Cecil Strafford, a genial and competent man who had been with the Company as resident engineer in the early 1920s and had more recently been assistant works manager. He was succeeded in that position by Mr. D.W. Munton who (like Donnithorne and Strafford before him) had been on the staff of Shewan Tomes and had later filled the post of executive engineer (Mains Department). This department, later renamed Distribution Department, was headed by Mr. I.N. Murray, while the senior members of the generating staff were Mr. W. Armstrong, resident engineer, and Mr. F.C. Clemo, station superintendent – both having come from positions with Kowloon Docks.

The chief accountant was Mr. W.J. Brown who had been company secretary in 1924 and subsequently took over the accounts. Mr. Noel Braga, one of J.P. Braga's sons, became secretary in 1925. Both Brown and Braga retained their positions until after the Pacific War. Mr. Brown formed the Kwong Wah Football Team in 1929 to encourage employees of his department in sporting activity, and he personally supervised all the training. This took place three times weekly and consisted of morning running and evening football practice outside office hours. Later on, the team took on Chinese staff from other departments and eventually was to become one of the more prominent participants in Hong Kong's football league.

At this time, too, the China Light Club was formed for local and foreign staff and a clubhouse put up on crown land near the Club de Recreio, in an area where nowadays the Queen Elizabeth Hospital stands. The club had a bar but no catering facilities, but whist drives, dances, and tennis all proved very popular. The club was completely destroyed during the Pacific War, and was not resurrected when peace came.

On 16 February 1931, the *Hong Kong Daily Press* carried an article headed 'Fifty Years in Hong Kong', which recounted the felicitations offered to Mr. R.G. Shewan 'when many friends called at his office to congratulate him on completing fifty years in the Colony [on 14 February]. The occasion was also one for sincere pride by the office staff and employees of the associated companies ... in some cases three generations being represented at the gathering.' Among a list of those present, most of whom were well known figures in Hong Kong, the name 'Fung Shiu Wah with his sons and grandchildren, Fung Ngan Chuen, Fung Ki Cheuk ... Fung Chik Man (compradore of Shewan Tomes)' strikes an almost forgotten chord. For Fung Shiu Wah is none other than the son of Fung Wah-chuen, Mr. Shewan's old compradore whose Canton power station China Light took over.

Two days before the report, the *South China Morning Post*, of which Robert Shewan was a director, gave prominence to the occasion of the

111

anniversary of his fifty years in the Colony, remarking with a certain irony that 'opinions may be divided as to whether this is a matter on which to offer congratulations. . . .'

The article then outlines his progress in Hong Kong since he arrived on St. Valentine's day 1881. Among the companies over whose 'destinies' he had presided were: The Green Island Cement Co., Hongkong Rope Manufacturing Co., China Light & Power Company, China Provident Loan & Mortgage Co., Sandakan Light & Power Co., and China Underwriters Ltd. 'All of these have at one time been, and three still are, under the management of the firm of which Mr. Shewan is the head, so that it can in truth be stated that he has very largely been the guiding hand in many of the principal industrial and commercial enterprises in the Colony. . . . By his kindly and generous disposition, Mr. Shewan has endeared himself to many and he will today be the recipient of a host of sincere wishes.'

The paper then prints under the slightly odd headline 'Valentines and Compradores' some reminiscences written by Mr. Shewan who, it is stated, 'only after much persuasion . . . consented to give the *Morning Post*' these words about his early days. He is a man 'who dislikes talking about himself.'

The reminiscences are as curious as the headline. 'It is 50 years,' he begins, 'since I was landed here on 14th February 1881 by the Messageries steamer "Yangtse". It was St. Valentine's Day, a great day with Mr. Samuel Pepys and his lady friends. People in those days were not above sending tokens of their affection and at this distance of time, I do not mind confessing that I too have tightened my belt and gone without my lunch for eighteen days in order to buy a Valentine which I am proud to say was the envy of all the female friends of the fair recipient.'

The statement strikes a strange note – what sort of a Valentine required the lunch money of eighteen days to purchase it?

'I had not been many days in Hong Kong before I was introduced to the compradore system, and a very pleasant help in time of trouble I found it. No visits to "Uncle"; all you had to do was to tell your creditors to take it to the compradore, who never said a word till Chinese New Year came round. Then, when he handed you a long account of receipts and payments, it invariably ended with the words "balance forwarded not got." As it was certainly "not got" we could only leave him to carry it forward.'

Mr. Shewan then recounts a series of slightly wistful, slightly nostalgic, and not very humorous anecdotes under headings such as 'Jesus's Pluck.' This latter tells the tale of a man called McCulloch of the firm named Turner who 'was another character. His clerk Jesus, in passing him at his desk, knocked down McCulloch's pen and was rather roughly compelled to pick it up. The way it was done seems to have ruffled Jesus, who retired to his desk to think it over. The result was that a laden inkstand came flying over the *punkah* above McCulloch's head drenching him with ink and, as McCulloch owned a shock of fiery red hair, he was a horrible sight as he rushed across to the club to get it washed. But McCulloch bore no ill-will; on the contrary he was full of surprise and admiration of Jesus's pluck.'

The flavour of these artless anecdotes seems to reflect a character that was certainly kindly, but one with rather small breadth in its appreciation of larger matters. Under the heading 'Thoughtful Solicitor' he wrote: 'Then there was the well known solicitor who was requested somewhat late at night to attend a sick lady who wished to make her will. The lady in question lived in a somewhat doubtful locality, and the lawyer friend, in telling the story afterwards at the Club, explained that he was somewhat diffident to undertake a mission of that kind at night. However, he dressed himself and went along, taking in addition to his paper a $100 bill. He found the lady suffering more from fright than any sickness giving the prospect of early death. One of his humorous friends, full of suspicion, asked him, "Why did you take a $100 bill?" To which was replied, "Well, I didn't know what would happen."'

Mr. Shewan ends his unrevealing tale with a sad enough little flourish. 'With all our ups and downs we lived joyous and even exciting lives and, if I now look back with sadness to those days, it is only because with two exceptions all the actors have left the scene, and but Mr. George Potts and myself remain to murmur "Superfluous lags the veteran on the stage."'

Later in that same year, 1931, the sad quotation from Samuel Johnson's *Vanity of Human Wishes* must have seemed even more appropriate to Mr. Shewan. For the Company began the process of divesting Shewan Tomes and its head of the positions of General Managers of China Light.

THE GREAT DEBACLE

By 1931, the board of directors of China Light came to the conclusion that it would be in the best interests of the Company if Shewan Tomes ceased to be its General Managers. This meant severing the Company from the guiding hand of Robert Shewan, the man who had in fact formed it long ago, and who had in large measure steered it through the troubles of the years.

There appear to have been two factors uppermost in the directors' minds in asking the shareholders to agree with them in this action. First was that direct management by the Company of its own affairs was much more in line with current thinking and practice in Hong Kong. Second, was the fact that as the Company's income rose, and it was then rising quite rapidly, the remuneration to which Shewan Tomes was entitled under agreements was getting out of all proportion to the services which that company rendered. Perhaps, too, there was another reason, not stated but known to those concerned – the increasing age of Mr. Shewan himself, with the infirmities that age brings to some, although by no means all, who have lived a highly active business life.

The agreements with Shewan Tomes were three in number. The first (in 1901) awarded them, on an annual basis, 5 per cent of the Company's gross receipts and a further $5,000 to defray office expenses. After the reorganization of 1918, a new agreement was made in 1919 whereby the annual commission was set at 5 per cent of the credit balance of the working account before allowances were made for depreciation, but after debiting that commission, plus the $5,000 expenses as before. Then, in 1927, a slight alteration in the terms was made – the $5,000 was omitted, China Light providing its own office and accounting services, and commission was fixed at 5 per cent of the working account before debiting depreciation or commission.

The last agreement resulted in payments to Shewan Tomes of $25,000 in 1927; $27,000 in 1928; $39,000 in 1929; $40,500 in 1930; and $42,800 in 1931.

The question of dispensing with the services of Shewan Tomes had arisen in theory during the proposed merger with Hongkong Electric in 1929, since that company had their own General Managers, Gibb, Livingston & Co. During the negotiations at the time, the sum of $500,000 was a figure mentioned as compensation to Shewan Tomes, one which that company regarded as far too small. They said then they would be satisfied with 10,000 Hongkong Electric shares which stood in 1929 at $55. Two years later, in August 1931, the same shares were at about $81.

Mr. A.H. Compton, about 1939

Seven months after his much-celebrated fiftieth anniversary as a businessman in Hong Kong, Mr. Shewan received a letter in mid-September 1931, signed by Mr. A.H. Compton in his capacity as senior director, offering $240,000 as compensation for termination of the relationship. This offer, on the face of things as they would have stood had Shewan Tomes taken the Hongkong Electric shares two years earlier, seems almost insultingly paltry. And Mr. Shewan replied on 26 September, stating that he was willing to accept $1,000,000 – a sum which was more nearly in accordance with what the Hongkong Electric shares would at that time have been worth.

Some further exchanges of letters failed to bring the two sides to an amicable agreement, and it was arranged that Shewan Tomes would cease to be General Managers as from 1 April 1932, the amount to be paid as compensation to be determined by arbitration.

This step had to be ratified by the shareholders of China Light, and they were notified of what was happening in a circular dated 15 February 1932. An extraordinary general meeting was called for 2 March. Since there were few premises suited to a gathering of what was expected to be a large crowd of shareholders for this important matter, it was decided to utilize a room in the offices of Lowe, Bingham & Matthews, the Company's joint auditors.

Addressing the meagre quorum on 2 March 1932, Mr. Compton explained the directors' certainty that they would be correctly interpreting shareholders' wishes by agreeing that Shewan Tomes must be compensated for loss of office as General Managers. While the 1927 agreement provided for settlement by arbitration, it was now felt that the usual method of two arbitrators, or their umpire, might not be the most satisfactory. The whole matter principally hinged on questions of legality – first as to the basis upon which compensation was to be paid, and second, as to the correct method of calculating that compensation. The directors had come to the conclusion that lay arbitrators would be unsuited to the task owing to the probability of appeals against their decision, first to an umpire and then to the courts. For similar reasons, direct legal proceedings were equally inadvisable. In the circumstances, and after considerable discussion, it had been decided that the Chief Justice, Sir Joseph Kemp, should be asked to take the case in chambers as a quasi arbitrator, which he was empowered to be if both parties concurred. Sir Joseph had been approached by the respective solicitors, and in principle he was willing to hear the case provided shareholders agreed, and if a writ were issued.

Mr. Compton stated further that the advantages of this method were considerable. There would be no question of appeal and there was no danger of the matter dragging on for a long period. And he thought that the case would be over even faster were it heard in chambers, thus reducing the costs in comparison with an action in open court. He promised that China Light would be responsible for Shewan Tomes' legal costs up to a sum of $7,000. 'And the last advantage is that your directors feel that there would be no possibility of either of the parties feeling dissatisfied with any award so obtained.'

The shareholders duly signified their approval of the plan, and they also passed a resolution changing the Company's Articles of Association

Sir Joseph Kemp

to provide for the elimination of references to General Managers, at the same time increasing the directors' fees from $10,000 to $23,000 per annum.

Lawrence Kadoorie, as a very young director, remembers sitting through the meeting when it was decided to go to arbitration. In an interview more than forty-five years later, he recalls how he noticed that the motion specified neither upper nor lower limits to the eventual award. Because he was young and felt himself inexperienced, he said nothing.

The Chief Justice agreed to hear the case. Notice of termination was served on Shewan Tomes, who at once replied by issuing the necessary writ (in Original Jurisdiction 80 of 1932). Mr. Compton's optimism, however, on the ease with which the matter could be settled, and indeed on the eventual satisfaction of the parties, proved unfounded. First, a great deal of time was spent on preparation for the case. Shewan Tomes assembled large amounts of evidence in support of their own cause and consulted a chartered accountant named S. Hampden Ross of the firm of Percy Smith, Seth & Fleming, and also Mr. E.R. Childe of China Underwriters, who was a qualified actuary. The upshot of this was a memorandum dated 8 July 1932, in which an opinion was expressed assessing the amount of compensation at about $1,200,000. This figure was arrived at in assuming reasonable profits over the years to come, and then obtaining cor-

117

responding present values with a discount of six per cent.

Hearings did not begin until 16 November. Mr. Eldon Potter, K.C. and Mr. H.G. Sheldon, instructed by Sir William Shenton of Deacons, appeared for Shewan Tomes. Mr. F.C. Jenkin, K.C., assisted by Mr. Leo D'Almada, represented China Light on the instructions of Johnson, Stokes & Master. It was in the course of this case that the young D'Almada made a name for himself as a junior to Mr. Jenkin, and in fact from the fees he received managed as a struggling counsel to afford to get married.

The arbitration process went on for over three months and involved 37 hearings, largely because the arbitrator preferred to record all the evidence and much of the submissions in long hand. Among witnesses for Shewan Tomes there appeared Mr. A.L. Shields who had been a partner in the firm since 1921, Mr. Hampden Ross, Mr. Childe, and Mr. James Carnegie, an American who had been superintendent of the Electric Power Administration of Canton.

For China Light, Mr. I.N. Murray gave much evidence. Various forecasts were offered, extending in range over a period of about fifteen years, and figures assumed by Sir Arthur Preece were also cited. Mr. Carnegie, using similar data to those of Sir Arthur, predicted a 1947 peak load of 47,000 kW, somewhat higher than Mr. Murray's figure. Such a peak load figure, once established, enables the calculation of electricity sales by multiplying by a known constant and then with the load factor; that is, the percentage of the average load in terms of peak load. For 1947, the load factor was estimated at about 39 per cent by Carnegie, and at about 29 per cent by Murray.

As a matter of fact, the estimate produced then, in 1932, for peak load for 1947 was very close to what, fifteen years and a World War later, actually turned out to be the case. Allowing for the wartime interregnum of five years and taking 1952 instead of 1947, the actual load was 47,800 kW. But none could foresee in 1932 the intensive post-war industrialization which brought in 1952 a load factor of about fifty per cent and sales of 211 million kWh.

The documents relating to the details of the hearing were lost in the war that was to come, and all that survives in terms of record of the proceedings is the typed copy of the Award by the Chief Justice on 24 February 1933, at the conclusion of the hearings. Sir Joseph pointed out that 'the appointment of a firm ... as General Managers of a company in perpetuity may be an undesirable contract, and it may be that a commission of five per cent on the balance of the working account provides, or would in future have provided, an excessive remuneration for the services actually rendered, but the present China Light & Power Co. (1918) Ltd. deliberately took over from the 1901 company the appointment of Messrs. Shewan, Tomes & Co. on those terms and incorporated it in their Memorandum and Articles in 1918 and again in 1927.... The undesirability of the contract, however, if it be undesirable, and the excessive nature of the remuneration, if it be excessive, are entirely irrelevant for the purposes of this arbitration, as is also the question of how the Company is to finance the payment of this award.'

Sir Joseph adduced arguments to the effect that Sir Arthur Preece's and Mr. Carnegie's data were on the high side. On the load factor, he accepted Mr. Murray's lower estimate of 29 per cent. Then he completed his summing up and made the award. 'The question of the period to assume for the purposes of calculation of the fund is a very difficult one. I am prepared to take a period of about fifty years. The Carnegie estimate for fifty years works out at $3,087,091. Making the correction for load factor and peak load indicated ... I award the sum of two million dollars.'

Lawrence Kadoorie's suppressed impulse to set limitations on the award they would pay had been the right one. China Light paid $1 million in March and the second million in April 1933. It was also required to defray costs of almost $125,000.

Lawrence Kadoorie recalls the shareholders' meeting held to inform them of the results of the arbitration proceedings. The large room in Ice House Street had been prepared and extra chairs brought in for the expected crowd. When the appointed hour arrived only nine people turned up – and ten were needed for a quorum. After waiting a little, the directors asked Noel Braga, the secretary, to go out and find a broker in the Stock Exchange, or some other shareholder. In due course Braga returned with an elderly Portuguese gentleman who was lame and walking with a stick. He was a shareholder, so the quorum was complete and the chairman began his speech. Suddenly, in the middle of it, the old Portuguese got up from his seat and, clutching his stomach, made for the door. Compton, the chairman, seeing his quorum about to disappear, cried: 'Stop him, stop him! Give him an inkpot or something!' And that was really the sole remarkable thing about the meeting.

Mr. Compton described the size of the award as 'a very severe blow.' But, he added: 'In spite of the fact that this amount was greatly in excess of anything that had been contemplated, I feel that I can say with confidence that this heavy charge will not in any way handicap the development of the undertaking.' That must have been euphoria, or self-deception. In fact the award amounted to about one third of China Light's issued capital. Paying it sent the Company deeply into debt.

Since then, at the insistence of Lawrence Kadoorie, China Light's balance sheet has continued to carry a debit of HK$1, a token of the written-down value of the award to the former General Managers.

'That $1,' he has said, 'does not represent the idiosyncracy of an ageing chairman,' as the auditors sometimes seem to think. 'It represents a basic step in the history of the Company, the day and the cost of its freedom and independence....' It is there to remind him and other directors that 'the price of success is constant vigilance. No detail is too small to be ignored....'

Subsequently, at various times, the financial directors on the board suggested that reference to 'compensation to general managers for loss of office' should be dropped from the report. On one such occasion, after an impassioned plea from the chairman that it should be retained, even if merely on grounds of historical record, one director remarked: 'Carried by a majority of one for reasons of *feng shui*'.

Movement of China Light Shares during Arbitration
Sept. 1931 – peak of about $26 (adjusted for subsequent rights issues = $32)
Nov. 1932 – about $16 (as hearings began – adjusted actual price $17.50)
Feb. 1933 – about $11 (recovered to $12)

Hong Kong Electric Shares (for comparison)
Sept. 1931 – $84
Feb. 1933 – $74

Note: The period coincided with the Depression in the Western world which, although it affected Hong Kong, was not a crippling blow

---

Thus, with shock to the Company, and – it is hard to see how it could have been otherwise despite the heavy compensation – with sorrow to Robert Shewan whose connection with it ended, this span of China Light's story came to its conclusion.

Shewan had retired in 1932 at the end of over thirty years with the Company, and returned briefly to his native Scotland. Then he came back to Hong Kong for reasons unknown.

On St. Valentine's Day, 14 February 1934, the eve of Chinese New Year, and exactly fifty-three years to the day since he first disembarked from the steamer 'Yangtse' in 1881, Robert Shewan was found dead in the garden of his house at 2, Conduit Road. *The Hong Kong Daily Press*, in an article on 16 February (no paper was published on the previous day which was Chinese New Year's day) remarked: 'His body was found at 6.55 a.m. ... and it is believed that he fell from his window while leaning out. The Police were immediately communicated with upon the discovery being made and Mr. Shewan was rushed to the Government Civil Hospital. On arrival, however, life was found to be extinct. Mr. Shewan was married in 1908 and is survived by his widow and a nephew Mr. I.W. Shewan.' I.W. Shewan was a director of the Company. Robert Shewan's wife never appears in reports of any social or other function; and with the statement from one who knew him that he was 'a lonely man,' we may assume that she was not in Hong Kong.

Mr. Shewan's will, dated 23 September, 1930, is signed 'Rob Shewan,' and there is no mention in it of his wife. He left various bequests – £5 each monthly to Miss Annie and Miss Maggie Shewan, of Peterhead, Aberdeenshire (perhaps his sisters); to a daughter of William Thomas Shewan, known as Eddie Shewan, England; to Mrs. George Eckley of San Francisco, about whom we know nothing. His trustee was his nephew I.W. Shewan (although a codicil to the will, dated 24 April 1933, after the award to Shewan Tomes, alters this to include Herbert Rothsay Sturt, the manager and secretary of China Underwriters Ltd., jointly with his nephew.) His real estate was left to his nephew with provision for trusts for the children of his brother Andrew Shewan, and his sister Marion Hogg. Brother Andrew, however, does not seem to have done well – for, something over a year later, he died in Poplar, Middlesex, leaving a total estate of £54.14.1 to his wife and son, a warehouse clerk.

Robert Shewan's funeral took place on 15 February 1934, and the principal mourners were his nephew and A.L. Shields, his former partner. A simple headstone marks the grave in the Colonial Cemetery in Happy Valley. Among others present at the funeral was Fung Chik Man, Shewan Tomes' compradore who was descended from the original compradore, Fung Wa-chuen, who probably started Rob Shewan in the electricity business so long ago.

BEFORE THE HOLOCAUST

ONCE arbitration was over and the Company had recovered, at least psychologically, from the financial blow of the award, the board of directors and the management began to work closely together in a new relationship in the running and planning of its affairs. Directors, of course, found that they had much more to do with the business of the Company on a day to day basis than previously, and it was probably with this in mind that it was decided that each (with some exceptions) should serve as chairman for a one-year period in rotation. They recorded in minutes their satisfaction at the wholehearted co-operation of the staff. The Company's manager, Mr. Strafford, retired in 1933, and to mark his term of service the Company, in acquiring a new building in Tai Po Kau for the residence of the New Territories district engineer, called it Strafford House.

Around the same period quite a number of other buildings were acquired: in Humphrey's Avenue a substation combined with a cash collection office and showroom; at Tai Po a cash collection office, and stores and quarters for Chinese employees. New substations were built at Ma Tau Kok and Lai Chi Kok, and that at Yuen Long was designed to house stores, cash office, and staff quarters as well.

The year 1935 saw the Silver Jubilee of Their Majesties King George V and Queen Mary, two of the best loved royal figures since the old Queen passed away. In London it was a glorious day of warm sunshine, memorable as one of the last royal events of moment before the King's death in the following year. This was followed by the short interregnum of Edward VIII, the abdication, the coronation of his brother as George VI – and the gathering of ominous clouds over Europe.

Hong Kong, in many ways still a very colonial place, celebrated that Jubilee in 1935, and China Light set up various 'illuminations' in Kowloon and parts of the New Territories, which seem to have been appreciated by the populace and especially by village elders and ordinary villagers. The acute flux of fortunes which characterized European life between the two world wars – the profound labour troubles of the 1920s, the Depression years, the political catastrophes of the 1930s with the rise of the Nazis and of the Fascists in Italy, had only rather pale reflections in Hong Kong. There seems not to have been a Nazi Party in Hong Kong, although there certainly was in Shanghai.

For the Company, the last few years of the inter-war period were generally years of progress. A new manager, Mr. D.W. Munton, ably assisted by Mr. I.N. Murray ran the technical side of things. The boardroom had lost the services of Sir Robert Hotung in 1933 when he relinquished his seat. He was replaced by Mr. Lo Cheung-shiu, for

Mr. M.K. Lo, about 1939

a brief period before his death, after which Mr. Lo's son, Mr. (later Sir) Man-kam Lo, joined the board.

Kowloon was growing. Large increases in population occurred in Yau Ma Tei, Mong Kok, Tai Kok Tsui, Sham Shui Po, and in Kowloon City. More and more factories were springing into being, not only in Kowloon but in the New Territories, and it was apparent that in due course more generating capacity would be required. The Preece reports had made it evident, however, that increased capacity, to be cost-effective, had to be achieved with the best new equipment obtainable to generate power. The report had indicated the desirability of a new power station. It was proposed to install initially a boiler and turbine yielding 12.5 MW, operating at a pressure of 400 lbs. per square inch, and therefore working at very much better thermal efficiency than were older units.

Sir Elly Kadoorie, looking ahead to a time of vastly increased demand, opted for a building big enough to house the plant capable of producing at least five times the power of the first machine to be installed. And the Company, as a preparatory measure, had acquired in 1935 the roadway which had previously separated the power station site from the newly reclaimed area, so that the land now extended all the way from the Green Island Cement Company to the beach next to Kowloon Docks. This, it was felt, would be enough room for whatever plant was required for increased production in the foreseeable future. As part of the new extension a modern workshop and store were put up on the new reclamation.

In 1934 a committee consisting of directors and senior staff was formed to deal with the extensions proposed. It met regularly for the next several years and made many important decisions based, quite often, on the advice of Preece, Cardew and Rider. The tenders for new plant numbered seven for turbines, and the committee took up the bid which, as far as could be seen at the time, offered the highest engineering quality. A 12.5 MW machine was ordered from Metropolitan-Vickers Export Co. of Manchester. The corresponding boiler was a three-drum vertical type with a capacity of 120,000 lbs. per hour, and the contract for this was signed with International Combustion Ltd. of Derby. The design of the necessary new buildings to house this and future equipment was by Mr. S.E. Faber, and the principal civil contractors were Hong Kong Engineering & Construction Co., Ltd. Mr. Faber had designed the power station in Shanghai and was well known to the Kadoories.

New generating capacity was one thing. To prove effective it had to be backed by an efficient and expanding distribution system. With the raising of the distribution voltage in 1922 from 2.2 to 6.6 kV, new switchgear was installed and new feeder cables laid. And in the same year a power line and special substation were constructed to supply electricity for the building of the Shing Mun Dam – an undertaking which took nearly four years to complete. This was the first time in Hong Kong that electricity from a central power station had been used on such a project. The usual procedure was for major constructions of this kind to provide their own generating equipment.

Right: Work on the foundations of Hok Un power station in 1937

In 1935 a high tension line (6.6 kV) was built to connect the step-down substations at Au Tau and Kwan Ti, and this new circuit also served Lok Ma Chau police station and the villages of San Tin, Mai Po, Nga Tam Mi, Chuk Yue, and Pok Wai. Simultaneously, it provided an alternative source of current in the districts of Sheung Shui, Fanling, and Kam Tin. In a period of intensive expansion even bathing sheds near various beaches were provided with light under special safety conditions, and the total area over which China Light operated was approximately 154 square miles.

Finances, in such a period, were obviously of great concern. The situation was complicated by several factors quite apart from the need for money to effect all the additions and extensions to the Company's services. One of these was the change-over by China in the mid-thirties from the former silver-based currency to paper currency. In the chaotic conditions of China in the decade before the Second World War the *yuan* had formed the guideline for the Hong Kong dollar which therefore fluctuated in relation to sterling in which most of the Company's purchases had to be paid. For some years before this change, the Hong Kong dollar had been high in relation to sterling, but it was now liable to drop. This would increase working costs but at the same time afford a competitive edge to young Hong Kong industries – thus encouraging the use of larger amounts of electricity.

The magnitude of the sums required for overseas purchases by the Company in its ongoing projects prompted the directors to authorize £85,000 sterling to be covered forward at $12.60 to the pound. And a fortunate move this proved to be when, about a year later, the Hong Kong dollar stabilised at around sixteen to the pound.

Another factor was the rising price of coal. Favourable contracts were made, ensuring delivery at old prices for the following twelve months. But after that it proved necessary to cope with costs continually escalating as the global catastrophe, which the wiser heads in the Western world saw approaching, was seen to threaten.

Costly coal provided an opportunity for some delivery contractors to use their ingenuity to add to income. The power station at Hok Un had no proper landing stage, and ships transporting coal had to anchor off at some distance in Kowloon Bay where they discharged into lighters that came alongside at the station yard. There, unloading was done by women labourers each carrying two baskets on the familiar shoulder-pole. As the lighters neared the landing stage in very shallow water, some of the coal would mysteriously fall to the bottom,

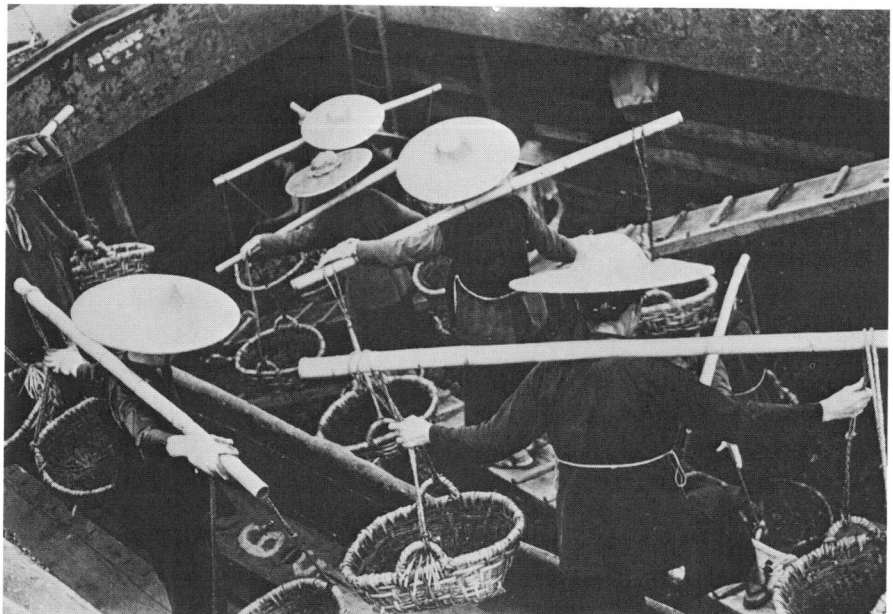

Hakka women unloading coal barges in the traditional way. This method was still normal when the photograph was taken in 1956

the lost weight being made up by water from hoses. At night the bulk of the dumped coal was salvaged by fishermen expert in this job. Unfortunately for this enterprise, the delivery contractors had reckoned without the knowledge that the Company's chemists could determine the water content of the coal supplied. So it was not as easy as it looked at first.

In 1936, Lawrence Kadoorie, the current chairman, surveying the scarcity of electricity supply in neighbouring Guangdong Province and the very high prices charged for supply, had the idea of providing power from Kowloon. At this time he made frequent trips to Canton, often with Mr. F.A. Joseph – a director who had joined the board in 1931. In Canton they were in touch with Mr. Sun Fo who was the leading member of the various political bodies which formed the local administration at the time.

The idea contemplated was that China Light should supply bulk power at low rates to a company to be formed by Mr. Sun Fo, which would then distribute it at a retail price competitive with the indigenous supply but still allowing a handsome profit. Meanwhile, the Hong Kong representative of Calendar's Cable & Construction Co., Mr. Barnes, was asked to make a survey for a line to transmit the current, to follow more or less the route of the railway from Beacon Hill to Canton.

The process reached the stage when an agreement was initialled by Mr. Sun and China Light, the occasion being marked by a luncheon given for Mr. Sun. This gargantuan feast of sixty-five dishes (not unusual, in fact, at this time in China) began at one o'clock and did not come to an end until four hours later.

Rumours of the impending deal caused a surge in price of China Light shares on the market, but the plans fell through because of a dispute between Mr. Sun and the local warload, General Chen Chi-tong. The general wanted to have a monopoly of the profits from opium shipments on the Pearl River in exchange for permission for Mr. Sun to operate the electricity monopoly. So what was a well-planned business venture eventually came to naught.

In a Colony in which, at that time, because of the size of share transactions, it was comparatively easy to manipulate the market, it is hardly surprising to discover that China Light shares were at one time the subject of just such manipulation – on one occasion by a well-known speculator.

In those days forward transactions on the Stock Exchange were permissible. The speculator, a man in the employ of a local company, who had been successful in a number of dealings in local shares, decided that China Light would be a stock on which to make a killing by selling 'short' – that is, selling at the price of the day with the shares thus sold to be delivered at a later day, known as 'settlement day.' This day was generally two or three months later when, by the speculator's calculation, the shares would have come down in value so that their purchase then to fulfill his obligation to deliver would net him a nice profit as against the price at which he sold them.

The speculator duly sold the China Light shares 'short.' Since his job by its nature involved personal contact with his employer's customers, he was able in the course of his duties (although it was no part of those duties) to wrap the purchase of each customer in a paper prominently printed with the words 'Sell China Lights'.

Not unnaturally, so small was Hong Kong in those days, the whole matter came to the knowledge of the chairman of China Light. He paid a call on the speculator's company and complained of an 'act of war' by the latter company. This put paid to these appallingly unethical, if highly ingenious, tactics by an employee.

Time was running out – for China, for Hong Kong. The Marco Polo Bridge incident near Beijing (Peking) on 7 July 1937, when the Japanese started their all-out war against China, was one formidable portent. During the following months Chinese coastal provinces fell one by one, forcing more and more people out of their homes, some of them into the Colony. It was in this period, with the fall of Shanghai and other heavily industrialised cities to the Japanese, that a boost of considerable dimensions was given to Hong Kong industry. Factory owners arrived, quite a number bringing the total equipment of their factories, and set up anew in the comparative safety of the British Colony. The combination of new industry establishing itself and the influx of refugee labour, proved to be the beginning of a radical alteration on the whole pattern of Hong Kong life and finance. Initially, this process was reflected in a substantial increase in China Light's sale of electricity. In 1938, the overall annual increase in sales was in excess of 30 per cent.

In a letter to a member of the Derby company supplying new equipment for the Hok Un station, dated 24 October 1938, Lawrence Kadoorie, after dealing with the business on hand, wrote in an apparently casual paragraph: 'Today Canton is reported to have fallen and, curiously enough, the reaction on the local stock exchange has been favourable rather than unfavourable.' And he added, prophetically, as it turned out: 'It is, of course, too soon to make any forecasts as to the future.' In fact, perhaps the majority of Canton's inhabitants had fled – some to Hong Kong – and by November there were Japanese faces on the other side of the border.

But, while the invading Japanese armies were creeping southward from Beijing in 1937, Hong Kong suffered another of its recurrent nightmares – one of the most severe typhoons for a long time. The storm arrived on 2 September with little or no warning – the Royal Observatory still apparently unable to predict such an event with any accuracy – and over ten thousand persons perished, casualties being disastrously high among the fisher-people. The damage to Company property was severe, and it took a great deal of money and arduous work to repair the ravages of that September day.

At this time, the construction of the new station at Hok Un was making good progress, and it was there that the station super-intendent, Mr. F.C. Clemo, was involved in an heroic rescue. Lawrence Kadoorie tells the story:

'I was living in the Peninsula Hotel at that time. When the typhoon was blowing hard, an old four-masted schooner called the *Shenandoah*, was anchored off, waiting to be broken up. She pulled her anchor and quickly drifted right up to the China Light wall where she carried away the water intakes and made a terrible mess. I was a director of the Kowloon Dock Company at that time, so I tried hard to get a launch or a tug. But no luck. The manager of the dockyard had a house on the Peak, and so did the deputy manager. In the 1937 typhoon they were stranded there.'

After some time Lawrence Kadoorie managed to get on to the police, but by the time their launch arrived on the scene the *Shenandoah* had drifted out from the Company's sea wall. Two officers from the police launch managed to board the vessel, and then a sound of hammering was heard coming from it. The officers then reboarded their launch and left. Later on, it was discovered that all they had done was to nail up a notice stating that unless the 'wreck' was removed within twenty-four hours the owners would be sued!

During the height of the typhoon, Mr. Clemo, hearing shouts coming from the *Shenandoah*, tied a rope round his waist and jumped into the turbulent sea. Somehow he managed to reach the vessel and by means of the rope managed to have her pulled in close. This manoeuvre resulted in the saving of eleven people from the ship, the party including some women and children. There was nothing to give to the rescued people to eat until Lawrence Kadoorie went off to the Peninsula Hotel and got hot food for them.

It was this typhoon which broke the anemometer calibrated for winds up to 150 mph, which the Hongkong Electric Company had recently installed. Its pen went off the upper end, and the eventual calculation was that the wind speed must have been over 166 mph. Tardily, the Royal Observatory ordered an instrument capable of recording winds of 200 mph.

With the new power station making quite rapid progress in construction, and with the load increasing faster than had been predicted, the company ordered another boiler from International Combustion Ltd. This one had a 200,000 lbs. per hour capacity and was again the tri-drum water tube type which, when complete, was to have the largest travelling chain grate stoker (the mechanism whereby coal was fed to the flames) in the world.

The 120,000 lbs. per hour boiler was commissioned in January 1939, and the 12.5 MW turbine in the following month. Thereupon intensive acceptance tests were carried out, proving that the new equipment fulfilled the range of requirements as guaranteed by its makers. This turbine was to have an eventful life, as we shall see.

The ensuing weeks saw the completion of the station, and preparations were then made for its formal opening which was to be performed by the governor, Sir Geoffrey Northcote. The preparations were quite elaborate, as befitted the occasion. The whole area of the boiler house, in which the second unit was nearing completion, which was as yet unoccupied by plant – indeed built to house future units as yet not ordered – was cleared, and many rows of chairs installed. Some fifteen hundred guests had been invited, some to arrive by ferry and some by car..

Many of the guests who attended the opening did not know the story of the perfectly ordinary wall near by. Around 1938, the Company asked permission of government to put up a wall between the stores and coal stocks, and the approach road and the station proper. Lawrence Kadoorie remembers that his father, who was on very friendly terms with the Chinese contractor who built the station, wanted to hurry on with it. Lawrence, however, replied that the board really did not have enough money to build it right then. However, at a meeting of the board shortly after that, Sir Elly suggested that some of the directors ought perhaps to pay a visit to the station. 'The wall you are all so worried about – it's already been built.' And indeed it had been. The engineers, Lawrence Kadoorie recalls, were so impressed by this somewhat cavalier action that they had a plaque cast which read 'Sir Elly's Wall.' Unfortunately it has been lost.

Some of the official guests from the Public Works Department must have been surprised by the wall since, because of their delay in authorising its construction, it was built without government permission. But nothing was said.

A system of coloured tickets had been devised so that guests would have easy access to seating in the boiler-house from the moment they arrived in the vicinity of the flag-bedecked building.

To the opening on 26 February 1940, all the shareholders, about a thousand of them, were invited, as well as a representative group of government officials and their wives, and of course many others connected with the construction and equipping of the station. There were two entrances to the boiler house where the opening was to take place, so arranged for convenience when such a large crowd was

Hok Un power station from the air in 1947. Sir Elly's Wall is by the oil storage tank. Staff quarters behind the station have drums of cable stacked between them

expected. One section of the crowd had been issued more or less at random with pink tickets for one entry, while the remainder had blue tickets for the other entry. No seats apart from those for the official party in the front row had been reserved. But, alas, when the time came and the crowds arrived someone had got the instructions totally wrong, and had placed several chairs as barricades and wired them together so that the pink tickets were divided from the blue, and the back section became hopelessly overcrowded – whereas there were rows of empty chairs in the front section to which no access was possible.

Lawrence Kadoorie, who was chairman that year, made the opening speech – part of which is quoted in the introduction to this account of the Company's history.

He underlined the progress made by the Company in difficult times in Kowloon when, 'what is Salisbury Road today ... was a fifteen-foot avenue skirted by two rows of banana trees interspersed with granite pillars surmounted with oil lanterns which shed their dim light on the few passers-by on their way to and from the single deck diminutive steam launch alongside the bamboo pier at Kowloon Point.... Not even the most lively imagination could have predicted that Banana Avenue with its soft sandy surface was leading to a future city destined to become the terminus of land, sea, and air communications of the first importance in the Far East....'

After outlining the history of the Company in Kowloon, the chairman continued: 'Today the Company's property at Hok Un comprises an area of no less than eight acres. The selection of the new site speaks well for the vision of those responsible. In a public undertaking of this nature, breadth of vision is an invaluable asset; and confidence in the future, backed by the judicious expenditure of required capital ahead of time is essential....'

The new station, on its reclamation behind a massive sea wall of granite blocks, had been designed for approximately 60,000 kW (60 MW) plant capacity (the demand in 1940 reached 13.8 MW.) 'The boiler house is 220 ft. in length and nearly 52 ft. wide, while the roof is 100 ft. from ground level.... The turbine room lies parallel with the boiler house and is 185 ft. long, 60 ft. wide, and 73 ft. to the ceiling...'.

The governor's reply took up the points made by the chairman. 'The story of the growth of this great Company, to which you have just been listening, cannot fail to make a deep impression on all of you who were not already in the know; and the first offer of congratulations which I shall make today is to the Company's able and courteous chairman, Mr. Lawrence Kadoorie, on his achievement in putting before us so simply and effectively his complex and absorbing tale. Doubtless, as we listened to Mr. Kadoorie, the thought struck other minds as well as my own: What would Kowloon have been today had it not been for the vision and the faith of Mr. R.G. Shewan and his fellow-directors during the first twenty years of this century? Suppose that instead of marching ahead as a standard bearer, the local light and power company had been governed by a cautious policy hesitating twice or thrice before each step forward; would we have had on the peninsula today the amazing development of shops, hotels, and factories which the last twenty years have seen and which is still, I am glad to say, in rapid progress. I think it very unlikely. The provision of light and power is essentially fundamental to sound progress, and the inhabitants of Kowloon are very deeply indebted – perhaps some of them in more senses than one! – to the China Light &

Power Co. for what the energy and foresight of its directors have brought into being.

'So much for the past: what of the future? The building in which you find yourselves supplies the best answer to that question. For this vast room is designed to house three times the plant which is now within it and which is adequate to all Kowloon's present needs; and the rest of the station is on the same courageously far-sighted scale. In the face of those facts can any of you doubt that the vision and the faith of the present board which sanctioned the huge expenditure necessary for such an enterprise is as clear and as strong as those which animated the Company's founders? There can be but one answer.' Sir Geoffrey's rhetoric is splendid, even if his English is ungrammatical.

'What is it that the vision foresees and on what does that faith rest? Obviously it is to a great manufacturing future for this town of Kowloon and its suburbs that the China Light & Power Co. is looking, and I readily take my stand beside them in that confidence. It is with the same end in view that Government must frame its schemes for the development of the port, and of the town itself, and I am happy to be in a position to reflect that all these problems are about to undergo close examination by experts. . . .

'Mr. Chairman and directors, I feel greatly privileged to have been invited to open this magnificent power station and to be the mouth-piece of those present. I assure you that all of your guests today join with me in wishing all prosperity to the China Light & Power Co. and with those good wishes I declare your new power station open.'

With that, Sir Geoffrey turned a switch on the dais. At once there was a blaze of light, and an illuminated sign came on, which read: 'The plant is now in operation.'

Despite the mix-up in arrangements for the function, when the speeches were over everyone mingled happily enough at the reception in the turbine room which was empty except for the one massive new machine. The Peninsula Hotel provided champagne and other re-freshments of which the centrepiece was a huge cake in the form of a scale model of the new station. It must be one of the few occasions in history when a turbine room has been carpeted wall to wall and decked in flowers and potted palms.

Two days later, the *South China Morning Post* carried a leading article on the opening. 'The tributes paid to the late Mr. Robert Shewan and his fellow pioneers found ready echo: all who were in Hong Kong forty years ago will agree that the Kowloon of those days, while it promised well, gave little hint of the great reward that awaited faith. The sponsors of the Company, and their successors, have been firm in their confidence and content to postpone their profit while they expanded their plant and built upon solid foundations a utility undertaking which for prestige and responsible service compares well with any.... Both His Excellency the Governor and Mr. Kadoorie emphasised the industrial factor.... The war in China has helped to demonstrate further that Hong Kong is an industrial centre, capable of supplying China with manufactures and of using China's raw materials to export goods abroad – to the benefit of China's economy as well as our own. Teaching the value of careful, confident building, Kowloon has also a lesson to offer in farsighted planning.... His

The opening ceremonies at the Hok Un 'A' station in 1940. The unfortunate area of empty seats is all too plainly visible

135

Excellency's reference to investigation is a reminder that the effort to step ahead still proceeds. It is, in fact, an open secret that Government is attempting to zone the whole Colony. This effort calls for public approval.... The peninsula itself would naturally be a shipping, godown and banking zone. The Shamshuipo-Mongkok-Kowloon City belt lends itself to factories. And in contemplating Kowloon's future it is necessary to include also the border. Promotion of industry there would establish a closer community of interest between Hong Kong and China and relieve the Colony of some of its traditional dependence upon its front door. Whatever the conflict of opinion on those and other points, Kowloon can count itself fortunate that the China Light & Power Co. stands ready to supply industry's essential motivating force in all parts of the mainland.'

References to 'the border' and 'the mainland' presumably meant the New Territories (the other side of the border being occupied by the Japanese when the words were printed). The article shows a prescience that was comparatively rare at the time, an almost prophetic approach reminiscent in fact more of Mr. Shewan than the generality of opinion. The Company had made a great step forward in providing for the future at a time when the war in Europe was going badly against Britain, and when there was every temptation for less venturesome minds to conserve rather than expand. In this, of course, as Lawrence Kadoorie and the governor remarked, the Company was still pursuing the line of policy formulated at its very beginning forty years previously.

At this time, the Company was about to receive a further 20 MW turbo-alternator and a second boiler producing 200,000 lbs. of steam per hour. The first unit of this size was commissioned in June 1940, and everyone hoped that the second would be installed by the end of 1941 – despite the probability of delays in a world at war in the West.

By the date of the opening of the new station, the war had made little enough impact on Hong Kong life. A previously tax-free society had accepted a war tax in order to bolster the British war effort, and this was to prove an irreversible step, as well as being the precursor of the Colony's post-war tax system. It was a time when many voluntary contributions were also being made for the same purpose. The Company itself gave $25,000 to the *South China Morning Post* War Fund in 1940.

As time went on, however, the effects of war began to be noticed. One or two industries suffered setbacks and did badly. But it was not until the summer of 1940 when general conflagration in the Far East looked as though it might break out at any moment that British women and children were evacuated – many of them to Australia. In common with other male members of the community, members of the staff were adversely affected by this separation from their families, and there were even moves to get the evacuees returned to Hong Kong, at one time and another.

But the moment was not far off when what had been feared, and what had been prepared for in various ways, was to happen. Still, before it did, the Company attempted to continue as if nothing much were in the way. The new administration offices at the intersection of Argyle Street and Waterloo Road were completed in 1940, whereupon the offices of the manager, the executive staff, and of most of the accounts department and a large portion of the distribution department were moved there from Kowloon Tong substation where, for many a year, they had been making do in improvised accommodation.

The numbers of staff had grown with the Company, and at the end of 1939 there were 900 employees, excluding casual labourers. The foreign staff accounted for 88, of whom 34 were contract staff and 54 non-contract. There were 27 Indians, mostly watchmen, and about 785 Chinese office and manual staff. The wages bill in that year amounted to about $1 million.

Conditions for the staff had gradually improved. The old provident scheme, long in existence, was upgraded in 1936 with provision for life insurance participation, and in 1940 the Company's contributions to the scheme were increased for those with more than ten years' service.

By the end of 1939, the transmission and distribution system, which then served an area of about 200 square miles, comprised roughly 220 miles of overhead lines and underground cables. In 1940, nearly $500,000 was spent in strengthening and extending this system, and further quantities of switchgear, cable, and ancillary equipment were ordered from overseas. This expansion was reflected in the Company's financial performance. While, year by year, the shareholders had been and were still called upon to provide more funds, profits and dividends rose steadily. The net profit for 1940 amounted to $1.23 million, and a dividend of $1.10 million was paid.

But as revenues rose, expenditure advanced inexorably, more rapidly than was comfortable – chiefly on account of the steep rise in the cost of coal. Its price doubled between 1940 and 1941. The

Company found it could no longer absorb the total additional cost of generation, and tariffs had to go up. On 1 April 1941, a fuel surcharge of ten per cent was introduced, but monthly meter rents were left unchanged at $0.50 (up to 5 amps), $1 (over 5 but not over 30 amps), and $2 (over 30 amps).

26 February 1940

'The Souvenir Brochure of the official opening of the Hok Un power station by His Excellency the Governor and Commander-in-Chief of Hong Kong, Sir Geoffrey Alexander Stafford Northcote, K.C.M.G.'

The brochure was designed by Technical and Power Publicity Ltd., and printed in London by W.P. Griffith & Sons Ltd., Prujean Square, Old Bailey, E.C.4. Prujean Square no longer exists on modern street maps of London, perhaps obliterated by the blitz of the Second World War.

The brochure has hard covers and is bound in what may be one of the very earliest spiral bindings, of a red substance that looks like a form of bakelite. The front cover is highly glazed and shows the initials CLP in a monogram within a circle in red, supported on either hand by a fancifully drawn Chinese dragon in gold with, below, a 'world' consisting of concentric gold lines floating amid Chinese-style clouds. Typically, in that still very colonial era, the sole colour reproduction in the brochure is devoted to a portrait of the governor in full regalia. This fine period piece nowadays ranks as a collector's item

THE WAR YEARS

As the threat of war approached Hong Kong in 1940 and 1941, efforts were made to prepare its defences, and to train the civilian population in the likely hazards to come. Frequent air raid practices were held, disrupting work and causing inconvenience to everyone. A blackout of the whole Colony was attempted and practised at ever shortening intervals. But it appears to have been impossible to enforce. Air observers during one blackout in 1941 reported that Hong Kong was 'a mass of lights.'

The usual Hong Kong scandals came to light – assaults in the blackout and blackmail of those showing a light in that dark. Considerable sums of money were voted by the government for civil defence, including the late but extensive digging of tunnels to shelter large numbers of people in an emergency. But the Air Raid Precautions Department came under fire for corruption when graft on a large scale was discovered. The architect to the Department, called to give evidence at an enquiry, was found to have shot himself, and an official in charge of tunnel construction was admitted to hospital with acute poisoning. The findings of the enquiry were never issued, the judge having taken the draft into internment with him in Stanley where he died before release; and that draft was never found.

The governor, Sir Geoffrey Northcote (who had opened the new power station) left Hong Kong on 6 September 1941, and his successor, Sir Mark Young, arrived four days later. The Colonial Secretary left, and his successor arrived on Sunday (7 December) the day before the Japanese attacked.

The sad story began to unfold of the brief but glorious defence of an essentially indefensible place. That tale has been well told in several books and many an article written by those involved. At 7.30 a.m. on 8 December, the frontier bridges were blown up. At 8.00 a.m. – exactly as their planes swooped on Pearl Harbour far away over the Pacific – the Japanese bombed Kai Tak airfield, destroying all five Royal Air Force planes and eight civil airline planes thoughtlessly left around on the tarmac. Simultaneously the invaders threw temporary bridges across the Shum Chun River and speeded into the New Territories. Ignoring the roads and guided by their spies they moved with great rapidity along paths and across open country. Gin Drinkers Line – the Hong Kong Maginot – suffered the same fate as its French equivalent, and by 11 December, Kowloon was being evacuated.

The historian of the period, G.B. Endacott, remarks with extreme brevity: 'The electricity generating station, the docks, and all military and other installations of vital importance to the enemy were made unserviceable before withdrawal.'

Lawrence Kadoorie plumps out the story. 'Some eight or nine months prior to the Japanese invasion, I was told that under certain circumstances I would have to give instructions for the power station to be blown up or otherwise denied to the enemy. So I said: "Look, I cannot give such instructions unless I'm given them in writing. I can't just blow up the shareholders' property, without written authority." Well, nobody gave me anything in writing; I couldn't get it. When at last the time came, the worst happened.'

The tale of what happened in Kowloon with specific reference to the power station and the personnel who ran it, can be pieced together, more or less, from various sources, not all of them agreeing on details.

Mr. J.W. Barker, who arrived with his wife in Hong Kong to take up the post of maintenance engineer with China Light in mid-March 1939, was surprised that the 'total output of the station was only about that of York Corporation Electricity Company' – his former employers. In June he was promoted to assistant distribution engineer. After the war in Europe broke out in September, Barker decided to bring his son and daughter to Hong Kong to avoid the bombing in England. 'Ironically, they came to Hong Kong in a Japanese boat and landed on a Monday in June 1940, and that same day government ordered all women and children should be evacuated by the following Saturday.... After the evacuation, all able-bodied males of British descent were conscripted, and we had two evenings a week of training in the use of rifles and machine guns.

'Apart from that, life went on as if the war had never started. The most important change was the installation of a new power station, and the introduction of a new post, that of executive engineer, in order to promote Mr. F. Clemo (then senior station engineer), and so as not to block promotions in the power station.... Mr. Cyril Wood was given a short vacation on medical grounds due to repeated attacks of malaria, and I became acting distribution engineer. Then

Mr. Clemo was given compassionate leave due to his wife's serious illness in Australia. The Japanese attacked before their return, and they both spent the next years in Australia.

'In early December 1941, all those eligible were ordered to report to the Hong Kong Volunteers Headquarters [on the Peak] except those in public services such as the power company. Later, we were told to leave Company headquarters [in Argyle Street] and congregate at the power station.

'Outside the offices many gangs of Chinese were looting and stopping people to rob them. They attempted to stop the car I was driving, but I just drove straight through them and eventually arrived at the station. The police and the Royal Navy were in charge and they refused to let me enter. They were removing important parts of the plant. I found out later that they were unable to carry them away so they just dumped them in the harbour, from where they were later gathered up by the Japanese with the aid of some Chinese staff.

'I then drove down to the Star Ferry and just caught the last one to leave Kowloon. We were told by the police to immobilise cars. I just lifted the bonnet of mine and invited the police to use their rifles, which they did, putting it out of action.'

Mr. E. Joffe, was charge engineer at the station when the invasion came. He recalls seeing from his flat in the staff quarters at Hok Un power station the Japanese bombs falling on Kai Tak airfield. 'There was an arrangement,' he remembers, 'that when the time came and the station had to be put out of action an army lieutenant would arrive with explosives to blow up the 12.5 MW turbine. We were told to strip and damage other machines. In the event, when we needed to put the station out of action, the lieutenant never turned up. At the last minute, I discovered that Mr. Gavriloff [assistant engineer] had some explosives. We fixed these up at the high pressure end of the turbine which we left running. Then we lit the fuse and ran for it. The big bang left most of the machine undamaged but the pedestal at the high pressure end was blown up, and the shaft was bent. Later on, the Japanese tried to make people believe they had mended the turbine – there was even a photograph in the papers – but in fact they had not managed, and had simply mocked the thing up with painted woodwork.' Mr. Joffe then reported to the Volunteer Headquarters on the Peak.

Mr. Barker arrived in Hong Kong from Kowloon when it was dusk and decided with others to try the Hongkong Hotel for a meal and a

Damage done to the 12.5 MW turbine at Hok Un before the Japanese took over

few drinks. They signed for them – as was the habit in those days – 'and then those of us who were lucky bedded down on the divans in the lounge. Others slept on the floor. The following day we went to Volunteer Headquarters, where we were supplied with rifles and ammunition and then sent to one of the batteries on the south coast to act as sentries. Three days later all China Light & Power engineers were ordered to go to Hongkong Electric power station – the idea being that we should take over in the event of the Hong Kong engineers being put out of action. In the meantime we were to act as sentries.'

142

While these movements were taking place, Lawrence Kadoorie appears to have been behind the scheme for the China Light engineers to go to the Hongkong Electric station. 'But before giving this instruction,' he recalls, 'I thought I should inform the Government.... So I went up the hill and walked through the Government offices – empty, not a soul in the place. There was some firing, but I thought it surprising all the same [that everyone had disappeared.] Then I met someone in the road and he said they were in the cave. I said: "What cave?" And he said: "In the tunnel just over the road." So I went into the tunnel – there were three levels in it – and walked right up to the top, which was under the dining room of Government House.'

After some shilly-shallying and futile attempts to raise Defence Headquarters on the telephones – all of which were dead because a shell had landed on the main cable as it came into the tunnel – 'they told me: "Look, you'd better go up to Volunteer Headquarters and they'll decide what to do with the China Light engineers." So I left the tunnel.

'At that time the Peak Tram was still running, and I got the last one to go up. It was a most extraordinary feeling because, as you know, the tram works on a rope from the top and the driver has nothing to do with it. We got in at the bottom and there we were going up, and the Japanese were shelling. A shell landed on Kennedy Road in a wall. I saw people fall over. It was just like fate, going up. You saw everything happening, there was no means of stopping, you just went right up through it all.

'So at last I got to Volunteer Headquarters which was in some flats just on the left up there. Of all the damn fool things to happen, they wanted to billet women and children above the H.Q. – which of course was being shelled. I was the Billeting Officer. For that honour, I had a red armband with the letters B O on it. Going round with B O on my arm struck me as being a bit too suggestive, so I put a T between the B and the O. However, it got me into wherever I wanted to go.

'I told the officer in charge that I wanted to get the engineers back to Hong Kong, but he said no. So I walked out. Down the hill a Japanese bomb had landed just below Barker road. We had moved out of our house on Mt. Cameron to Barker Road, to a house that belonged to the Chartered Bank. There I found a bomb splinter had gone into the amah's temple, but fortunately she was not seriously wounded.... My daughter, who was a year old, had her clothes burned by what turned out to have been an incendiary bomb – it had a horrible stink. . . .'

Back again down in the tunnel he was told: ' "You go and get these people from Kowloon." So I went on my way. I met a Russian engineer who had been working for us. . . . he seemed not to know what to do, and hung on to me. . . . We went to see the Defence Secretary who said: "I want you to go over and give instructions for the turbine to be blown up." I said: "I have nothing in writing." He said: "Don't argue about it. You just go. And here are two passes to enable you to get across." I said: "I'm not going if I only get two passes. My father is over on the other side. I need a pass for him and passes for all the China Light engineers. I'm not going over there and giving instructions to blow the place up, and then coming back on my own. That's not me." So I refused to go. An argument started. His secretary was there, a Miss Angus whose brother was our assistant station superintendent. She gave me a whole bundle of passes. But then I said: "They're not signed." She said: "You sign them." So on the ferry, with the Russian engineer holding them, and giving them to me one by one, I signed them – "Government Official authorising Lawrence Kadoorie. . . ."

'I remember I had no transport. I commandeered a small bus. I rescued two American sailors and three nurses from La Salle College who had been abandoned by their doctors – they were in a terrible state. I got them all into my bus. But just then, a Portuguese chap came up and said: "Can you look after this lady, Mrs. Wookey?" I asked: "Who is Mrs. Wookey?" He said she was the common-law wife of a sergeant-major. She had a small baby. I said "Fine, get in the bus." And I got them across the harbour.

'We crossed on a launch with shelling going on all the way across. Then by back streets to the Post Office where we sheltered for an hour and a half. Then I got hold of the American consul and told him I'd got two sailors. After some problems we got them off there, and the nurses to Dr. Selwyn-Clarke, head of Medical.

'Now what am I going to do with this Mrs. Wookey and baby, I thought. It seemed the best thing was to take them home. So I went back to the house but it was empty as my family had been moved to my wife's aunt's house. I eventually arrived there, complete with Mrs. Wookey and baby. I don't know what my wife thought – a hidden part of my life, perhaps, from Kowloon. . . !

'We put the baby in the same cot as my young son Michael, who was then eight months old. That night came the biggest explosion I ever heard. Two barges transporting ammunition from Green Island to Hong Kong were inadvertently shelled, and blew up.' It was the night of 12 December. 'The kids fell out of their beds. The windows were smashed by the terrific explosion. . . . I don't know what eventually happened to Mrs. Wookey and her baby. She stayed with us until we were interned in Stanley.'

Japanese shelling in those days is remembered by a director of China Light, a gentleman of regular habits. 'After breakfast, I would usually take my newspapers and retire. We had a house on Robinson Road at that time, and had dug a tunnel shelter into the hill at the back of the house. This particular morning, I picked up my papers and glasses as usual. And then it occurred to me that the shelling was getting worse. So I changed my mind about where I would go and went into the shelter. Shortly after, a shell, which did not explode, scored a direct hit on the lavatory.' The director is happily still with us in Hong Kong today.

'Hongkong Electric [the power station at Electric Road] had two Lewis guns,' Mr. Joffe (who had worked with the Company since 1932) recalls from those now far-off days forty years ago. 'We asked for them. It took two days to clean them up. One day we saw the Japanese crossing the harbour near North Point. Our officer in charge didn't believe it. In a nearby house we could see, one evening, the Japanese establishing a gun emplacement over the road. We were told to hold off, probably because it was felt the Japanese might blow up the station. Eventually a shell hit the turbine at Hongkong Electric, and we were told to evacuate to a British pill-box. On the way we passed burning tanks and, approaching the pill-box, we were fired on. The Japanese had taken it in the meantime. We surrendered later and were taken back to Hongkong Electric. Then we were all put into a large garage for twenty-four hours without food or water and with no sanitary facilities – it was very smelly by the end. After that we were moved into the open where we could wash. The Japanese front-line troops were bastards. They burned most of our belongings. My passport had a Japanese visa in it. They were so surprised that they gave it back to me with all the money they found.

'Then those of us from China Light [there were about thirty of them at the Hongkong Electric station] were taken over to the station landing at Hok Un. The workmen there were horrified to see us. Finally they took us to a Catholic school in Waterloo Road and the sisters let us spend the night and gave us books. We started our internment in a camp nearby and were there for six months. From there it wasn't far to the Sham Shui Po Camp where we spent one and a half years before, in my case, being sent to Japan to spend two years at Sendai, a hundred miles north of Tokyo, at the coal mines.'

Mr. Joffe was better off than many who were detained in Hong Kong. The Japanese needed miners, so he was better treated than those whose fate was to spend years in the vile Sham Shui Po camp or in the Stanley civilian camp. The Sendai camp was newly built, it had *tatami* floors and Japanese hot baths. Joffe managed to set himself up as bootmender, repairing the rubber soled shoes issued to all. 'So I established myself in a nice little cubby-hole between the main gate and the kitchen. One morning I managed to get the Commandant's newspaper and read it before it was delivered to him. And that was how I learned of the end of the war.'

The Kadoorie family, including Sir Elly who, by this time, was seriously ill, were taken to Stanley camp. 'The Japanese, knowing that he had done so much for education in this part of the world, and trying at that time to press forward their Co-Prosperity Sphere idea, seemed to think that it was a good idea to get rid of him. On some excuse, Lawrence Kadoorie recalls, 'I was called upon. They said I was a Canadian newspaperman. Well – I am not Canadian, neither was I a newspaperman. But who was I to argue about it? They told me I could buy tickets to Shanghai on a boat. Then they let us out of Stanley and we were supposed to go to the Hongkong Hotel. But my father.... said: "I am going to the Peninsula. I don't care what you say. It's my hotel.... I suppose to keep him quiet, they said alright. We were all put up on the second floor under guard....' The Japanese reiterated the offer that if the Kadoories bought their tickets they could go to Shanghai. 'I have no money. Let me get hold of my secretary who is a Russian.' But this was not allowed. After twelve hours a Japanese came along with money provided by a Parsee friend, Mr. Nemazee, and said: "Here are two thousand dollars, four 500-dollar notes." The passage was $1,875 so I said he should go and get change, or else take the whole $2,000.' But the Japanese said he could only get the tickets if he had the exact amount. At last, however, he took the money and got the tickets.

'So we got on to a ship called the *Taiwan Maru* – a very small ship, together with members of the Consular Corps. There were two thousand people on this ship. The Japanese had lifebelts, no one else had. We were packed solid. It took nine days to get to Shanghai and we weren't allowed on deck except in the evening. We went to Taiwan but they didn't allow us off. We managed to get a little fruit.... So we went to Shanghai, to find our house had been taken by the Japanese.'

Those days, and months, and years – in Shanghai and in Hong Kong – were filled with misery. Admittedly they did not compare in hardship with some in Thailand, Singapore, and Japan. But death, disease and malnutrition reigned. Brutality was commoner than normality. The survivors from the ranks of China Light, in common with everyone else, waited and hoped. In the limbo of the camps there was little else to do.

And slowly the depraved processes of world war worked themselves out in a welter of cruelty, bloodshed, torture, deprivation, and horror. Hong Kong, the formerly self-satisfied, venturesome, rather smug little pre-war Colony, was reduced to a cowed rabble of half-starved inhabitants (many had long ago fled), with hardly a service still running. The trams and the Peak Tram had long stopped – one tram driver remembers how he and some friends cannibalized a couple of axles and four tram wheels, built a wooden platform on them, and provided a cheap hand-pulled service along the length of the rails in Hong Kong during part of the occupation. Little electricity was generated in Kowloon at all, and the supply from Hongkong Electric was curtailed. The feeder to Taikoo had been taken up and laid across the harbour to China Light where part of the plant was running.

The Hongkong Electric station at North Point had surrendered several days before Christmas, and on that fateful Christmas day the surrender of the Colony was announced. The Japanese established in Hong Kong the *Denki-sho* – an electricity authority that took the place of the two companies. Military personnel managed to gather together many of China Light's workmen, and some of them were forced to recover the portions of equipment that had been cast into the harbour. A number of machines – but not the 12.5 MW set – were repaired, and a restricted supply of electricity was maintained.

When the Japanese had succeeded in connecting the two sides of the harbour by cable lying on the seabed, Hong Kong Island could then be supplied from Hok Un. But as time went on and the supply remained minimal, electricity was made dearer, with the intended result that not many could afford to use it. Coal, also, became scarcer and was eventually unobtainable. The Hok Un boilers were then fired with wood obtained by wholesale felling of New Territories trees, depriving many a hill and valley of its natural beauty. Finally, the supply was restricted to users whom the Japanese thought to be essential, and the ordinary civil population was cut off altogether.

It was from this situation that there stemmed the gentle art of power-stealing which became prevalent not only in Hong Kong but in many another country in the East as a result of the privations of the war. The method was essentially simple. One way was to alter meter connections – but this was readily discoverable and not the favoured way. Easiest of all was the long bamboo with a wire running down its centre, hooked to hang conveniently on overhead wires. This could be easily (and rapidly, which was the point) removed when authority threatened to come by. These and other methods became part of a way of life, necessarily so in the horror conditions of Japanese occupation. But it proved hard indeed to eradicate the practice after the war was over.

The lights of Hong Kong, Kowloon, and the New Territories were effectively dimmed by the Japanese occupation, and gradually most of them went out. It seemed, in the general hopelessness of the situation, that all the Company had worked for and achieved over the forty years of its existence was effectively negated. At the time, none could predict the term of the Japanese occupation, and indeed all the news in the first years of Hong Kong's defeat was of Japanese victories in every part of the Orient. The Rising Sun, paradoxically, cast a dark shadow over all.

BEGINNING AGAIN

A city occupied by the enemy, raped, systematically pillaged and looted by both occupiers and its own half-starved people, a city in which the essential services that underpin urban life – electricity, gas, water, and transport – have more or less ceased to function, becomes a desert, a nightmare, a shambles unfit for human habitation.

All this had happened under the Japanese in Hong Kong as a whole. Chaos was a fitting description of the place as the atomic bombs fell on Hiroshima and Nagasaki; and chaos cannot easily be resolved.

The rule of Japanese terror – it is a paradox that the armies which had swept with ease and high efficiency through the Orient seemed unable to achieve the necessary administrative order which their victories demanded in order to be consolidated – was suddenly deprived of the last remnant of its tottering power by the Emperor's acceptance of defeat on 14 August 1945.

But the peace that followed in Hong Kong revealed a lamentable state of affairs. The Company had lost many a familiar face from the ranks of its staff, and many a tragic story came to light. Sir Elly, having reached Shanghai with his family, suffered a further deterioration in health. Lawrence Kadoorie and his family were put in a camp and were only allowed out to see Sir Elly just before he died. The Kadoories were eventually confined to the staff quarters of their own house, Marble Hall.

When the war ended, Lawrence Kadoorie was asked by the general commanding British forces in China what he would like to do immediately. He replied: 'I'd like to get back to Hong Kong.' A.G.N. Ogden (now Sir Alwyne Ogden KBE., CMG.) who was British consul-general, had just arrived from Kunming on a D.C.3 – the first British plane to reach Shanghai. The consul general was a guest of the Kadoories' at Marble Hall until such time as the consulate was ready for occupation once more, as indeed were many others who recall with happy memories the Kadoories' hospitality. Lawrence Kadoorie, modestly, does not mention this at all.

'Well, it was after midnight as we were talking, and Ogden said: "If you could leave at four o'clock in the morning, you can take my plane to Kunming." General Hayes commanding the British Forces was present, and he gave me letters saying how important it was for me to return to Hong Kong. There was also a young engineer from the Dock Company, and he joined me on the plane.'

In Kunming, a request to the Royal Air Force to take him to Hong Kong was turned down. '"We don't take passengers," they said. So back I went to the British consulate where Mrs. Ogden was very nice to me.' Lawrence went several times to the R.A.F. with his letters from General Hayes, but met with refusal – no passengers. One day, 'I got thoroughly fed up – impossible to get out. Somebody offered to take me round the town in a jeep. But there happened to be a nail in the seat of this jeep, and as I got out it tore a large rent in my trousers. So there I was standing on the steps of the British consulate, feeling utterly miserable. Another jeep passed with some GIs in it, and someone asked me: "Say, buddy, what's wrong?" So I replied: "If you had only one pair of pants, you'd know what's wrong!" So they took me in their jeep, and forty minutes later I was a GI – all my clothes abandoned. I asked: "Who do you salute?" They said: "Nobody salutes nobody around here." So I said: "That suits me fine."''

Finally, rejecting an offer from the G.O.C. American forces in Kunming to go to Canton by plane (being unsure how he would get from there to Hong Kong) Lawrence Kadoorie tried the R.A.F. again. This time he suggested he could go as freight, if they insisted they didn't take passengers. '"Ah, that's different," they said. So, I arrived back in Hong Kong wearing GI uniform, classed as freight, and sitting on a pile of banknotes.' These were the notes which Hong Kong desperately needed to replace the Japanese military currency.

Reading the stories and listening to the tales of many China Light men – and of course others – who were interned and in many cases suffered brutal treatment, one thing that stands out is the determination of so many to get back to Hong Kong, back to the job, as soon as possible.

Sir Elly had passed away in Shanghai on 8 February 1944, as it happened, within a few days of his old friend J.P. Braga who had spent the occupation years in Macau. Two of the oldest, and wisest, heads in the Company's affairs were missing from the first meeting after the trauma of the occupation.

From the staff there were grievous losses. Mr. I.N. Murray, the deputy manager, was one of the thirty who, it seems, went to the aid of the personnel of Hongkong Electric at the North Point station. In the heroic battle there – a resistance that must seem futile as we read the fragmentary and often contradictory accounts of it now, but which at the time had its justification (like the resistance of the forces in general to the invasion of the Japanese) in the urge to defend what they saw the Colony as standing for in their lives – Murray was wounded. Taken to Sham Shui Po camp where conditions were the worst among the internment camps of Hong Kong, he became progressively weaker. His condition was such that he was unable to wash, and a colleague paid an orderly in cigarettes – six cigarettes was quite a princely sum – to have him cleaned up. Near to death, he was shortly afterwards taken to Bowen Road Hospital where he died.

The assistant station superintendent, Mr. G.I. Angus, was also with the defenders of the power station at North Point. He too was put in Sham Shui Po camp. Later he was transferred to Japan where he died before the war was over.

Mr. H.A. Samuel, the Company's statistician, was a member of the 1st Battery, Hong Kong Volunteer Defence Corps (known as The Volunteers) and was killed in the last ditch battle at Stanley on Christmas Day, while Mr. C.H. Mackay, a power station engineer, who was serving with the 2nd Company of The Volunteers, was killed at Chung Hom Kok not far away on the same day. Mr. A. Reed, an assistant in the Distribution Department, died from injuries sustained with the Volunteers when on duty at Wong Nei Chong Gap, and Mr. W. Brown Jr., an accountant with the Company and son of the chief accountant, succumbed in the military hospital on 17 December from wounds received in fighting at Lei Yue Mun.

Mr. H. Wong, an Australian Chinese who had been the power station electrical engineer and was a civilian at the time, was executed by the Japanese on suspicion of treason. The Company's chief cashier, Mr. Chung Shun-cheung, who is remembered to have been taller and broader than most Chinese, died in Macau during the occupation of Hong Kong, as did Mr. Chan Man-kai, a senior clerk in the Accounts Department audit section, who stayed on in Kowloon and passed away before the defeat of the enemy.

Mr. J.W. Bertram, power station maintenance engineer, survived his term as a prisoner of war, only to pass away shortly after he returned to Australia on recuperation leave.

The death toll of the Company's men includes another seventy members of the staff – the details of each one not always ascertainable. But certainly many died as the result of brutal treatment by the occupying forces. Others were killed in air raids, and perhaps a larger number succumbed to malnutrition.

The survivors of the almost four years of Japanese rule, half starved, suffering from various more or less untreated diseases, suffering too from the psychological effects of that dark time in life, found themselves in many cases in indifferent health. In many a case lives that had seemed assured before, were now irretrievably blighted by illness and the effects of deprivation. A story told of Mr. J W. Barker perhaps strikes a note to which all would respond. Many years after the war, when he was the Company's distribution engineer, Mr. Barker had a visit from a Japanese who was seeking an order for some of his firm's products. As a conversational gambit this man asked if Barker had ever been to Japan. 'Yes,' said Barker, 'as a guest of the Emperor.' After which the visitor departed as quickly as he could.

Only a few weeks before the Emperor's surrender many technically skilled personnel had been transferred by the Japanese from Stanley prison camp to Ma Tau Chung camp. Precisely what the Japanese intended to do with them is uncertain, but doubtless some not particularly edifying fate was in store for them. But with the surrender came acquiescence to command by virtually all the Japanese troops. The Emperor's word was really a divine command, and was obeyed in letter and spirit.

On the surrender, internees were allowed some freedom of movement. Mr. C. Crofton – station superintendent when the Japanese took over, and last seen by Lawrence Kadoorie just before he crossed over with his mixed crew of American sailors, an unmarried mother, and others, to Hong Kong all but four years before – left Stanley Camp, together with Mr. H.V.C. Randall, district engineer. By what seems almost miraculous good fortune, each managed to find the senior foreman of his department. Crofton arranged to guard the power station, while Randall took over the Argyle Street administrative offices, in order to prevent looting and sabotage.

The threat from looting was a serious one. Conditions for Chinese, as for foreign residents, were appalling. Food was scarce and prices high. All the conditions for a black market were present. There was scarcely any fuel of any kind. The population had been reduced by the Japanese to 600,000 persons, but the scarcity of accommodation was a major problem. During the occupation and in the Allied bombing prior to the end of the war every single untenanted building had been thoroughly looted, and stripped moreover of everything that could be burned as cooking fuel. Floors, window-frames, doors, stairways – all were gone. And in Hong Kong's rainy season this meant that to rehabilitate such buildings was an expensive and time-consuming procedure. Nearly 2,000 European-style houses had been destroyed, and about 400 damaged. About 600 Chinese houses 'of the better class' had been destroyed, and many others badly damaged. Over 8,000 tenement houses were destroyed and the same number damaged. Nearly 300 factories were destroyed. In all, a total of about 160,000 flat dwellers were homeless. And worse – people were arriving

The workshop and stores at Hok Un gutted by fire during the occupation

in considerable numbers from China every day.

Against this backdrop of a ruined city, its utilities and industries virtually at a standstill, surviving staff and employees of China Light went back to work.

Mr. Crofton, who had stayed behind in Kowloon as the Japanese arrived, and who had been interned, returned to Hok Un station to find the Japanese still in charge. The whole place was a shambles, suffering from years of neglect and misuse. A rice mill had been installed in No. 2 block and outsize rats were scurrying among the husks.

He found the Japanese had been unable to repair the 12.5 MW

generator and that two other machines, the 5 MW and the 3 MW, were in very poor condition due to lack of maintenance. Two others had apparently not been in use at all and were in fair condition. Yet another two machines were missing, and were later discovered in the Kowloon Wharf & Godown Co., whence they had doubtless been destined to be shipped to Japan. These two were taken back and put together again

The boiler plant was in similar condition. Four units had been steamed on water with a heavy percentage of salt in it. One boiler had had its front removed, and fuel in the form of wood had simply been dumped on to the grate by women workers. The control room, once the pride of the station, had been used as a wash house and kitchen, while blast from a bomb had damaged the low tension switchgear and the carbon dioxide fire-fighting apparatus. Fire pumps and other equipment had been hopelessly abused and rendered useless. The new turbine room had been hit by three bombs which burst inside it, doing considerable damage, and two bombs which luckily failed to explode had hit the old station. In addition, the workshop and store had been completely gutted by fire.

Another problem was posed for returning staff by Japanese alteration to the distribution system during the war. Connections had been made and severed in such a way that when a switch was closed the results could be totally unexpected – power reaching completely different areas from those for which the action was intended. Many of the Company's transmission plans were rendered completely obsolete.

Fortunately, just prior to the outbreak of hostilities, China Light had taken on a German engineer named Dr. Steinschneider. Since he was not technically an enemy, the Japanese kept him with the Company during the war years working in the distribution department and, thanks to his knowledge of what had been done, the Company was able to restore some order in the chaos rather more rapidly than would otherwise have been possible.

The first step taken was to get rid of the rice mill and the rats – one and the same operation – and clean the place up. The help of the Royal Navy was asked in the first days, and the small naval contingent was replaced by Royal Air Force men under Flight Lieutenant Malloy who signed documents as Commander of the China Light & Power Co., Ltd. The R.A.F. rendered invaluable assistance in maintaining the supply of electricity and effecting some repairs during the time when the Company's engineers were still in such places as Japan, or in some instances had gone on recuperation leave.

George Gavriloff, formerly chief civil engineer, returned from Japan where he had been interned. 'I had three or four hundred Japanese assigned to me. They came at the double when told to do anything by their commanders. After four years in a Japanese camp, with all that that meant, the way these Japanese tried to please us made me unhappy. Yesterday like tigers, today with spirit gone. It didn't take too long to clean the place up. The Japanese were so eager to please that they'd pick up anything with their bare hands.'

Another engineer who returned, Mr. Joffe, had been repatriated from Japan, via Canada, to England where he was joined by his wife who had been interned in Stanley camp. He now came back to Hong Kong by air via Calcutta and was put in charge of the station on his arrival in April 1946. Lawrence Kadoorie recalls him as 'the man who really rescued China Light after the war. His eldest daughter ... was the first baby to be born in Stanley camp. Joffe returned to the power station. In spite of all the troubles he had been through in Japan, he stayed there. He was sick and at one time covered in boils until at last we managed to get some cases of oranges. He was really the man who took over in the early days after the occupation.'

'Oddly enough,' Joffe recalls, 'it was not until many months after my release from Japan that I became very sick. The tedious journey out from London made things worse.'

Mr. Joffe, now retired in south London, tells how he 'converted the boardroom in the power station as quarters for myself. My wife was not permitted to travel out to join me. It was a 24-hour-a-day job for a long time. I came back out of loyalty to the Company. The R.A.F. had done a damn good job, but whereas we were short of trained staff, the ordinary Chinese staff that returned was actually bigger in numbers than before the war – they had brought relatives with them to share the rice bowl! The Company tried to cut down the numbers. All of them wanted a big rise in pay. The engineers were all on pre-war salaries.'

Apart from the question of how much money was the problem of how to find the *actual* money to pay the employees now reporting back for work. The reason for the difficulty was that when Hong Kong was overrun at Christmas 1941, the Japanese military yen was introduced as the currency. It was given the arbitrary value of HK\$2 = Yen 1. This was changed on 24 July 1942, to HK\$4 = Yen 1. On 1 June

1943, the use of Hong Kong dollars was finally prohibited. Early in September 1945, there was an acute shortage of the Colony's currency, and this was not relieved until 13 September when the Hong Kong dollar was, by proclamation, formally restored and the military yen declared worthless – two days after Lawrence Kadoorie had arrived sitting on the new banknotes and saved the day.

During the hiatus of two weeks when insufficient currency was available to pay the Chinese workers, the rice mill established by the Japanese at Hok Un proved itself invaluable. Thousands of bags of rice were stored there, and workmen who at first were disturbed and anxious at not receiving their pay were soon receiving four catties of rice a day – something that they found very acceptable.

At the time it was re-occupied, Hongkong Electric's power station was completely out of action and the whole Colony had to be supplied from Hok Un station – the island via the cross-harbour cable laid by the Japanese. At Hok Un, up to four hundred tons of wood were consumed every day in the effort to keep up the supply. At one point, a member of the power station staff recalls, he saw several Chinese women each carrying on her shoulders a huge beam a foot square and many feet long. He could not imagine how it was they managed such a weight. But enlightenment came when he discovered the wood was balsa, and the women thought it a good idea to get the lightweight stuff out of the way first. The insubstantial balsa, unfortunately, did little to augment the heat supply to the boiler.

Then, toward the middle of September, the cross-harbour cable was fouled by a ship's anchor and had to be abandoned. Hong Kong Island was thereafter in darkness until 4 October when Hongkong Electric managed to get a generator working at North Point.

Evidently, besides rehabilitating the existing machinery, the paramount need was to obtain *new* generating equipment. By good judgement, a Hong Kong Planning Unit had been set up in London during the course of the Pacific War, its aim being the restoration of British administration and local services as soon as that war came to an end. A former China Light manager, Mr. Strafford, had been advising this unit on matters concerned with the power supply to Kowloon and the New Territories. In June 1945 his place was taken by the Company's executive engineer, Mr. F.C. Clemo, who had spent the war years in Australia. Preece, Cardew & Rider, well known from former days, acted as consultants.

In December 1941, when Hong Kong fell, the 20 MW generator

Mr. Albert Raymond, about 1939

ordered had been ready for shipment. It was then taken over by the British government and, in the interests of the war effort, shipped instead to Russia. The Planning Unit, after extensive consideration, and recognising that if new plant were not ordered at once it might take as long as five years to obtain, ordered replacements of the machine that went to Russia, the outstanding 200,000 lb. boiler, and a quantity of 11 kV switchgear. This was done with the assistance of a guarantee from the Hongkong & Shanghai Banking Corporation. The Unit also made plans for a permanent cross-harbour cable connection between China Light and Hongkong Electric.

Three days after his return to Hong Kong on 11 September, Lawrence Kadoorie attended the first post-war board meeting, at which Mr. Albert Raymond was elected chairman, a position he held until his death in 1955. Present also was Mr. M.K. Lo, while Mr. A.H. Compton, the only other surviving director, was unable to attend. The Company's manager, Mr. Munton, summarized recent events, and Mr. Clemo gave details of the Hong Kong Planning Unit's actions. The orders placed by the latter for the generator and boiler were confirmed, but it was thought that the 11 kV switchgear was not yet required.

In this and several subsequent meetings many of the immediate problems facing the Company in terms of staffing and generally putting the physical aspects of its operation back to something like normal were planned and approved. There was plenty to be done. Strafford House was unfit for habitation, the Kau Pui Shek substation had been removed by the Japanese as they made a new runway at Kai Tak airport. The general deterioration of the distribution system had to be remedied, as had the ticklish problem of losses from illegally used current, which proved a very hard nut to crack in the miserable circumstances of the population as a whole.

With the return of the governor, Sir Mark Young, on 1 May 1946, military control gave way to civil administration. The attempt was made in all spheres to return to peace-time conditions. But, something the other participants in the war discovered also, prices never returned to the pre-war level. And rice, the Chinese staple food and the item with which other costs could most properly be compared, rose from its pre-war price of about 14 cents a catty to 30 cents in February 1946, and to $2 in May. This was a serious situation.

Electricity charges also rose. In October 1945, the charge was arbitrarily set at 1.5 times that of late 1941, and when the revenue from this proved to be insufficient, it was raised again, in March 1946, to twice the former level.

China Light reverted to full control by its own board of directors on 15 June 1946, after a period when military administration had assisted in its rehabilitation and had also paid rental to the Company. At this time the rates had again to be increased in the face of rising costs, high fuel consumption (the most efficient generating set was still out of action), and of massive power-stealing. The rates were then set at 2 to 3.6 times the 1941 levels, which meant that one kWh of lighting cost 71.2 cents in Kowloon and 99 cents in the New

Territories. The tariffs were arrived at in consultation with the government, and they were, naturally, highly unpopular. But it was promised that they would decrease as circumstances allowed.

It was precisely at this point that mounting dissatisfaction among employees of various essential services and undertakings culminated in a strike at Hongkong Electric beginning on 15 May 1946. This was followed (a week after the reversion to its own control by China Light) by workers' demands for higher wages, followed by strike action. In the grossly uncertain climate of the times, it was perhaps not surprising that workers voiced their anxiety about prices and income in this forceful manner.

One problem in this area was that after the end of the war the old staff had returned quite quickly – they needed full employment; but, as Mr. Joffe recalled, everyone's rice-bowl being rather meagrely supplied with rice, they had brought with them brothers and cousins and uncles whose presence on the staff swelled the ranks of those the Company was employing to about 900 – many more than pre-war. This figure was much above what was required. Talks which were held showed the workers opposing any reduction in numbers, and they gave notice of strike. The engineers had to take over the complete running of the power station.

Mr. Joffe recalls Lawrence Kadoorie coming to him one day in the station to tell him that all he could promise was some blackleg labour to help handle coal and ash from the boilers. 'Soon we had five charge engineers and some apprentices running the boiler house, and Mr. Wong – all of them prepared to stay and work. I said that if it was for the good of China Light, I'd try my best. I personally adjusted all the automatic equipment, often with the help of people about to go on strike. When the strike hit, we carried on for the whole thirty-four days. We had executives driving lorries with coal. The boss of the blackleg labour employed was a fierce woman who said she had been a pirate in Bias Bay, and she certainly got her men moving.'

With this tiny work force in the station on a tight schedule of shift work, and the eighty-three labourers shovelling coal and ash, the station managed to keep running, and necessary work including cable-laying and jointing was carried out by teams of senior employees, even in the face of a severe typhoon as well as acts of sabotage when cables were cut, substations broken into, and relays damaged. It was something of an epic. The very fact that electricity supplies were kept up and factories did not have to stop and lay off workers throughout the period of industrial action did much to assist the rehabilitation of what was still a very tentative new order in the Colony.

The strikers, in discussions with one of the directors, the Hon. M.K. Lo, gradually yielded on various points. Finally, after a long meeting at the Labour Office, a settlement was reached on 26 July 1946 on terms quite close to those offered by the Company. And 500 superfluous men were paid off. It was a very polite strike, politely ended. There were to be no further strikes for the next twenty-one years.

Rice was far from being the sole commodity in short supply and highly priced in the early post-war years. The old bugbear of the Company, coal supplies, and more especially coal prices, came up again. The alternative was oil which at that time and for many a year to come was not only available but, on a heat value basis, attractive in price. The Company decided to order new equipment to convert the boilers to oil burning. But there came the rub. In the difficult manufacturing situation at the time in the West, it seemed likely to be about three years before the new plant could be expected to arrive. A start in conversion to oil burning had been made by Lieutenant Crone of the R.A.F. (who stayed on to work with China Light.) He carried out modifications to the 60,000 lb. boiler so that it could maintain a partial load on oil. But this was a drop in the ocean.

A suitable excuse for conversion was provided by the fact that during the strike the backhoppers of the 120,000 lb. boiler burned out beyond repair. Replacements would take years. But luckily there was a ship in the harbour waiting to be scrapped which had suitable oil-burning equipment. On the recommendation of Mr. Joffe, this plant was purchased. The nozzles and steam pumps so obtained were, however, only part of the total hardware needed. So everything else had to be locally made. 'I designed and modified all the equipment to suit our boiler,' Mr. Joffe recalls. 'A local engineering firm had been working with China Light for many years, and now we asked them to help out in this work. Their manager, Mr. Law, used to sit with me as I made sketches in chalk on the power station floor of the parts he had to make. A draughtsman followed up with proper drawings, and the new parts were made in record time.' Mr. Joffe was particularly keen on a control valve they made which permitted very tiny adjustments in the quantities of fuel to suit different loads required. 'That boiler was still functioning when I left on retirement in 1969,' he recalls.

In fact the operation was a good deal bigger and harder than that. The Company's stocks did not contain enough tubes to convey the oil, so a number of old boiler tubes had to be pressed into service. It was not the first time such makeshift tactics had to be resorted to – at one time some street lighting standards were used to convey steam in the absence of the correct tubing. And at first there were no oil tanks, a barge tied up alongside the sea wall serving as a reservoir until an ex-army oil tank was discovered and put up on the hillside outside the station's main gate. This provided a gravity flow to the burners. Eventually more tanks were installed to ensure sufficient storage capacity.

Engineers – the fact dawns on the observer as the tale of those arduous post-war years unfolds in its almost superhuman effort – seem to be a special breed of men. If it can hardly be said they are born, at least it appears they grow into a pattern in many respects very similar from one to another. They are distinguished, first of all, by an extraordinary attachment to their machines – attentive to the very sound of those machines, to the look of them, to their health, rather in the manner that other men respond to their horses or their loved ones of the human species. The ruling passion of the engineer is the deep throb of power, the continuous hum of the station's generators, apparently before all else.

The second characteristic of engineers is that even today, a hundred years after the tendency was first apparent, a very large percentage of them tend to be Scotsmen – men whose accents stay with them after a lifetime of foreign service with their beloved machines under an extremely un-Scottish sun in the various mad-dogs-and-Englishmen climates that prevail in un-Scottish latitudes.

And the third aspect of the engineering breed is the high proportion of what, even in Scotland, are called 'characters' among them.

Listening to the talk of the Company's engineers, a close camaraderie is obvious. The talk, when it is not of the beloved machines' health, turns often enough on the frailties of former colleagues; and

161

reminiscent laughter – tolerant, kindly mirth – breaks out among them. They remember one who was both engineer and Baptist preacher – naturally called John the Baptist – whose frequent homilies on foreswearing blasphemous words in times of stress fell, as some seed must, on stony ground. They recall another whose energies seemed so boundless that he managaged a second job in his spare time – one as close to the Scottish heart as machines, if more liquid: and yet another whose abundant energies led him a pretty dance round the resorts of the town until at last he was enmeshed by the most notorious female of them all, a temptress known as the Black Panther.

These are tales without unkindness. And the telling of them reflects in some part the comradeship of the machine-lovers that characterises a great deal of the power station's story down the years.

The years immediately after the catastrophe of war were a time of immense effort on the part of all concerned, reflecting the general picture in Hong Kong of deeply changing circumstances and the lively response, both Western and Chinese, to the emerging new conditions of life and business. One factor in Company history at this period was the rapidly rising load. This applied also to Hongkong Electric over the water. The problem was compounded by the impossibility of getting new equipment except after long delays. Hongkong Electric at one time had to stop connecting any new consumers, and it was then that the link made by the Japanese with cannibalized cable across the harbour, had to be reinstituted. Agreement on terms was reached between the Hongkong Electric chairman, Mr. H.V. Wilson, and Lawrence Kadoorie, and in a carefully planned operation the cable was laid in just under an hour.

Alas, like its predecessor, the cable rested on the bottom of the harbour, at the mercy of tide and current, and more especially of ships' anchors. Predictably, in due course, it was put out of action by a dragging anchor. This happened no less than five times, with re-laying after each event. But the connection remained until the 1960s even though the exchange of current stopped in 1958 when both companies had sufficient generating plant for their needs.

The first shareholders' meeting after the war took place on 14 December 1946, confirming the constitution of the board of directors and what they had done in the Company's name since the war ended. The accounts for the period of war and occupation were presented, a doleful document showing losses of $5.4 million. In fact a large part of the pre-war records of the Company was lost during the period under review, and the problems in making up the accounts had been severe. The acting chief accountant, Mr. G.A. Noronha, had done the best he could in the circumstances. He recalls the task as an arduous one that kept him and all his staff working at full pitch.

Naturally there was no dividend forthcoming. Later the same day, at an extraordinary general meeting, the authorised capital of the Company was raised from $15 million to $25 million, enabling funds to be called up as and when needed.

Another meeting took place on 12 April 1947, at which the accounts for the thirteen months ended 30 September 1946 were approved. The net profit was $1.17 million, but losses carried forward and contingency reserves more than swallowed this, with the result that there was a net deficit of $0.76 million.

Mr. Raymond, the chairman then and for long after, began at this time to prove his mettle. Lawrence Kadoorie, one of his admirers, recalls him as 'the leader of the Jewish community in Hong Kong. He was a very imposing chap, white hair, tall and slim, and very intelligent – a clever man altogether. For a hobby he studied ancient Greek, made comparative studies of that and Hebrew.... One of the fine people of Hong Kong.'

At the April meeting Mr. Raymond announced that serious theft of current had been brought under control while with the impending arrival of spare parts the 12.5 MW machine would soon be repaired. A tariff reduction of 10 per cent was to take place at the end of the month, a first reduction that was followed by many others in the coming years as generation of current became more efficient.

The month of July 1947 was a date of some significance. In it Hong Kong got a new governor, Sir Alexander Grantham, who was to continue in that post for the next eleven years. Simultaneously, the Company at last got the 12.5 MW turbo-alternator working again. And the saga that started in late 1941 came to an unusually happy conclusion as the machine began churning out current more efficiently than any other had done since the explosion just before the Japanese charged into the Hok Un station.

Hong Kong itself was by now a different place. The numbers of people had grown once more to the pre-war figure of 1.6 million. The civil war in China was quite evidently being won by the forces of Mao Zedong (Mao Tsetung), and as the prolonged upheavals on the mainland gradually drew to their climax in one of China's periodical cataclysms, more and more Chinese fled to the comparative calm of the Colony.

This movement was significant in two ways. Numbers swelled the workforce (and of course also the ranks of those with no home to go to), and industrialists swelled the actual and potential opportunities for work, for profit and for the consumption of current to run their factories in Hong Kong instead of in Shanghai and other mainland centres as before.

In this immediate post-war period the powerful roots of the industrial future were striking down into the Colony's being. And the future was to prove more extraordinary by far than anything which could have been imagined at the time.

China Light's head office in Argyle Street decorated for the Coronation celebrations in 1953

INDUSTRIAL EXPLOSION

Few power companies in the world can have experienced a rise in sales of electricity of the order experienced by China Light between 1948 and 1951 when the output grew no less than five times. The following years saw substantial increases in sales continuing. The 1957 figures had risen by 280 per cent by the time the 1964 figures came to be announced. A simple table demonstrates these dramatic increases:

Sales

1947 =	36 GWh	
1948 =	60 GWh	(increase of 67 per cent: rise on pre-war record of 58 GWh in 1941)
1949 =	96 GWh	(increase of 59 per cent)
1950 =	146 GWh	(increase of 52 per cent)
1951 =	182 GWh	(increase of 25 per cent)
1957 =	423 GWh	(increase of 11 per cent)
1964 =	1347 GWh	(increase of 16 per cent)

Demand (annual maximum)

1947 =	14 MW
1951 =	43 MW
1957 =	87 MW
1964 =	297 MW

In order to achieve a generating increase on such a gigantic scale in a short time it was obviously imperative to implement a programme of unprecedented expansion. But to understand the astonishing build-up of demand for power, it is essential to understand the human and political changes which were taking place in the world, insofar as they affected Hong Kong, and to take a look at the nearer events in neighbouring China.

China had emerged from the Second World War with a position, more theoretical than real at that time, as one of the four big powers. In fact China was a country ravaged not only by the Japanese occupation of portions of its territory, but by at least a century and a half of dire internal struggle. The two Opium Wars with the British, far back in the early and middle years of the nineteenth century, the extraction by force of the 'unequal treaties', the siege of Canton, the sacking of the Imperial Summer Palaces outside Peking – all these acts of foreign aggression, and others, served only to weaken further the central control of the last dynasty. The Chinese saw their own rulers helpless to control foreign depredations and even, it seemed at times, aiding and abetting them in the Treaty Ports up and down the coast and along the major rivers.

It is hardly coincidence that the huge and bloody Taiping Rebellion of the mid-nineteenth century was started off by a Cantonese and eagerly joined by the southern Chinese who had at that time more experience of the foreigners (and more detestation of them) than others further north in China. Both the Taiping and the later Boxer rebels (in the last years of the century) had as one of their aims to 'drive the foreigners into the sea.' That they failed was the failure of China to progress with the industrial times, its failure to modernise, its terminal confusion before the death of the last corrupt dynasty.

China's partial emergence from the ignominy imposed by foreign

The Kowloon Peninsula in late 1946. At Hok Un, No. 12 boiler chimney is in position, and the foundations for the new stores building are being laid (extreme left foreground). In the distance, the Peninsula hotel is the tallest building near the ferry pier

domination and semi-colonization, came with Dr. Sun Yat-sen and the Nationalists (Dr. Sun was another Cantonese educated in Hong Kong, and a qualified doctor), at about the same time as the formation of the Chinese Communist Party under its first leaders. These events gave political form to the reactions of men who were patriots first and politicians second. But both Dr. Sun and Mao Zedong realised that to succeed in changing a nation you have to be a politician first and a patriot all the time. Both of them were – to the end of their lives.

Thus began the polarization of force in China between the Kuomintang and the Communists, the situation that was to be hopelessly confused by the brutal semi-conquest by the Japanese, and by the Second World War.

Once that conflagration had ended and the Nationalists were recognised by the world as rulers of China (which was far from being true), the divide deepened and the struggle turned into outright civil war. The conventional warfare of the KMT was countered by skilled guerrilla tactics of the Communists, and the upper hand was gained and lost by both sides many times in different parts of China. But, despite foreign arms worth three and a half billion US dollars between 1941 and 1948, the bankrupt strategy of Chiang Kai-shek, the deep corruption in his administration and the banditry of his armies which divorced them from the people at large, placed the Nationalists on the losing side. By 1948, Communist forces probably had as many men in the field as their opponents, but were far less well equipped.

One other factor in Nationalist defeat was the failure to manage finance, and the subsequent runaway inflation which made complete nonsense of the currency. This was perhaps one of the last and most powerful factors in their loss of what popular support was then left to them. Even capitalist city-dwellers could hardly be expected to like a government which permitted a doubling in basic commodity prices no fewer than sixty-seven times between early 1946 and August 1948; and after that August prices rose an estimated 85,000 times in the following few months, wiping out the value of money.

The decisive battle of the civil war (the Battle of the Huai-Huai, so called from its location around the Huai River and the Lung-Huai Railway) began in mid-November 1948, when four separate Nationalist armies were trapped and surrounded on the Hsüchow Plains. Together with numerous divisions which arrived to try to break the siege, these eventually surrendered on 10 January 1949.

About 200,000 Nationalist troops were killed in the battle, and 325,000 were captured. Chiang Kai-shek and his government were driven down to Canton whence they fled to Taiwan on 8 December 1949. Mao Zedong proclaimed the People's Republic of China in Peking on 1 October 1949.

For the first time in a century and more, the forces on the China side of Hong Kong's short border represented something like a regime controlling all China. And for the first time in as long a period, the government of China was capable of exercising power to remove foreign influence in the country. This they did with a vigour reminiscent of that displayed in the same process several times before in Chinese history. What was left by that time of foreign business and industry was ejected. Much of it landed on the Hong Kong doorstep, and soon began to reorganize in the Colony.

With the foreigners and their industries came Chinese owners of similar ventures, which were also set up in Hong Kong. And with both came legions of ordinary Chinese to swell the problems of the Colony which had still not fully recovered from the ravages of war and occupation.

But the coincidence of capital, both Chinese and foreign, arriving and wishing to establish industries in Hong Kong, with the simultaneous arrival of a suitable labour force to work these industries, produced one of the most astounding booms that the world of industrial production has ever seen.

Meanwhile, before the civil war came to an end, Hong Kong had built up an extremely powerful garrison to defend itself from what was seen at first as possible intervention in the Colony by the forces of Chiang Kai-shek. The Concessions at Shanghai and at Shameen on the Canton riverfront had reverted to China under an agreement signed by the U.S.A., Great Britain, and China. There was now only Hong Kong for the foreigners. Some parts of the New Territories had the appearance of an armed camp – a situation which, apart from its other consequences, meant that China Light was under pressure to extend its supplies as and when required.

The character of business and trade in Hong Kong began at this point, when the Communists took power in China, to alter fundamentally. The history of the Colony's trade had been one of entrepôt – meaning, operatively, trade with China, whose vast, even if mostly impoverished population, formed a market of very large proportions. Now the Colony turned to manufacture, and its imports (since there are virtually no raw materials in Hong Kong) radically changed in character. The main import need was now material to be processed by the Colony's burgeoning factories. The traditional industries of Hong Kong were few but well established: shipbuilding and ship-breaking, sugar refining, cement and rope manufacturing; and sub-sidiary industries such as the making of electric torches, rubber shoes, cigarettes, and matches. These were now suddenly joined by textile mills, most of them owned by former Shanghai entrepreneurs. And very soon the spinning, weaving, knitting, and finishing factories – initially mainly for cotton but later dealing with wool as well, and then with man-made fibres – took first place in the ranks of the Colony's industries. Later still, as if this first big bang innovation of textile manufacture and export had set off a chain reaction, industry diversified as world need and world fashion demanded plastics, wigs, transistors, and a string of other consumer goods.

The unrivalled capacity of Hong Kong industry and its workforce to meet each new demand with the right product, however different, and to counter each new restriction on its exports abroad, and each failing market with diversification into another, was ably matched by the future planning of China Light. The overwhelming majority of the new and expanded industries were located in Kowloon and the New Territories, and the challenge to produce enough power for them therefore fell largely on China Light's shoulders.

The driving force behind the Company's rapid expansion after the war was in part the dedication of the staff, old and new, and this has been acknowledged generously by the chairman and the board at various times. But a company requires a pilot in difficult waters such as those of the post-war years. In Albert Raymond, and later Law-rence Kadoorie, China Light was fortunate in having two inspired men. Raymond had retired from long-time residence in Bombay where he was in charge of Sassoon's cotton spinning mills – a vast undertaking, at that time probably the largest of its kind in the world. The total number of spindles in the mills under the control of Albert Raymond certainly outnumbered all the spindles in Hong Kong. Raymond is remembered as a distinguished figure, courteous, bril-liant, a leader of the Hong Kong Jewish community for many years, a man commanding the respect of business as of other communities.

As to Lawrence Kadoorie: 'He was so self-assured, so certain that we were all going to put our companies back together again.' Thus Elmer Tsu of Island Dyeing and Printing Company remembers him, and the particular atmosphere of enlightened determination. He goes on: 'That kind of confidence was contagious. After the war, I was moving my factory to Hong Kong from Shanghai and I couldn't decide whether to put it on the Hong Kong side or Kowloon side. What finally helped me make up my mind was that Hongkong Electric couldn't guarantee its power supply. Lawrence Kadoorie promised he would supply my factory – and he did.'

There were immense problems involved for the Colony in the tense and often dramatically threatening events of the post-war years. No sooner had Hong Kong recovered and begun to see industry starting to boom in response to the urgent demand of a world picking up the pieces of life after the appalling damage and losses of the Second World War, than the Korean War broke out in June 1950. Initially this tended to act as a spur to Hong Kong development and trade, but then, with the intervention of Chinese forces on the side of the North Koreans, the United Nations put an embargo on all trade with China. Probably no country in the world was harder hit than Hong Kong by this measure. Overnight, the booming new industries of the Colony supplying the newly-established Peoples' Republic of China were deprived of their major customer, and in that year Hong Kong had its industrial feet more or less cut from under it. As things turned out, it took a decade before full recovery could be achieved.

It was during the 1950s, however, that the new Hong Kong – and with it a new-look China Light – really formed, rather as an embryo forms from an apparently shapeless bundle of cells and in a short time looks like what it will be at birth, and what it will grow to be in times to come. Hong Kong was a place born of what may fairly be defined as rapine in 1841, and it grew up as something of a problem child in the long decades of the nineteenth century. The first Hong Kong met its death in 1941 at the hands of the Japanese.

At that time death was not suspected – only a severe setback, a kind of enforced hibernation. But, watching the post-war Colony develop, it could hardly be doubted, and certainly is not now in doubt, that what happened then was death and a new birth. For the new Hong Kong is fundamentally unlike the old one. It has at least one new parent – massive industry – and the other, British rule, is a deeply altered person.

In the first year of this new city and this new Company, the figures for industrial expansion and those for demand and capacity to supply it on the part of the Company tally with remarkable accuracy. The struggle to equip and re-equip the power station at Hok Un in such a manner as to meet and anticipate the growth of Hong Kong's industry was something of an epic. The success of the struggle, by all relevant standards, was a resounding victory.

China Light stated early on that it would supply electricity when and wherever it was required; and it fulfilled that promise. In days when most countries in the world were suffering from lack of foresight, and consequently were unable to increase their capacity to generate enough electricity for a newly emerging style of life and work in a new world, and when blackouts and brownouts were common in the most highly developed states, China Light has a very good track record.

To achieve this a prodigious amount of work and a prodigious sum in capital had to be put in. In November 1948, the first 20 MW turbo-alternator was commissioned, and it was followed in July 1952, July 1954, and May 1957, by three more, each of the same capacity. All these sets were bought from the same makers, now known as Associated Electrical Industries (A.E.I.). Matching them, the first post-war boiler of 200,000 lb. capacity, arranged exclusively for oil firing, began operation in June 1950. It would have been sooner at work had it not been for the huge shipping delays inseparable from the immediate post-war period. A further two boilers of the same size, also oil-burners, were added in March 1952 and March 1954 respectively, both manufactured by the usual suppliers, International Combustion Ltd. (I.C.L.)

Meanwhile, the generating units of the 'old' station were gradually sold as and when space was required for the modern equipment. But rapid increase in demand soon made it apparent that more physical area was going to be needed. The Company managed to buy 130,000 square feet in three contiguous parcels of land, part of which was owned by the Green Island Cement Co., but the majority of which had to be reclaimed from the harbour. With this new land the Company acquired a new, and as it turned out somewhat difficult tenant, Star Textile Company, which operated on part of the land a mill producing grey cotton cloth. For reasons doubtless valid in their own eyes, this company refused to budge for a long time, causing much inconvenience to China Light.

By 1950, the change-over to oil firing was virtually complete, and after that hardly any more coal was used. In finishing off the coal stocks at Hok Un, an event took place, unrecorded in official minutes. As the coal heaps were slowly diminished, the workers driving the

The half-way stage in the erection of the 20 MW unit at Hok Un, carried out between August 1946 and July 1948

excavators which loaded the trucks continued work. There was no clear dividing line between coal and what was beneath for, after many a year sitting there the coal had dyed the ground a good black colour. The workers went on, and it was not until the fires in the boilers began to go out that the engineers discovered they were 'burning' what amounted to ordinary earth.

At this point, too, the engineers living in the Company's accommodation on the Hok Un grounds lost their free supply of coal for fires in winter months. Two coolies (as they were universally called in those days) were regularly detailed in the cold months to proceed each morning to the quarters and collect the empty coal scuttles from the flats there, to take these over to the coal stock where nicely shaped lumps of coal were selected one by one, washed, and placed in the scuttles which were then returned to the living quarters. Now this daily pantomime had perforce to cease.

The station required a good deal of maintenance work after its rehabilitation, and this resulted in improved thermal efficiency. The governor, Sir Alexander Grantham, visiting Hok Un in 1952, expressed in characteristic manner his approval of the place by writing in the visitors' book: 'Hurrah for private enterprise!'

The rise in demand from industrial private enterprise was of such magnitude that for long spells the whole plant was in operation, only rarely allowing for one or other unit to be taken off load for repair or maintenance. Minor work on plant had to be done at night when load was lighter. In the circumstances, the Company was lucky (even with the assiduous care taken by the station staff) to get away with rather few breakdowns. One such instance was due to a typhoon in 1954 (named Ida) which drove the ship *Dona Lourdes* against the cooling-water intakes and caused extensive damage to the installation and loss of vacuum on the steam side of the condensers. This required the shedding of load.

By the end of 1957, Hok Un had achieved a generating capacity of 98 MW. This total included the capacity of the last remaining 5 MW set from the 'old' station which was dismantled soon after, in April 1958.

Those who had been present when the station was opened in 1940 would have found it hard to squeeze inside by this time. The station building now housed machines with a 73 MW capacity which with extensions added since the opening, totalled 93 MW – over seven times the original capacity. From this time onward it was to be known as Hok Un 'A' station. Meanwhile, a new station, Hok Un 'B', was being built on ground previously occupied by the 'old' station. This

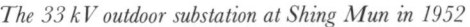

The 33 kV outdoor substation at Shing Mun in 1952

structure was designed and built entirely by the staff of China Light.

Orders had been placed in 1955 for one new set comprising a 30 MW machine with steam pressure of 600 lbs. per square inch and a temperature of 850°F., and for its boiler with a 315 klb. capacity. This was in commission by June 1958, and formally inaugurated by the governor, Sir Robert Black, on 6 August. The next set was installed by January of the following year, and the next by July 1959. With the third set installed, the first stage of 'B' station was complete. The generating capacity stood at 183 MW, doubling that of fourteen months earlier, and allowing of a measure of spare capacity – not to say a little time to take breath.

These very large efforts were, however, only the beginning. For the second stage, the Company's plans were for even larger sets and another improvement in thermal efficiency so vital to keeping generating cost low. By October 1962, four sets of 60 MW each with 900 lbs. pressure per square inch and temperature of 900°F. had been ordered. Construction of the necessary buildings was done by the Company's own staff under Mr. George Gavriloff who was construction and maintenance engineer. Surprisingly, in the context of Hong Kong, several items of archaeological interest turned up in the excavation for the foundations. Down to a depth of 19 feet below the silted bed of the sea, pottery and porcelain, all of it domestic and humble, turned up, along with the bowl of a clay pipe, a large stone weight, and various fragments of cheap late-Ching overglaze enamelled wares. The dates of these pieces range from somewhere in the Tang dynasty (7th–9th century) to the present, and tell something of the boat people anchored there, in sight of the entry to the harbour at Lei Yue Mun, and dropping their possessions casually over the side down the centuries.

The first of the four 60 MW sets was taken into service in October 1962, but its related boiler had a more difficult time in finding a home. The Star Textile Company still occupied their premises, and negotiations to induce them to move out proved longer and more tedious than was expected. The Company pleaded, truthfully, that more electricity was a *necessity*, and in the public interest. But the textile company, doubtless feeling that a measure of self-interest motivated the plea, refused to move. Various concessions had to be made before access was gained in April 1964. Meanwhile the boiler had had to be sited on the projected location of the fourth 60 MW set. The third boiler was not affected by the recalcitrant textile company,

Above: This photograph was taken on 26 September 1955 and shows Hok Un station at the end of a now vanished beach. The barn-like structure served as changing rooms for the Hung Hom Fai swimming association. Overleaf: The station about September 1963. Work on 'C' station has not yet begun

and was put up on the correct site in July 1963. But two months later a unique engineering feat began under the direction of Mr. J.F. Coombes – later to become station superintendent. The second boiler was dismantled, its parts stored in an area on the Hung Hom reclamation. Starting from September 1964, it was reconstructed on its proper site, and was finally at work in August of the following year.

Boiler number four had been commissioned in January 1964, and turbine number three in March of the same year. 'B' station was at last completed in March 1966, when the fourth turbine came on stream, bringing the generating capacity to 423 MW.

This was not by any means the end. By May 1963, when there seemed no sign of demand abating, the board authorised the construction of Hok Un 'C' station which would house another four 60 MW sets. Initially two sets were bought (turbo-alternators from A.E.I. and 550 klb. boilers from I.C.L.) at a cost of $80 million.

The work at Hok Un was but one part (if a major one) of the Company's effort to update the whole of its operation. As early as

1948 a start had been made on replacing obsolescent mains as well as plant, and a new substation had been built at To Kwa Wan in view of that area's heavy industrial load. This was followed rapidly by more substations at Prince Edward Road, Kau Pui Shek, Kimberley Road, Rutland Quadrant, and Anhui Street – all of them operative by 1950. A lot of new street lighting was installed – the whole of Yau Ma Tei, for example, being converted from gas to electricity. The last of the 60 cycle supply – to Kowloon Docks – had to be converted to 50 cycles, and the equipment ordered effected this change in 1951. The new stores building at Hok Un, ready in 1949, was commandeered by the army and not handed back until 1954.

Above: The completed new stores building at Hok Un. Overleaf: Laying the submarine cable to Tsing Yi island in 1953. Compare pages 232–233

Meanwhile, more substations were built in urban areas, supply was extended to Sai Kung district for military and villagers' use. The 22 kV overhead line was extended to Au Tau, establishing ring main facilities for the whole area. The system was further enlarged later, and by August 1953 Tsing Yi Island was connected by submarine cable.

The transmission voltage was raised in 1954 from 22 kV to 33 kV,

and a new line was laid to Ngau Tau Kok, then scheduled as a new industrial area. This line was soon extended to Kwun Tong.

The New Territories supplies came in for big new development, to match the rapid opening up. Two 33 kV underground cables were laid from Lai Chi Kok to Tsuen Wan and further. Lantau Island, formerly supplied only by small Diesel engines, was connected by submarine cable linked with overhead lines to Silvermine Bay and also to Shek Pik where a new reservoir was being built. Later the lines went on to Tai O and to Chi Ma Wan; and later still to the islands of Peng Chau, Hei Ling Chau, and Shek Kwu Chau, by submarine cable.

Demand in the New Territories increased even faster than in Kowloon. The decision in 1960 to raise the normal distribution voltage in urban areas from 6.6 kV to 11 kV (in order to avoid saturation), was followed the next year by a similar rise as 66 kV feeders were laid from Hok Un via Cheung Sha Wan to Kwai Chung and Chai Wan Kok. Later still, two 66 kV cables were laid from Hok Un to Fanling. And then in 1963 the 132 kV system was inaugurated.

Meanwhile, electricity for pumping water from China was made available near the border at Lo Wu to boost the supply to Tai Lam Chung reservoir.

The Rural Electrification Scheme sanctioned by the board was begun in 1961, the aim being to bring electricity to many small isolated communities – although in the short run this would be totally uneconomic for the Company. By the end of 1964, almost four hundred villages had been connected.

At that time the Company's transmission and distribution system consisted of lines with total mileages:

Line	Mileage
132 kV	7
66 kV	55
33 kV	274
11 kV and 66 kV	456

The aggregate capacity of transformers was 1,655 MVA. Primary substations numbered 30, and secondary ones 626.

The expansion in those years of both transmission and distribution systems was such that it required an immense amount of dedicated work from the staff at all levels. The long hours of overtime are remembered by many members of the staff of those days, together with the emergencies occasioned by such diverse events as typhoons, lightning striking the overhead wires and insulators, and other sudden interruptions to supply. Automatic reclosing gear, first installed in 1955, helped to minimise breakdowns. Typhoons such as *Susan* in August 1953, severely tested the Company's newly installed radio-telephone equipment which proved very useful in shortening time required for repair work. The severest typhoon of the period – *Wanda*, which struck in the early morning of 1 September 1962, scoring a bull's-eye on the Colony – caused havoc to many installations, most especially in outlying areas. The 1,600 calls for assistance were all dealt with as expeditiously as possible, but in some cases supply was off for two days. The severity of *Wanda* will long be remembered by all who were in Hong Kong at the time.

The steep rise in demand obviously meant a rise in numbers of consumers of electricity, apart from a rise in per capita consumption in certain fields.

Year	Consumers
1941	33,000 plus
1946	24,000 (just post-war)
1948	30,000
1955	65,000
1964	289,000

These figures include data from the New Territories, although the main rise there came somewhat later on. In the New Territories the rise in numbers of consumers was startling, as skeleton figures show:

Year	Consumers
1946	3,000
1953	5,000
1960	18,000
1964	61,000

Such vast and rapid increases meant phenomenal amounts of hard work on the part of the Meter Department and also the Distribution Department in supplying all comers and in calibrating the necessary meters. And the fact that in many a household not one but two meters had to be installed to cope with lighting and separate power tariffs, hardly eased the burden. The total number of meters in service rose from 27,000 in 1946 to 461,000 in 1964 – a reflection of the prodigious effort put in.

Myriad meters meant myriad meter readings, and an equivalent number of accounts. It is hardly surprising that the Company found it needed a computer. Whatever may be thought by the public at large about those temperamental pieces of hardware, they can be made to take some of the sweat out of routine work. The NCR 315 which was installed in 1963 was the first electronic computer in Hong Kong. By 1964 it was printing the majority of bills – not, it must be confessed, always with total accuracy. But perfection takes time to accomplish, even in the best regulated computers. Its functions were pressed into service in other departments of the Company's work. The chairman, with his usual humorous sagacity, remarked about the new equipment: '... lest we expect too much, it is well to remember that a computer is but the servant of the human brain.... Man has not surrendered his duty to think, and your board and staff have not been rendered obsolescent.'

Probably every company has a computer story, and China Light is no exception. One Thursday, the chairman recalls, the machine refused to work. NCR who installed it averred that there was no need for alarm since there was another example in Hong Kong which was compatible. But when China Light's programmes were fed into this one, it returned the answer that, in effect, it did not speak the same language. The suppliers then said they had several in Japan from where a spare part would be sent – their office in Tokyo promising for the following day. Their expert visited the British Consulate in Tokyo for his visa, but it was a holiday in Britain and the office was closed – and Saturday and Sunday were also holidays. On Monday he got his visa and came to Hong Kong – but the part did not fit. A phone call was then made to the factory in the States and on Tuesday the part was airfreighted. At San Francisco someone saw that it was addressed to the China Light & Power Co. Ltd., and decided that as far as China was concerned the contents of the package were 'classified' and 'strategic' and could not be forwarded.

It took all that Tuesday to persuade the authorities that Hong Kong was not part of the People's Republic of China and that no harm would come to America if the package reached our shores. By the Thursday evening it arrived and was fitted – exactly one week after the initial breakdown. The computer started to work again – a quarter of a million accounts behind. And the arrears had to be 'guesstimated.'

In 1963, the year of the computer's installation, the provident and retirement fund, updated in 1952 after a review of wages and salaries led to a new grading scheme and the consolidation of cost of living allowance into pay, was further modified in the light of the recommendations in studies begun in 1958, which resulted in a report in 1962. The new provisions were for guaranteed retirement money dependent on years of service and final salary. The Inland Revenue Department approved the scheme as from 1 January 1963, and this implied that payments from the fund to employees on retirement would not be subject to Hong Kong taxation. A second scheme existed already for meeting retirement benefits of hourly paid staff, and sufficient funds were assured to supply it.

The number of Company employees in September 1964 was just under 2,500 – equivalent to 7 persons per MW of generating capacity. The staff in 1939 had been about 900, equivalent to 28 persons for each MW of generating capacity. There were numerous changes in personnel during this period of expansion.

Board and Staff Changes 1947–1961

The able chairman since just after the Second World War, Albert Raymond, died suddenly toward the end of 1955, and was succeeded by Lawrence Kadoorie who has retained the chairmanship up to the present. The board was strengthened by the addition of Mr. H.D. Benham in 1947, and by Mr. Leo D'Almada, Q.C. in 1955 – the young counsel involved in the arbitration dispute. Mr. W.A. Welch became a member when Sir Man-Kam Lo died in 1956. Sir Man Kam's place was taken by his brother Mr. M.W. Lo. In 1961 Mr. Y.C. Wang joined, but in the following year the number of directors was reduced again by the death of Mr. H.D. Benham.

1950	E. Joffe confirmed as station superintendant
	J.W. Barker appointed distribution engineer
1954	F.C. Clemo retired after 34 years service
	C.F. Wood appointed manager
	E. Joffe appointed deputy manager
	A. Macdonald appointed station superintendant
1957	P.W.A. Wood left the Company
	A.A.M. Onslow appointed secretary and chief accountant
1959	C.S. Rolfe succeeded Mr. Barker as distribution engineer
	J.W. Barker appointed executive engineer

The capital requirements for all this mushrooming expansion and development were obviously extremely heavy. For the twelve years 1947–1958 inclusive they amounted to $143.7 million, of which $21 million was financed by shareholders' subscription and the remainder very largely by retained profits and by depreciation. In the ensuing six years, 1959–1964, capital expenditure came to $360.4 million.

During the period, authorised capital was increased from $25 million to $100 million in December 1950, and to $150 million in May 1959. The issued capital, amounting to $13.2 million just after the war, rose to $21 million in 1949, to $42 million (after the 1950 revaluation of assets) in 1951, to $55.2 million in 1958, and to $110.4 million in 1964.

By this time it was becoming apparent that the Company could not forever rely on its shareholders to raise the kind of money that the future appeared to require in order to finance greater schemes that would almost certainly be needed.

Meanwhile, another brew of circumstances and events, related to but separate from the rapid growth of the Company and its services, was simmering, and was destined to reach an angry boil in the not too distant future.

THE NATIONALISATION FIASCO

O<small>N</small> 9 April 1959, the government, without prior intimation, sent letters to both electricity companies informing them of its intention to set up a commission to enquire into how some form of statutory control could best be arranged to cover their operation. The announcement was not entirely a surprise. But in order to understand what caused the government to act in this manner, a brief glance over the shoulder at the then recent past is necessary.

The finger that gradually increased its pressure on the trigger, and which eventually fired the commission gun, was the introduction in late 1951 of a surcharge on the bills of ordinary consumers, coupled with the continuation of the bulk supply fuel surcharge which was initially based on the rocketing price of coal. When coal was no longer the energy source, the surcharge was still applied, but with an arbitrary discount granted to the consumer.

For the ordinary user of domestic electricity the percentage increase was at first 19.1 per cent. It rose to a maximum of 23.1 per cent in April 1952, declining to 9 per cent in August. Thereafter the surcharge varied between 18 and 4 per cent until (after the long crisis was resolved) the tariffs were put on a different basis on 1 July 1965. The figure for bulk consumers varied between 3 and .75 cents per kWh over the years.

As the efficiency of production by the Company improved, rates in the New Territories were lowered to the level of those in Kowloon which, in January 1956, expressed in cents per kWh, were: 29 for lighting, 14 for ordinary power, 13 for special domestic heating. And these rates remained in force until a new system took effect in 1965.

Complaints about tariffs had been voiced as early as 1946, but at that time the government, after consultation with the Company, sent a letter from the office of the Financial Secretary to the chairman of the complaining party, the Kowloon Merchants' Association. This stated that 'there can be no question of Government instructing the China Light & Power Company to reduce their electricity rates. The Company is a private enterprise, and Government cannot interfere unless it considers that the Company is acting against the public interest. The conduct of [the Company] has been consistently cooperative with Government policy and we are satisfied that as soon as it is economically possible for them to reduce their rates they will do so.'

This, naturally enough, hardly mollified the complainants, and in the ensuing years other protests appeared in the newspapers and elsewhere. While many of these complaints were based on an obvious lack of knowledge of how an electricity company has to be run, there was an insistent undercurrent that would appear to have had some justification.

Long after the dust of the whole issue had settled, Lawrence Kadoorie, who had been a major participant in the dénouement, freely admitted that 'we didn't preserve the best of public relations.' Consumer complaints were often channelled to government departments when in fact the Company would have been wiser to deal with them by explaining in some detail the nature of its operations and the means by which the fuel surcharges (particularly those on bulk consumption) were computed. Looking back, it is easy to be wise. But in the extreme pressure of those days as the Company strove with quite extraordinary force and perseverance to .expand at least as fast as its market and potential market, the question of public relations was not uppermost in anybody's mind. The omission was unfortunate, and almost cost the Company dear.

By the end of 1948, the government considered necessary some measure of control on tariffs and dividends, and the board of China Light sought the opinion of a British lawyer, Sir Valentine Holmes, on the subject. He affirmed that the Company was registered as an ordinary company free of any statutory control, that it had conducted business on that basis, and that control of its dividends would be tantamount to confiscation of shareholders' interests. After an exchange of letters with the government, the matter was allowed to drop.

In 1957, the running fire of dissatisfaction among large consumers was highlighted in a petition sent to the governor by the Kowloon Chamber of Commerce. Another, by the Chinese Chamber of Commerce, suggested a commission of inquiry. Surcharges were also opposed by committees of industrialists from Kowloon and the New Territories who, it seemed, failed to understand that the Company's rates actually favoured them against smaller consumers. Eventually the Secretary of State for the Colonies was requested to take action. The criticism was mainly that while the electricity companies were making steadily increasing profits, the surcharges remained. There was little appreciation that very large parts of these profits were channelled back to finance the heavy and ongoing programme of expansion of the generating capacity by the purchase of new plant. In fact, the arguments about how such expansion was to be financed consumed a lot of time later on, and were in the end inconclusive. The *Hong Kong Standard* carried a weighty editorial on 11 December 1958, headed 'More Power to You.' 'There are those in Hong Kong,' it began, 'who believe that public interest and concern on the problems of power supplies and rates are seasonal phenomena which will fade away quietly if one merely pretends that they don't exist.

'Unfortunately ... this approach is useless in solving problems, and in the case of Hong Kong's power rates and supplies question, procrastination merely compounds the difficulties....

'Currently there has been a renewal of civic concern ... as a result of the disclosure of the comparative rates of industrial power, and the fact that during the last two years there have been more than 3,354 minutes of power disruptions of supply to our industries in the New Territories.

'... what is needed is a strident civic outcry.' And the crusading *Standard's* editorial went on to delineate the general aims of such an outcry, disassociating itself from 'irresponsible soap-box orators' and offering help to the government 'in its formulation of a constructive policy.' And much more to the same effect. This was in continuation of a leading article of two days previously in which the power cut disclosure was made, and its details analysed. The Company was accused of, on most occasions, not informing the factories to be affected, and one manufacturer vowed that he had lost $15 for every minute without power, in overhead expenses alone.

This article had been followed on the next day by one from civic leaders and industrialists arguing that from the 'huge profits' of the Company a 'special reserve fund' could 'easily be set aside to meet unexpected increased costs of fuel and freight.' The writer favoured 'raising fresh capital for modernising the plant of the two companies.' The money, he said, should not come from consumers. Many industrialists and others expressed similar views.

The extent of the Company's lack of public relations was (or perhaps should have been) evident then; for many of the lengthy arguments put forward by the complainants, and the solutions proposed were far from revealing understanding of what the issue was all about in terms of generating and distributing electric power.

On 12 December 1958, a lead article on the front page of the

Standard was headed 'Committee Suggested to Investigate Hong Kong Power Setback.' This argued from the industrialists' point of view for some form of control over the power companies, and Mr. Dhun Ruttonjee, a leading business figure, endorsed the suggestion.

The following day the Civic Association was reported as having made the first move to get the government to set up a special committee. And Mr. Chu Shek-lun, president of the Chinese Manufacturers' Association, said the CMA had approached the companies on the question of surcharges, but that the response had been 'slow-motion sparring' on their part.

On 14 December, Lawrence Kadoorie replied, the story headlined in the *Standard* by: 'Kadoorie Says Hong Kong Industry Subsidised by Power Company.' At a meeting the day before, he was reported to have said that it was the Company's policy to subsidise industry by supplying part of its bulk power below cost.' It had always done so and 'only two factors can lead to improvement – greater efficiency and lower fuel costs.' He pointed to the rising efficiency of the Company's operation with the continuing installation of new plant. But the cost of fuel was beyond Company control. In any case, '2,000 minutes of the 3,354 power stoppages were arranged shutdowns.'

At the meeting in question, the Hon. C.E.M. Terry, who appears to have had his head slightly above cloud level at the time, 'was at a loss to understand why anybody in the commercial and industrial world should ever advocate government interference with the operation of a commercial company.' He failed to confront the actual problem – that the industrialists (whether rightly or wrongly) were baying for blood. And he failed, further, to understand that their reasons (whatever justification these had) were given a powerful push in the direction of government interference by the prevailing climate in Britian at that post-war time in favour of nationalisation of all big companies, especially those which were in public utilities fields. Since then it has often been asked in tones of wonder, as did Mr. Terry, how it was that industrialists in Hong Kong actually came to support nationalisation of the electricity industry. But this would appear to be the answer – lack of Company public relations, and the heady atmosphere in England in favour of what seemed a logical way round the problem of conflict between shareholders' rightful interests and the public benefit.

On 16 December, the *Standard* was back in the fray with a headline: 'Statistics to Back Kadoorie Statement on Subsidies.' Lawrence

Kadoorie, having bitten off quite a mouthful with that statement, now came to the tribune to justify himself and what he had said.

'Selling electricity,' said he roundly, 'is different from selling tins of tomato juice. An electricity undertaking sells a service. One unit of electricity will light a 15-watt lamp for 66 hours; the same unit will operate one of our more modern cotton mills for approximately one and a half seconds. Therefore it is obvious that the charges for the service of supplying electricity must vary according to the purpose for which it is being used.... The China Light & Power Company has always been industry conscious, knowing that the livelihood of a large part of our population depends upon employment. It is this reason that has motivated preferential rates to industrial users even to the extent in the case of large bulk consumers of supplying a part of their requirement at prices below actual cost.'

He continued: 'It must also be remembered that electricity must always be available to meet the highest demand made on the system at any time of the day or night and, unlike commodities such as tins of tomato juice to which I have referred above, it cannot be stored. This is another factor which plays a most important part in costs, and is the reason why every effort is made to obtain what is commonly called a balanced load.' By balanced load he meant a more or less even demand over the twenty-four hour period – a state of generating bliss that is indeed hard to achieve, and was harder at that time before the wholesale use of such items as air-conditioners.

'Incidentally,' Lawrence Kadoorie continued, 'this is one of the reasons why in England and in many other parts of the world power companies base their rates on true cost and maximum demand. In this way the supply undertaking minimizes the risk of losing out on the average because of abnormally high demands from any particular sections of the community.'

Both before and after the remark about the Company's role in subsidising industry and the follow-up 'tins of tomato' speech, the press was full of a flurry of letters, articles, and statements by people of every shade of opinion, including those 'irresponsible soap-box orators' the *Standard* had vowed to eschew. The controversy raged furiously and, in the manner of such *causes célèbres*, often without the benefit of understanding on the part of participants. There were among all the rantings, however, just a shade too many of the 'customer-be-damned' accusations about the Company's conduct to be altogether ignored.

The long exchanges in the press had their lighter moments. Hong Kong is, even today, a place in which letters to the editor tend quite often to be couched in Verse or Worse (to quote the apt title of a book of such material). A letter from Mr. W. Stoker, General Manager of the Hongkong Electric Company, in the *China Mail* averring that all explanations of the electric companies' positions had been fully given, incited a correspondent signing himself 'Two Little Sparks' to verses under the title: 'Poetic Musings on the Surcharge':

'In darkness we sit without any light,
Mr. Stoker has turned our day into night,
He's made a surcharge that's left us broke,
We think he's a cruel cold-hearted bloke.

Our profits have gone with his half per cent
We wonder where the other half went,
Our own small business is busted wide,
We sure have been taken for a ride.

If only we'd been supplied in bulk,
Our wives and children would no longer sulk,
But our lights have gone out, and so's the kitty,
Oh, Dear Mr. Stoker, please have pity.

He said the surcharge is to pay,
For the high cost of fuel today,
But we who moan, we get the kick,
His Company's profits make me sick.

O Scrooge, O Stoker, hear our plea,
And give us Christmas light for free.'

The editor noted that he had deleted 'two questionable stanzas.'

Undoubtedly the best piece of verse among a somewhat tedious lot came from a gentleman signing himself A.G.

'To get this brawl i' proper focus,
Between accountant, cranks and stokers,
Why don't they think of saving brass,
And turn instead to using gas?'

It turned out that the initials stood for Arnold Graham, the sporting and well liked head of the Gas Company.

The government's eventual response to years of controversy and bickering took the form of the letter of 9 April 1959, addressed to both electricity companies. The press had the story the next day. The government, according to the letter, after long and careful consideration of their position, had come to the conclusion that it was undesirable that the operations of the two electricity supply companies should remain entirely free from statutory control. A commission would be appointed and would make recommendations in regard to such control. The government proposed that the chairman of the commission should be a leading member of the Central Electricity Authority in the United Kingdom, and that one of the members should be an independent accountant capable of dealing with allegations of overcharging and excessive profit-making.

The news was greeted with approval by the Chinese Manufacturers' Association. Both China Light and Hongkong Electric pledged assistance to the commission, and the chairman of the former company affirmed the opinion of his board of directors that the policy of the

A new cash register for the Company's accounts office at Tai O on Lantau island arrived by sampan in 1960

One of many villages supplied under the Rural Electrification Scheme – 1961

Company in endeavouring to anticipate the needs of industry for electrical power must be continued.

The Electricity Supply Companies Commission was formally constituted on 16 July. Its chairman was Mr. John Mould, retiring chairman of the East Midlands Electricity Board in England; the other two members were Mr. C.J.M. Bennett, chartered accountant and partner of the London accounting firm of Barton, Mayhew & Co., and Mr. Dhun Ruttonjee whose endorsement of the idea of an investigative body had been voiced the year before. The legal adviser was Mr. O'Reilly Mayne, and the secretary was Mr. D.S. Whitelegge.

The Commission's terms of reference were stated: 'Whereas it appears to government undesirable that the operation of the electricity supply companies in Hong Kong should remain entirely free from any statutory control; to advise, in the light of –

    a) the past record of the Hongkong Electric Company Limited and China Light & Power Company Limited

    b) the control now exercised over the other public utilities in Hong Kong, and

    c) any other relevant circumstances

on the form and extent of control which government should impose, and on the method of assessment of any compensation which may become payable in the event of any such control being imposed.'

Looked at dispassionately, the terms of reference were so poorly drawn up, so loosely worded, that it is perhaps permissible to wonder what amateur translated government intentions into such a cloud of verbal vagueness. The members of the Commission evidently thought much the same, for they decided, before proceeding, to attribute a basic meaning to their terms of reference. Their opinion was that what they had been asked to do should be viewed in the light of a government decision to impose some form of control. Whether the government actually had decided, at this point, is debatable. But the assumption was warranted.

The secretary of the Commission, David Whitelegge, wrote to the Company on the day after the body was set up inviting it to give evidence and to make submissions on all aspects of its activities, and sought detailed information on these under forty-seven headings. The Company promptly forwarded answers from a whole volume of data which had been compiled for the purpose. Hongkong Electric did likewise.

The Commission then called for representations in writing from organisations and members of the public, to be followed up by evidence taken at public hearings on those submissions. There were over twenty responses in the form of complaints and comments, among which were those of the Hong Kong Cotton Spinners' Association, and the Chinese Manufacturers' Association. The latter expressed discontent at what they termed the companies' monopolistic and arbitrary attitude, and made several accusations: that new generating units were outmoded and too small, therefore inefficient and costly; that rates and especially the surcharge were too high, making for unreasonably large profits; that rates in the New Territories were needlessly higher than elsewhere; that stoppages in supply, often without warning, were costly to factories; that deposits were too big and interest on them too small, and that meter rents were unfair and capital contributions for service in outlying areas excessive; that requirements for transformer rooms on private property were unreasonable; and that technical aspects, such as variations in voltage and insufficiency of the feeder system, demonstrated inadequacy.

This range of complaints was representative of that voiced by most other parties.

Altogether fifteen public hearings were held in the Legislative Council Chamber, the first serving mainly for identification purposes. The second, third, fourth, and fifth sessions were occupied by complainants commenting and enlarging on their submissions. The sixth and seventh sessions, on 22 and 23 October, saw China Light presenting its case. The Company was represented by the chairman, Lawrence Kadoorie, the manager, C.F. Wood, the secretary and chief accountant, A.A.M. Onslow, and the statistician, E.M. Laufer. Counsel for China Light was D.A.L. Wright, instructed by Messrs. Lo & Lo; and Sidney S. Gordon (now Sir Sidney) acted as adviser on financial matters.

Lawrence Kadoorie began with an address in which, after outlining the Company's history, he stressed what must be the theme of any consideration of its policies and achievements – the identity of its interests with those of Hong Kong industry, the interdependence of each with the other. He then considered the Hong Kong investment climate in which, as he pointed out, not only private companies' projects, but also government expenditure are self-financing. Capital expenditure comes out of revenue as far as possible. Finally, Mr. Kadoorie described the significant progress made in post-war years in the absence of restrictive controls.

Mr. Wood replied to technical questions which had been raised – those of interruptions of supply, new installations requiring capital contributions, and aspects of the tariffs in the New Territories. Mr. Onslow clarified such subjects as depreciation, bulk rates, deposits, meter rents, and the controversial surcharge, as well as other related matters.

In what remained of the seventh, and in the eighth and ninth sessions, the Company's representatives were cross-questioned by various parties on aspects of what they had said.

Hongkong Electric's case came up in the tenth session, on 30 October, and was presented by the manager, Mr. W. Stoker. He strenuously argued against any form of control other than what already existed: and at the conclusion of his speech he was cross-examined at some length.

The following three sessions were taken up with detailed questioning of the China Light and Hongkong Electric representatives by the legal adviser to the Commission, while the final two days' business on 16 and 17 November consisted of further addresses by various participants – the last two by Mr. Kadoorie and Mr. Stoker.

After refuting several allegations, Lawrence Kadoorie continued: 'I am not here to talk of others, but since our Company's record of service has been impugned I have no alternative but to make comparisons, some of which may be odious. Inadequate water – a four hour supply after one of the wettest summers on record and at a cost 220% higher than pre-war. Inadequate telephones, inadequate buses, inadequate piers, inadequate ferry services including vehicular ferry services to the outlying areas of the New Territories. Inadequate hospitals, inadequate staff, inadequate planning. To borrow a phrase from the Sunday Press, centres of frustration controlled by desk-bound administrators. Too little, too late, and at too high a cost. Why? because of lack of foresight and delays in implementation inherent in bureaucracy and government controls.

'In contrast the China Light & Power Co. has built in record time and at the low cost of £40 per kilowatt one of the finest power stations, for its size, to be found anywhere. We have taken our power lines to remote parts of our area and have always been ready to supply electricity to industry and to the public where and when needed, at an average price less than double that of pre-war, a price which is decreasing as steadily as our size and efficiency grow'. This state of affairs would not have been possible 'had we had to work under the same restrictive conditions as those I have criticised.' He went on to affirm that if controls were introduced there must be provision for fair, prompt, and effective compensation. His concluding remarks are worth quoting in full:

'We ask to be judged by Hong Kong standards, and this demands an understanding of local problems entirely alien to anyone who has not lived here for some time. Looking back, it is almost impossible to imagine the ruin that was Hong Kong immediately post-war, and one can only wonder at the work, the strain, and the spirit that has made Hong Kong what it is today. The secret has been to put first things first. Our duty has been and is to supply the community with a basic need. That we have not yet attended to a few of the more formal requirements of a well-ordered electricity supply company does not mean that we will not in time become more orthodox. It certainly does not mean that we are a disorganised concern without the knowledge or ability to do this. What it does imply is that our board has an intimate knowledge of the Company's requirements and fully recognises the paramount importance of employment to our community. That this knowledge has been put to good use is apparent to all who have seen the industrial development of Kowloon and the New Territories, a development which has become the wonder of the world and in which the China Light & Power Company has played the major and indispensable part. I can only hope that in the short time the members of the Commission who have come from England have been in the Colony, they have been able to grasp what this outpost of the British Commonwealth stands for – a free port, free from prejudice, free from interference, and free from unnecessary controls, where a free people can go about their tasks to the benefit of the community as a whole. No one should treat the responsibilities of this heritage lightly, lest in destroying these fundamental freedoms they destroy the Colony itself.'

Speaking for Hongkong Electric, Mr. Stoker agreed that they too had an obligation to the public; but he pointed out that, as a private company, Hongkong Electric also had an obligation to its shareholders, like that of any other utility company in Hong Kong. He outlined his board's intentions to finance the company by the present methods. A continued reduction of tariffs was intended. He firmly believed that control of the company's operations would be detrimental to consumers and shareholders alike, but that outright purchase was the only alternative to the present basis.

Thus, on 17 November, what had been – by Hong Kong standards – a brief commission of enquiry, concluded with special thanks from its chairman to the companies who had at all times, in his opinion, been forthcoming, helpful, and ready to produce a great volume of information – which was a testimony to their administration.

The commission now had before it a large body of evidence. It then began to examine the physical structure of the companies' plant, and their commercial organisation, inspecting administrative offices, power stations, and transmission and distribution systems. Much supplementary information was called for. And prior to the hearings the commission had paid familiarisation visits to industrial undertakings on both sides of the harbour, and to the New Territories as well – even to Lantau Island.

When the report of the commission was published on 20 January 1959, it had the effect of a massive explosion in the Colony. What the commissioners recommended was nothing short of outright nationalisation of the electricity companies.

Given the year in which this recommendation was made, and the constitution of the commission, it was perhaps less surprising than it seemed at the time for such a decision to have been taken. Britain was riding the flood-tide of nationalisation, legislation for which was carried through in an outburst of post-war new-broom policies such as generally erupt after major national trauma. The honeymoon with the new and (often) brash is ecstatic and, depending on the participants and the environment, longer or shorter lived, before the crude reality of experience begins to show how intractable is human nature, and how hard to alter. And then some sort of backtracking has to be set in motion.

What was proposed by the commission was:

a) the establishment of a government authority responsible for generation, transmission, and distribution of electricity in Hong Kong, since in this way the competing interests of shareholders and consumers would be eliminated.

b) to achieve this, the two companies would be taken over by compulsory purchase rather than by acquisition of their share capital.

On 9 April, just prior to the appointment of the commission, that capital was valued on the stock market at $192.2 million for China Light, and at $168.9 million for Hongkong Electric. The shareholders of the latter had contributed a further $10 million since that date. The purchase was to take the form of $6\frac{1}{2}$ per cent interest stock with an ultimate redemption date of about thirty-five years from the date of issue. The amounts allotted were to be $220 million for China Light and $208 million for Hongkong Electric. These levels were to insure that income derived from the stock, after 12.5 per cent tax, would be about the same as the dividend paid or forecast prior to 10 April 1959, that is, the 1958 dividend of 12.1 million of China Light and the 1959 dividend forecast of 11.4 million of Hongkong Electric. The government was to undertake responsibility for compensation, guaranteeing both interest and principal of the stock, and maintaining appropriate sinking fund installments.

It was estimated that, all things being equal, in the years 1960 to 1964 the surplus on revenue account, together with depreciation, would be sufficient to meet the $358 million covering the combined capital requirements as forecast by the companies.

Riggers and others who worked on the first 60 MW unit at Hok Un, commissioned in 1962. Left to right: Law Kin, Lo Siu-pui, Chui Kau, Leung Kuei and Lam Shing

The commission believed that the integration of the companies, and the resultant pooling of their generating resources, would make for a substantial reduction in investment on new plant, and there was a hope that the new situation would facilitate the building and operation of a desalination plant in conjunction with the production of electricity – something that the chronic water shortage problem of the Colony made desirable.

The commission found the conflict of interest between shareholders and consumers could only be removed by elimination of the former, which was in their view confirmed by the 'intransigent attitude of the companies' that admitted of no compromise on the question of control.

In general, the commission had very little fault to find with the companies, which it commended for many positive contributions to

196

the rebirth and growth of Hong Kong after the destruction of the war, and for augmenting their plant in line with the needs of the community. These aspects were said to compare very favourably with the record of similar undertakings elsewhere in the world. The companies' policies on other matters were slightly criticised, only China Light's policy on bulk tariffs coming in for strong objection as offending two basic principles in rate fixing. These were that there ought not to be undue preference shown to one group of consumers against another; and that the rates charged to each group should broadly reflect the actual cost of production of the current supplied to the group in question. The outdated fuel clause, offset by an arbitrary discount, was condemned if only because it was detrimental to good consumer relations. But the commission took the view that an adjustment in times of rapid fluctuation of fuel prices was a perfectly proper procedure. Concerning the uneconomic development in supplying outlying areas, it was agreed that this had been taking place and that the programme reflected great credit on the companies. But on public relations there was a communication gap. 'Many of the representations and submissions made to us displayed an ignorance of the essential facts. This illustrates ... the extent to which consumers are in the dark with regard to the companies' operations. We feel that there is room for improvement in this aspect....'

The single major and substantive conclusion of the commission was that – despite the evidence of continual reasonable growth which they had heard and indeed commended, and despite the fact that they found no dire fault with the management of the companies, the only sure way for an electricity utility service to be run more efficiently was by the plastic surgery of nationalisation. Doubtless, in the political and emotive climate of the times, they had what they felt to be their reasons. Many more august bodies were of the same opinion then. History overturns many an idea that once appeared right.

The government then wrote to China Light about interim measures to safeguard assets, and also restricting the rate of dividend for the current and succeeding years to 'the latest rate adopted or publicly forecast prior to 10 April 1959,' and forbidding dividends or additional shares from being paid, or assets distributed. The Company pointed out that this would restrict the 1960 dividend to the 1958 figure of $1.10, while for 1959 $1.25 was paid – an increase in no way affected by the appointment of the commission, and accompanied by a tariff reduction. It alleged discrimination against China Light since, because of fortuitous circumstances, Hongkong Electric was able to pay its current dividend at 1959 rates. Government disallowed the request. The Company took advice of a leading London Queen's Counsel and tried again, but again failed to alter the government decision.

Meanwhile – absurdly, having gone to the trouble of appointing an expensive commission to back it up – the government showed definite signs of reluctance about a policy of nationalisation. It was apparent that having asked for advice and paid heavily for it, government was rueing the day it started the process. On 3 February, the Financial Secretary spoke in favour of 'the principle that a public utility should be operated by private enterprise in collaboration with government, contrary to the principle recently enunciated by the Electricity Supply Companies Commission.' It appeared that the government was now open to reasonable suggestions from the companies on these lines. Lawrence Kadoorie went on holiday to Russia at this point. When asked by the press why, he replied: 'So as to learn how better to deal with the Hong Kong government.'

March saw the Colonial Secretary opine that 'the two electricity supply companies ... with the government's consent are now exploring all possibilites to find a formula which might cover most of the recommendations of the Commission, short of nationalisation, the aim being to ensure that government is given a maximum degree of control consistent with the retention by the companies of incentive to efficiency and expansion.' But government insisted that any such compromise be formulated against a background of amalgamation of the companies and integration of their generating facilities.

The first such proposal came from the companies after a great deal of work and lengthy discussion with counsel, with economists and technical experts from England and elsewhere, and was submitted as a draft agreement on 24 October 1960.

In his annual review dated 24 November 1960, China Light's chairman, remarking that the obvious nationalisation solution ran counter to the Colony's interests, and that the Company's success story had been accomplished by private enterprise, went on to propose a scheme in which for each unit of electricity the Company sold it would be entitled to a certain margin of profit and, within that margin, to a certain margin of dividend. Dividends were to be limited to a standard margin and the difference between this dividend margin and the standard margin of profit would allow for a standard margin

The commissioning ceremony in 1962 for the Company's first 60 MW unit. Left to right: E. Joffe (deputy manager, CLP), Horace Kadoorie (head only), Lawrence Kadoorie, an unidentified person behind, C.F. Wood (manager, CLP), C. Wilcox (AEI), Michael Turner (Hongkong and Shanghai Bank)

of retention – broadly in line with the needs of normal expansion.

This scheme aroused widespread disapproval, and the government rejected it, while explaining that it was still reluctant to carry out the full proposals of the commission if a suitable compromise formula could be found.

The ensuing spate of proposals and schemes, and their universal rejection by the government, do credit to the ingenuity of all concerned. During this long, tedious process it was always evident that as far as was possible and compatible with its dignity the government wanted to slide out from under the suffocating mantle of the Commission's advice which it had intemperately sought. The various permutations and varying weights given to the essential elements of the problem were all tried unsuccessfully, and China Light shareholders were at all times kept well informed of what was going on. They were naturally impatient from time to time, and expressed their opinions forcefully on the issue.

Late in 1963, the government came to the conclusion that it was not possible to devise merger terms between the two companies as it had all along insisted, and that in the near future it would introduce legislation to impose controls on each company separately and to grant franchise rights without charging royalties. The dividend restraint was relaxed for 1963, allowing a return per share of $1.80 for Hongkong Electric shareholders, and $1.35 for those of China Light.

Two problems then faced the Company, as formidable as any in its history. The first was, how to obtain the right conditions of control so as not to stunt the growth which it was felt lay ahead of it: and second, how to find the funds to finance that growth potential – forecast in the next five years to require $525 million.

Lawrence Kadoorie takes up the story. 'Before the war I had a friend, Mr. George Bell, who was manager of the Standard Oil Company in Hong Kong. We used to meet with a few others once a week over lunch for informal discussions on the local scene. After the war, when we were all very busy getting China Light going again, there was a definite neglect of public relations. And then the Commission made its recommendations which in part were unpalatable to the government. The Company was stuck, we couldn't move. It seemed that we might as well go ahead and spend all we could on development. Appetite came with the eating. The Company was growing rapidly, but no one quite knew what to do about it. Our money was blocked, and there was little hope of attracting new investment.

'At this point, by chance, my friend George Bell came on the scene again. He was on a round-the-world tour on retiring from Standard Oil – now Esso – drumming up some business for them as his parting gesture. "Can I sell you any oil," he asked me. "Not the least chance," I replied. "We are in a mess here, the government has tied our hands."

'The upshot was that he suggested that Esso possibly could be of some help. At that moment I was on my way to London, and he suggested that I might return via the States. When I was in London I got a call from Esso in New York who said the same thing. So I stopped off at New York, where I was introduced to the Standard Oil Co. (N.J.) chairman, Mr. Michael Haider.

'In our discussions, at one point I said: "Really, I've been thinking, the only worthwhile part of the Company that I can now control is the contract for the oil. We use forty per cent of the total oil import to Hong Kong. The idea might be attractive to Esso?"

'Esso then made a loan offer, which I turned down flat. They said they'd never seen a loan turned down so rapidly before! I said: "What I want is a strong partner to share the profits and losses. But of course you Americans are scared to death of the word Communist. We're a company situated twelve miles from the border with the largest Communist country in the world, and if I could sell electricity to them, I would. Besides probably half our customers are Communists anyway!"

'Esso consulted the United States government, and of course it was confirmed that they could not take shares in China Light as we might be dealing with the Communists. So that was no go. Then the idea, which eventually became PEPCO, formed. If a new company could be formed to make electricity and sell the product to China Light – China Light could then do as they wished with it.

'I remember as we were going to lunch at the University Club in New York, thinking how odd it was that I was one man and they were numerous top echelon people. And, just as we were going into the restaurant, I had one of those flashes I get of being on a satellite and looking down on myself. Here I am, I thought, going in to talk with one of the most powerful companies in America on investing about forty million US dollars in a power company right on the doorstep of the Communist bogie. I suddenly stopped. "Gentlemen," I said, "I have something to say. It seems quite extraordinary that I'm talking to you on this question at all. If you want to be polite and give me lunch and say "go home" afterwards, I won't mind. On the other hand, if you want me to go home now, I'll also understand!"'

'The negotiations were one of the best-kept secrets in Hong Kong. At the time we had a drought and four hours of water once in four days – so when Esso were in the Colony finalising the deal we pretended that they were here to work with me on the question of a desalination plant. The agreement was a considerable surprise to Shell: one of our directors described their reaction as severe shellshock.

Lawrence Kadoorie goes on: 'When PEPCO became a reality, Lord Shawcross, from Shell – the company we had abandoned in favour of Esso – came to visit me, obviously with the intention of hauling me over the coals. But it so happened I had a curio dealer in the office at that moment. He had brought three huge jade *pi* [discs of a ritual nature with a central hole] – so we got talking about them. I bought one and Shawcross and an influential oil man with him from the Middle East bought the other two. So we never got round to talking about Shell.'

The Financial Secretary, John Cowperthwaite, indicated his interest in the PEPCO idea, and very soon three-cornered negotiations were held between the government, Esso, and China Light. By late October a plan had been hammered out incorporating a scheme of control that was to prove acceptable to the government, together with another scheme covering a number of understandings between Esso and China Light, later to be embodied in relevant agreements. On 27 October, Mr. Kadoorie and Mr. Leet, Vice President of Esso Eastern for manufacturing operations and one of the Esso team which put together the joint venture with China Light, forwarded a joint letter to Mr. Cowperthwaite outlining the plan providing for a form of tariff limitation as well as for the injection of $220 million of Esso capital, and with China Light shareholders offering to provide a further $40 million in new capital as and when needed. The plan was outlined in a submission accompanying the letter.

a) The annual permitted return of China Light and the new company would be 13.5 per cent of the combined average of fixed assets

b) any difference between permitted return and profit after taxation to be transferred to or from a development fund which would represent a liability of China Light and would not accrue to the interest of its shareholders

c) an annual charge equal to 8 per cent of the average balance of the development fund would be credited to a rate reduction reserve to be liquidated by reduction in charges to consumers

d) the net return – the permitted return, less the sum of the charge on the development fund and interest on longterm loans – to be shared between China Light and the new company as agreed by them

e) China Light to reduce tariffs at a rate that would amount to $18 million when applied to the revenue for 1965 – with certain provisos

f) the combined dividend payout to China Light and the new company not to exceed 50 per cent in each of the years to 30 September 1967; thereafter, a dividend limitation would come into effect if the balance of the development fund exceeded ten per cent of net fixed assets

g) these arrangements to be applied from 1 October 1963, and to remain in force for fifteen years. After twelve years, discussions with government to be held on revisions

The essential aims of the joint scheme can be stated quite simply:

a) China Light, with Esso, proposed to form a new company which would produce electricity to be sold exclusively to China Light
b) this company would initially install four 60 MW units at Hok Un on land leased from China Light, and then four 120 MW units, or the equivalent, on some other suitable site, the whole of this generating plant to be constructed and operated by China Light
c) the financial structure of the new company would be: China Light 40 per cent; Esso 60 per cent
d) net returns, as defined by the scheme of control, would be shared between China Light and the new company in proportion to their respective shareholders' funds, these to include paid-in capital, free reserves, retained earnings, and shareholders' advances
e) both China Light and the new company would as soon as possible purchase all their existing petroleum requirements from Esso under long-term contracts at competitive prices

On 17 November 1964 the long struggle for a solution was over. (Hongkong Electric remained without a scheme of control until 1979). The government approved the scheme of control subject to the agreement of the shareholders of China Light and Esso. Agreement was readily acquired at the extraordinary general meeting of China Light on 29 December 1964. After the motion to approve had been passed, the seconder of the motion, Mr. Shum Wai Yau, addressed a few remarks to the meeting. He could not do better, he said, than quote from the governor, Sir Geoffrey Northcote's, observations on the occasion twenty-four years ago when he opened the new power station at Hok Un. And he went on to do so: 'Obviously it is to a great manufacturing future for this town of Kowloon ... that the China Light & Power Company is looking, and I readily take my stand beside them in that confidence.

'What would Kowloon be today had it not been for the vision and the faith of Mr. R. G. Shewan and his fellow directors during the first twenty years of the century? ...' (see pages 133–134). What indeed? The results were now apparent to all. The agreement of Esso had already been obtained, and the new company, named Peninsula Electric Power Co. Ltd. (PEPCO), was incorporated on 31 December

1964, with an authorised capital of $400 million.

Thus one of the major challenges that ever faced the Company was successfully met and overcome. The scheme of control, accompanied by the benefits of the new partnership, would ensure ample generating capacity, reasonable tariffs subject to limitation, and an adequate return to the shareholders. The Company's successful conclusion of the long negotiations set the course for what – even then in the mid-sixties – could not wholly be imagined in terms of the future expansion of the enterprise.

From the point of view of Esso (the trade name for the overseas operations of the parent company Exxon, which owns Esso Eastern Inc., which in turn owns Eastern Energy Ltd. in Hong Kong), the joint venture with China Light was initially a means of re-entering the Hong Kong petroleum market after the split in which Standard Vacuum (a joint venture between Esso and Mobil) broke up. In

One result of typhoon Ruby in September 1964 – the chimney of a boiler at Hok Un broke off at roof level and came to rest on a generator transformer

Hong Kong, Mobil took the assets, excluding Esso from the market. Sir Lawrence's proposal of a partnership between Esso and China Light was seen by the former as just the opportunity they had been looking for. Thus Esso's first agreement with China Light was a twenty-year fuel supply contract. This formed the basis for the relationship that developed as time went on and became a commitment to future participation in the power industry.

The fuel sales incentive was the driving force at that time – Esso still supplies 45,000 barrels of fuel a day to China Light and the generating companies – but as the need for more generating capacity continued to rise there came a time in 1977 when it was evident that additional capacity would mean the construction of a new power station – a station that was to be coal-fired due to the uncertain world situation regarding oil supplies and cost.

Exxon thereupon decided on a commitment to invest in this new station, an investment that was ultimately to prove one of the largest among all its worldwide operations. Exxon regards this as investment in the energy business, even if petroleum sales are not involved – that business being the conversion of fossil fuel into a variety of forms of energy.

THE PRESENT AND THE FUTURE

THE history of Hong Kong after the Second World War will probably seem as dramatic and astonishing to future historians as it does to those in whose lifetime it took place. For Hong Kong had the geographical, the demographic, and other types of good fortune to be in the right place at the right time, and with something like the right ingredients added to the mix, which sparked off what might almost be termed a chain reaction. In a decade, what had been a comparatively sleepy entrepôt situation, admittedly torn apart by Japanese occupation, changed to one of fundamentally different character.

In a world hungry to restock with the goods that war had destroyed, or whose production it had stopped or severely limited, Hong Kong suffered neither the constraints of new political solutions as did Britain, nor lack of manpower, skilled and unskilled. The misfortunes of civil war in China drove the manpower and the capital and the managers of industry there into the Colony, eager to start work again in comparative stability and political calm. The success of the Communists in 1949 in China virtually sealed these Chinese capitalists and also their opportunity-hungry workforce within the Colony. The Korean War gave a first fillip to new trade and industry, and the lagging economies of Europe, the developing purchasing power of the underdeveloped countries, and the appetite of the American market for goods that Hong Kong could make cheaper than the Americans could – all contributed to a unique set of motivating forces which transformed Hong Kong's life, its urban and even its country landscape, and its significance in the worlds of East and West, in such a small space of time as to give rise to many profound internal problems. Housing, transport and the alteration in traditional Chinese attitudes forced by rapid and deep changes in living, made life hard for government and governed alike.

The world communications revolution set in motion by the development of the transistor, later to be followed by the satellite, and by numerous other quite new elements of technology, all contributed to the amazing burst of construction and industrialisation in Hong Kong. Within a decade, all those who remember the fifties and sixties will recall, the actual look of Hong Kong changed as if by magic. The physical structure of its industrial, commercial, and residential premises was renewed in a frenzy of building that must in many ways be unique. Probably more concrete was poured in Hong Kong between the late 1950s and the end of the sixties than in any comparable city in the world at any time.

The major significant effect was a transformation scene in which a colonial backwater became one of the world's greatest ports, greatest industrial producers, greatest exporters and, latterly, greatest financial centres – well within the lifetime of a teenager born in 1950. By far the greater part of this growth took firm root in Kowloon and the New Territories. Initially, the newly arrived Chinese tended to think that Hong Kong Island was a better bet for them than the Kowloon Peninsula, which was contiguous with China just over the border: but pragmatism won, and the Island's geographical restrictions were soon seen to be too confining. By and large, industry took Kowloon and the countryside around as its new base. The figures relating to this industrialisation are astonishing. Taking even a rough guide in the yearly increase in number of establishments in the manufacturing industry, the table below gives a surprising picture of growth.

Number of Manufacturing Establishments

Year		
1947	833	(pre-war 418)
1948	1,266	
1950	1,752	
1952	2,088	
1956	3,319	
1960	5,599	
1964	8,215	
1970	17,239	
1974	25,250	
1975	31,034	(slightly different categorisation)
1976	36,303	
1978	39,606	
1980	45,409	

And by comparing the major manufactures of the Colony at the beginning and in 1980, the lists, in order of number of establishments for each category, demonstrate the profound change in the picture of manufacturing Hong Kong.

Main Industrial Groups

Year 1947	Year 1980
Cotton textiles	Wearing apparel
Rubber shoes	Fabricated metal products
Dockyards	Plastic products
Preserved ginger	Textiles
Tobacco, matches	Printing and publishing
Paint	Electrical machinery, apparatus
Cement	Machinery (non-electrical)
Ropes	Furniture

The whole scene, except for the perennial textiles, has changed. One further table demonstrates briefly the way in which China Light kept up with and anticipated demand for electricity over the same period. The numbers of manufacturing establishments are in parentheses.

Maximum Demand and Installed Capacity

Year	Maximum Demand (MW)	Installed Capacity (MW)	Year	Maximum Demand (MW)	Installed Capacity (MW)
1947 (833)	14.0	30.5	1974 (25,250)	1005.0	1612.0
1948 (1,266)	18.9	30.5	1975 (31,034)	1086.0	1812.0
1950 (1,752)	37.2	50.5	1976 (36,303)	1232.0	2012.0
1952 (2,088)	46.1	67.5	1978 (39,606)	1572.0	2152.0
1956 (3,319)	79.0	82.5	1980 (45,409)	1980.0	2416.0
1960 (5,599)	145.0	182.5			
1964 (8,215)	297.0	362.5			
1970 (17,239)	709.0	870.0			

The increase in numbers of factories was 54.5 times, and that of the Company's maximum generating capacity, 79.2 times between 1947 and 1980.

The new generating company, PEPCO, had its own board of five directors. The first chairman was Mr. F.C. Westphal, Jr., a senior Esso executive familiar with Hong Kong. He was invited, *ex-officio* as it were, to join the board of China Light. Two other PEPCO directors were Esso men, while the manager and the chairman of China Light represented that Company.

An operating service agreement between PEPCO and China Light was concluded, under whose terms China Light would render all necessary assistance in the construction, operation, and maintenance of its electrical generating facilities. The selection of new plant was stipulated to take standardisation into account, and to give preference to long-term suppliers.

Hok Un 'C' station, already under construction, was to be developed and owned by PEPCO, and the materials already in hand were therefore transferred.

The structural work in construction of Hok Un 'C' station was again in the hands of George Gavriloff, and the building was erected by China Light staff. Four 60 MW units were commissioned in July and December 1966, in May 1967, and January 1968; and the new station was inaugurated on 13 October 1966 by the Hon. S.Y. (now Sir Sze-Yuen) Chung, who also joined the China Light board. The combined capacity of Hok Un station when 'C' station was completed, amounted to 662.5 MW.

Before 'C' station was finished, it was quite evident that Hok Un would soon be saturated, and as it was unable to accommodate any further plant of the necessary capacity a site for a new station would have to be sought elsewhere – and as quickly as possible.

In the early 1960s the demand was rising at about 20 per cent per year, and it was obvious to anyone who thought about it that in the remarkable dynamism of those expansionist times such rises would probably continue for long enough. This reasonable prediction, together with the fact that bigger generators are more efficient than numbers of smaller ones totalling the same capacity, but take longer to install, boiled down to the necessity of finding a new site, and then making a start on ordering the plant.

After careful study of all the factors involved – where, for example was the new growth located, and likely to be located? – a site was found on Tsing Yi Island close to expected load concentration. It had abundant cooling water, was suited to construction of tanker facilities, and was relatively cheap. The area purchased from the government was 3.4 million square feet, and PEPCO took possession on 1 January 1966. Site formation involved cutting more than 5 million cubic yards from the hillside and reclaiming about 2.2 million square feet from the sea, together with the building of a sea wall 3,600 feet long. Of this land, about 1.1 million square feet was subsequently leased to Esso for a petroleum terminal to ensure continuity in fuel deliveries.

The first planned station – Tsing Yi 'A' – was to house six units, each of one 120 MW turbo-alternator set with a hydrogen-cooled generator, and an 840,000 lb. boiler with main steam at 1800 lbs. per square inch pressure and 1000°F., with reheated steam at the same temperature. The exhaust gases from each pair of generators would go to a common stack 425 feet high.

This station was again in the hands of Mr. Gavriloff as far as its construction was concerned, and erected by China Light staff. Great savings were achieved by constructing the whole station in one continuous operation – every building required for boiler-house, pump bay, turbine room, and switch-house, as well as an adjacent office block containing staff amenities, main control room, station laboratory and test rooms, in addition to the actual offices, went up as part of an integrated, planned operation.

Orders for the first two turbo-alternators were placed with A.E.I. and I.C.L. respectively in 1965, and the first 120 MW set was commissioned in April 1969, the second in November of that year. The station itself was officially inaugurated on 22 April by the

The governor, Sir David Trench, with Lawrence Kadoorie (left), and Mr. F.C. Westphal, Jr., Chairman of PEPCO, after the opening of the Tsing Yi power station in 1969

governor, Sir David Trench, who arrived in a helicopter – an event then still sufficiently unusual to cause comment. The company present included Mr. Michael Haider, chairman of the Esso parent company, Standard Oil Co. of New Jersey (now Exxon), and Mr. W.B. Cleveland, president of Esso Standard Eastern Inc., together with several hundred others prominent in Hong Kong – so many people, in fact, that special ferries were laid on by the Star Ferry Company to bring them to what was then still an island, unconnected to the mainland.

Tsing Yi 'A' had a capacity of 720 MW when it was finished with all six 120 MW sets in place, and was commissioned by April 1973. But it was evident, several years before that date, that further capacity was going to be needed. 'B' station was therefore designed for four units of 200 MW capacity and the plant was ordered from the same suppliers as before. The construction of the buildings was again entrusted to Mr. Gavriloff. He retired in 1973 and the job was then taken over by Mr. C. Mitchell. The completed 'B' station was ready in March 1977. The total capacity of Tsing Yi station, including a 42 MW gas turbine unit, was then 1562 MW.

By that time the formerly quiet Tsing Yi Island had been joined to the mainland by a bridge, jointly financed by China Light and other industrial organisations, which was opened by the governor, Sir Murray MacLehose, in February 1974, and then handed over to the government.

Steam driven turbines, economical to run as they are, require hours to reach maximum efficiency from 'cold.' In order to provide quick-start facilities at both Tsing Yi and Hok Un the Company installed gas turbines. The first at Hok Un replaced the two oldest boilers there in 1972, and the first at Tsing Yi was commissioned in September 1974. The gas turbines function very much as do the jet engines of a 'plane, and in fact the most modern variety is a variant of the jet developed for the supersonic Concorde – an example of the profitable industrial spin-off from a venture that was doomed in the air by escalating fuel costs, and perhaps by its rather small passenger capacity. By pressing a button, the gas turbines come on load in a matter of minutes.

China Light had a total generating capacity of 362 MW in 1964. By the end of 1977, the combined capacity of China Light and the associated generating companies stood at 2,212 MW. This consisted of 410 MW (80 at Hok Un 'A' and 330 at Hok Un 'B'), plus PEPCO's 1802 MW (240 MW at Hok Un 'C' and 1562 MW at Tsing Yi). In a matter of thirteen years more than five times the former capacity had been added to the system.

Between 1964 and 1979 there was a vast expansion of business, not only in the industrial field but in every other. In that period the number of customers all but trebled – from 289,000 to 843,000. Within this figure is concealed the staggering increase in numbers of customers in the New Territories – from 61,000 to 281,000. The yearly consumption of electricity per capita went up from 580 to 1956 kWh. This, of course, reflects the increasing use of electrical gadgets in the home, increasing affluence enabling their purchase and also the payment of the electric bills. The age of the electric iron in virtually every household, of the refrigerator in a majority, of forests of cooling fans, and a proliferation of lighting that is basically decorative instead of merely functional – had begun to arrive.

Thinking back to those early days of the century when lighting was generally reckoned by the number of lamps – those hot little properties that produced quite as much heat as yellow light, and looked like the twentieth century's answer to the common firefly – it is obvious that the expectation from life of the vast majority of the Colony's citizens has today profoundly altered. The day of the charcoal cooking fire has gone (except in the service of the pandemic fad of barbecuing on the beaches and in the country). It was replaced by the rice cooker from Japan, possibly to be counted one of the fundamental domestic inventions along with the electric light itself, and perhaps the telephone. Lower down the priority list came the hair-dryer – a boon in a humid climate. And lastly television. Probably most users little realise that when they switch on their medium-size TV set they are doing the equivalent of switching on perhaps three lighting bulbs of 100 watts each. Although the rice cooker is probably rated at 1,000 watts, it is not in non-stop use in the home, as TV is in many a household. So the bill for TV in terms of electricity consumed must form a large part of the family's total account. In 1980, over ninety per cent of Hong Kong households possessed at least one TV set. In the same year there were not far short of a million households in Hong Kong.

The seemingly unending task of bringing light and power to all those families in all but the most remote of the Colony's areas, is obviously a very big one. In densely populated urban places, the question that is posed is the load on the transmission system and on the distribution. Too much load – that is, too much electricity being used at one time – is liable to cause load shedding which results in a drop in voltage and a 'brown-out'. This is a rare occurrence in Hong Kong, something that both electricity supply companies can take pride in – when neighbouring countries suffer almost daily from just that event.

In the distant villages of the New Territories, the task is compounded by the need to build overhead lines from the nearest substations, sometimes to build new substations also, with all the transformers and switchgear required ancillary to this operation of supplying current to a group of people who may number not more than a hundred in isolated places. The operation is uneconomic in the short term, but has been persistently carried out under the rural electrification schemes. In turn, the sum of the load from literally hundreds of small places adds up to an increase in load on the distribution system, and eventually on the transmission from power station to major substations, from which the distribution network fans out.

A milestone in Company history was passed in April 1966 when the first 132 kV underground cables from Hok Un to Tsun Yip Lane substation were put into service. In the same year the change-over from 6.6 kV to 11 kV was effected in the distribution network of all urban areas, as well as at Tsuen Wan and Sha Tin districts. New 132 kV overhead lines were put up between the Kwai Chung control centre and Sha Tin, Hammer Hill, and Castle Peak Road, reinforcing the system for the New Territories. Another 132 kV overhead line went from Hammer Hill to Kwun Tong later, and in 1973 a 66 kV ring main for the New Territories was completed, thus extending flexibility in the transmission system to all parts.

At the same time the Company was enhancing its network of communications, converting its VHF radio links from AM to FM, and erecting a repeater station at Golden Hill to improve reception. Micro-wave equipment was installed in 1974, and this system was integrated with the Company's own private automatic telephone exchange systems in 1975.

In the middle and late seventies many another line was laid, and many another substation was built, reflecting the rise in population, in load, and also the changing distribution pattern of population and industry with the blossoming of vast new industrial and residential towns at Tuen Mun, Tsuen Wan, Sha Tin, and elsewhere.

In 1976 the ambitious project to build the Colony's first underground railway – or at least the first part of it – brought an agreement with the relevant authority to supply the power. This involved both Hongkong Electric and China Light. The facility of using the railway's power distribution system in the event of failure of supply from either source was also agreed on.

By the end of 1979, the Company's network of lines was impressive indeed.

Voltage	Kilometres
400 kV	101
132 kV	259
66 kV	228
33 kV	531
11 and 6 kV	1883

The aggregate capacity of transformers stood at 11,339 MVA, and there were 108 primary and 2,674 secondary substations.

It would be reasonable to think of this ramifying system of transmission and distribution as fairly proof against the hazards of even the Hong Kong climate. Yet, in 1971, when typhoon *Rose* struck with winds at times reaching over 150 m.p.h., an explosion devastated the substation at Tsun Yip Lane in Kwun Tong, in the heart of one of the most heavily industrialised segments of Hong Kong. The ensuing fire completely destroyed the 132 kV switchgear and ancillary plant. And due to freak conditions and a concurrent failure of various protective devices, the fault could not be contained in the immediate area. For the first time in many years there was a complete blackout. Power was restored initially in a couple of hours, but it took a week of gruelling work to bring the system back to normal.

In the fifteen years up to 1979, the number of employees of China Light just about doubled. The period as a whole was comparatively harmonious, with two short interregna in 1966 and 1967 when widespread unrest – even rioting – gripped the Colony.

One of the side-effects of the Cultural Revolution, then in full swing over the border in China, was the much disputed and argued-over social unrest that blew up in Hong Kong. The ostensible trigger was the raising of fares on the Star Ferry from the Island to Kowloon but, like that proverbial last straw, this was but one of a series of wider irritants that so inflamed the popular mind that the balance was tipped and violence broke out. While it is easy for readers of histories, even for their writers, and for those who guide the destinies of power and any other companies, to sit back and enjoy their anger at the profound disruption to life caused by violent protestors, it must be remembered that people do not protest about *pleasant* circumstances. Apart from the ferment in China at the time, some of the tensions of which did indeed spill over the border, the quality of life for the majority of the lower-paid workforce in the late sixties in Hong Kong was not enviable. The mood of the times may perhaps be illustrated by a small incident involving Horace Kadoorie who was then living in the New Territories. As he was driving into town, he noticed a large metal box, with what he took to be a clock attached to it, lying by the roadside. His immediate thought was that the object must be a bomb, and he called the police. In due course the bomb disposal unit arrived, covered the object with sandbags, and blew it up. Unfortunately, to the consternation of all concerned, the object turned out to be a valuable piece of equipment recently arrived from England for use in testing.

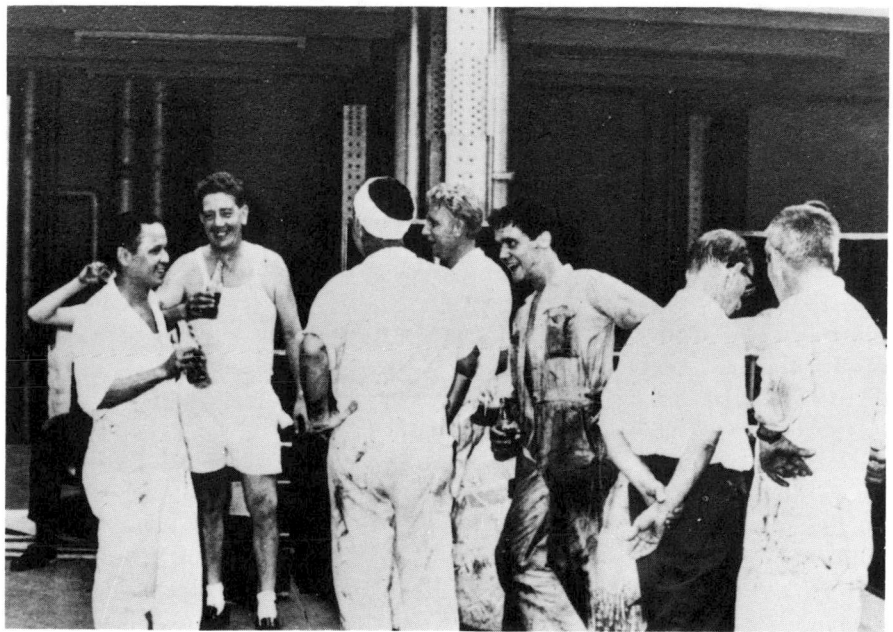

On the first night of the 1967 riots the 60 MW turbine, commissioned a year previously at Hok Un, shed a blade. Almost no labour being available, a team of engineers buckled to and started repairs. Left to right: Sunny Gomez (CLP), Bob Wallis (AEI), W.E. Derbghossian (with headband, CLP), J.F. Coombes (CLP), John Glennan (AEI generator engineer), L. Martland (CLP), and Bob Swan (AEI)

One result of the riots was the speed with which amenities such as playing fields, swimming pools, and entertainments of various popular sorts were instituted in rapid succession, once the active protest died down.

For the Company, the events meant that the workers union called on the total labour force to down tools. Sixty-three per cent of the power station workers and twenty per cent of the distribution employees – a total of 665 persons – walked out, many never to return. Engineering and clerical staff were not affected, nor were those working on building construction. But at the power station shifts had to be extended to twelve instead of eight hours, and dormitory accommodation, meals, and transport facilities had to be provided. In the event, continuity of supply was maintained, and when the unrest died down new employees were taken on and trained.

In the same year, conditions of employment in the Company were adjusted to underline equality of opportunity, and job definitions were made more clear, rather in the manner advised by the government; and wages scales and conditions for employment were improved in an effort to encourage a greater sense of belonging, of corporate spirit. One other lasting result of the disturbances is that the Company still provides meals at the station for those who work there.

Numerous changes in the board of directors took place during the period 1964 to 1979. The board was strengthened in 1965 when it was joined by Mr. G.R. Ross and Mr. F.C. Westphal, Jr., who was chairman of Esso Hong Kong and also of PEPCO. In due course it was felt that further enlargement of the board was indicated and, with shareholders' approval, the maximum number of directors was raised from nine to twelve in 1966, and then to eighteen in 1975. Mr. Westphal was to return to the United States on retirement in 1971, his place being taken by the new chairman of Esso Hong Kong, Mr. C. Howard Duncan. Mr. Duncan in turn, on his retirement in 1978, was succeeded by Mr. Roy W. Smith, Jr.; and in the same year Mr. J.S. Dickson Leach was appointed a director, bringing the strength of the board to sixteen in all.

The death in 1966 of Mr. W.A. Welch left a vacancy, filled by Mr. K.H.A. Gordon. In the following year Mr. Michael D. Kadoorie – Lawrence Kadoorie's son – and Dr. S.Y. (later Sir Sze-yuen) Chung became members. Mr. Leo D'Almada resigned in 1968 on leaving

Right: Conductor stringing at the Rambler Channel overhead crossing in 1969

Hong Kong for retirement in Portugal, and in the same year Mr. R.J. McAulay became a director. After retiring as general manager of the Company, Mr. C.F. Wood joined the board in 1970.

Mr. S.S. (now Sir Sidney) Gordon, lately retired as senior partner of Lowe, Bingham and Matthews, had joined the Kadoorie interests and was welcomed to the board early in 1971 and appointed deputy chairman – an office he has continued to hold until the present. He was knighted in 1972.

The role of Sir Sidney Gordon, a jovial and modest man, is as important in the modern history of the Company as his dislike of talking about it. Lawrence Kadoorie has described him as 'the link between the generations,' obviously referring to the continuity of the Kadoorie family and interests in China Light. And he has gone further than that. 'It was he who advised me during the arbitration proceedings, it was he who dealt in vast detail and masterly fashion with the complicated financial minutiae involved in the scheme of control formulations and negotiations; it was he who coped in a very fundamental way with the subject of the very substantial loans raised for the development of PEPCO, KESCO, and CAPCO.' Anyone with some knowledge of any one of these long and taxing problems and processes will be able to assess broadly the vital role played by the personality as well as the expertise of Sir Sidney.

It is generally a truth that it is both easier and more comfortable to assess persons who have passed out of the mortal realm and can neither be hurt nor embarrassed by the assessment. There are a number of such men in China Light. The Company has been fortunate, and also well advised in its choice of senior executives in recent years, just as it was, with only minor exceptions, lucky (more than well advised) in its choice in the early days.

But the contribution of these modern men is one that is perhaps a little hard to delineate without the risk of appearing fulsome in the pages of the Company's own history. They therefore tend to get less than their due. There is also the very real point that everyone in the Company moves, consciously or unconsciously, in the ambiance of the chairman – a figure of quite awesome stature in the world of business at large, apart at all from his impact within the Company. Lawrence Kadoorie himself, however, is at pains to voice his admiration for those around him who have taken with him and on their own the brunt of the hassles, the abrasive circumstances, the frustrating concatenations of events, and the painful jabs of the unforeseen.

Kwai Chung Control Centre

Before the commissioning of Tsing Yi power station (above) in 1969, all electric power was supplied from Hok Un station. Monitoring the power flow in the system was therefore a comparatively simple operation. With the advent of a second station, however, introducing two-directional flow, more stringent methods of monitoring became essential.

Various other factors, improving operational safety and consumer emergency services, indicated the need for centralised control of the power system. Kwai Chung, where a major substation was being planned, was selected as the most suitable site because of its geographical relationship both to the power system and communication network.

The system is a computer-based data acquisition and supervisory control system (Supervisory Control and Data Acquisition – SCADA). Data are received at the central processor from, and commands issued to, the remote terminal units, mainly via the Company's micro-wave system. A training facility is included in the installation, complete with a simulator evolved for this purpose by Company engineers. By the use of this, engineers with experience in distribution are trained quite rapidly in transmission and generation control, thereby enabling them to use the complex facilities of the Kwai Chung Control Centre. Overleaf: Part of the control panel at Kwai Chung

A portion of Hok Un 'C' turbine hall in 1981

In the ranks of a Company that is on the whole singularly happy in its personal relationships among senior executives, there are numbers of men whose services have been exceptional, mention of whom is in no sense an implication that they alone are responsible for the Company's achievements or occasional failures. In the structure of a large international company, the responsibility must necessarily be corporate, and in general the contributions – positive or not so positive – are known basically to a mere handful of senior executives.

Nonetheless, in the decades since the Second World War and perhaps even more narrowly in time since the partnership with Esso and all that this entailed in the complete restyling of what was hitherto a local organization as an international operation of the first class, the mettle of numbers of those concerned most intimately has been severely tested time and again.

221

Repair work in progress inside the furnace of a boiler at Tsing Yi power station

Cyril Wood, for long general manager, is one of those men. Michael Kadoorie recalls him from his childhood, tirelessly active on the Company's behalf. In those days the New Territories was still deeply rural. You would hardly meet three vehicles on the road to or from Kowloon. During the construction of various overhead lines Lawrence Kadoorie often spent Sundays with Cyril Wood and, accompanied by Michael, toured the routes, preoccupied entirely with the ongoing possibilities and problems of transmission – transmission actually in the field. The pioneering spirit of Wood was a good match for the same sort of approach in the chairman. And this spirit is visible in Michael Kadoorie today.

On another plane, that of directorial capability, no one in the Company would overlook the contributions of Mr. M.W. Lo. Now well over eighty years old, he still plays a game of tennis, and has a breezy, entirely characteristic outlook on life. This sporting good nature overlies an acute mind. His occasional incisive statement in comment on proceedings at meetings is worthy of note, and his sensitivity to general Chinese public opinion is also valuable.

M.W. Lo's nephew, Mr. T.S. Lo, is the latest representative of the family on the board of China Light.

Another director, Sir S.Y. Chung, a member of the Executive Council and a man of tremendous experience in public and business life, is remarkable for his political acuteness. And both these men, in their expressed views from time to time, open new windows on the questions under discussion, revealing possibilities that might not otherwise have been envisaged. This is a valuable asset to any board.

The general manager, Dean Barrett, came to China Light after a ten-year stint in Shanghai from 1947 to 1958. There he was manager in charge of a large textile company which was taken over by the Chinese at Liberation in 1949, and with whom he remained until the company had been satisfactorily handed over to the new rulers. 'My time in Shanghai taught me several things, among which were to be tolerant, to be patient, to be understanding,' he says. And these are valuable qualities in a man in his position with the Company.

Dean Barrett arrived in China Light at the end of 1966 shortly before the retiral of Cyril Wood. He and John Osborne were at that time appointed joint managers. Osborne unfortunately passed away not long afterward, and Mr. Barrett eventually became general manager in 1974. His field is strictly in the financial and administrative aspects of the Company where he has in many ways been

Above: In a remote part of the Sai Kung Peninsula a handful of villages such as the one above, and a few hundred people, benefit from quite extensive networks of power lines. Left: An aerial view of a New Territories village supplied by the Company

required by its phenomenal expansion and changing nature to make sweeping structural financial changes.

The extent of the Company's financial operation is implicit in a few figures. Spending in one year, currently, on plant is equal to what the whole company was worth a matter of two years ago – $3–4 billion – which was the book value of China Light then. In terms of the peak demand dramatic figures come up also. In 1966 when Barrett joined, this stood at 400 MW, whereas in 1980 it was 1,980 MW. The estimated peak for 1990 is 5,000 MW – a positively quantum-size leap in a quarter of a century.

Some other figures offered by Dean Barrett to demonstrate the need he found for complete financial revamping of the Company's operations makes equally astonishing reading: The Company's billings to customers each month are in the region of $300 million, and there are

Above: Hok Un station from the air in 1980. A comparison with the photograph on page 166 shows the huge development not only at the station but on the Kowloon Peninsula and on Hong Kong island also. Right above: A ceremony marked the opening of the gas turbines at Hok Un on 26 November 1980. Left to right: John Weedon (managing director, GEC, Hong Kong), Roy W. Smith, Jr. (chairman, KESCO), Sir Lawrence Kadoorie (chairman, CLP), John Coombes (station manager), A.J. Dawtrey (gas turbine engineer, CLP), Albert Lam (mechanical projects engineer, CLP). Right below: Sir Lawrence Kadoorie with Mr. P.W. Read (manager, transmission projects, CLP) unveiling a plaque at the Tze Wan Shan EHV substation, 22 December 1980

about one hundred new customers each day of the year. The monthly cash flow of China Light is between $500 and $600 million.

With Sir Sidney Gordon, Dean Barrett was heavily involved in what in the secrecy of some of its decisions one might be tempted to call the cloak without the dagger arrangements effected by China Light and Esso in the formation of KESCO. Mr. Barrett emphasises the close involvement of Sir Sidney as a financial adviser – a matter of crucial importance since KESCO was formed, as the Company has since that time been borrowing very large sums in contrast to its former policy of trying not to borrow money. One example is of course the loan of $10,000 million for Castle Peak 'B' station. He quotes Lawrence Kadoorie as saying: 'If we're going to borrow, let's borrow big!'

The 400 kV Transmission Cable

In order to joint sections of the 400 kV cable, a complicated procedure (above and opposite page) has to be adhered to in controlled conditions. This requires many hours of skilled work. The cable consists of numbers of copper wires bunched in its centre as the core and immersed in oil. These are insulated with various materials (impregnated papers and tapes) and covered by an outer sheath. Jointing is complicated by the fact that oil has to be allowed free flow in and out of the core from tanks at intervals along the length of the cable. As load increases the copper core heats up and expands, expelling part of the oil; and when the load decreases the reverse occurs. The 400 kV cable runs between Tze Wan Shan and Hok Un, for most of the approximately seven kilometres under road and pavement surfaces, passing through some of the most rapidly developing and highly populated areas of the earth's surface.

Such is the fever of demolition and construction along virtually its whole length, and the eagerness with which sometimes irresponsible contractors and others delve into the ground in or near their site areas, that it has been necessary to design and construct special protective environs for the cables. The vertical section (page 230) shows a typical protective environment for cables running under tarmac at ground level.

Despite massive protection afforded by depth under the surface, layers of earth, concrete, tiles, and the presence at various depths of warning marker tapes and coloured concrete, since the cables were laid there have been several instances of damage from excavation. Each of these necessitates costly repair in the form of jointing. In order to minimize such interference – which, paradoxically when the extremely high voltage is considered, may not damage human beings since the circuits break in a few milliseconds from the time of interference – the Company employs a man to inspect the whole route continuously during daylight hours. His job is to give warning of possible excavation work which might affect the cables (page 230).

The approximate length of the cable is 42,300 metres, and the cost per metre is HK$750 at 1978 prices. The cable is immensely heavy, weighing 35.72 kg per metre

1   *At the junction of the two ends of the cable, either a plug is inserted to stop the flow of oil past the joint, or a small tube is placed so that oil can flow through after compression of a ferrule connecting the two ends together*

2   *A copper ferrule surrounds the opposed ends of the core*

3   *Impregnated paper and tapes wound round the core*

4   *Brass flanges are bolted together to seal the parts of the covering of the joint*

5   *A lead sheath covers the layers of impregnated paper and tapes*

6   *Oil enters to impregnate the cable*

7   *The copper core of the cable which conducts the current*

8   *The duct running inside the copper core, permitting flow of oil in and out as the core contracts or expands with heat*

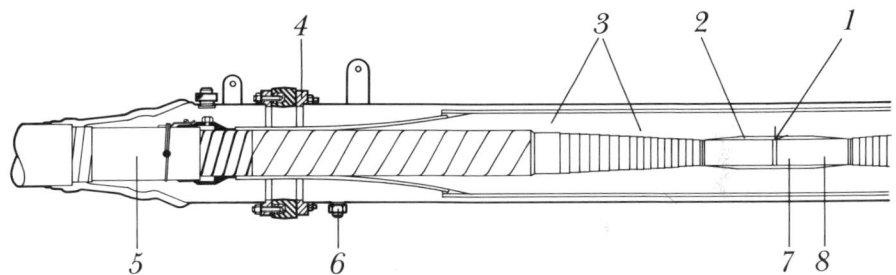

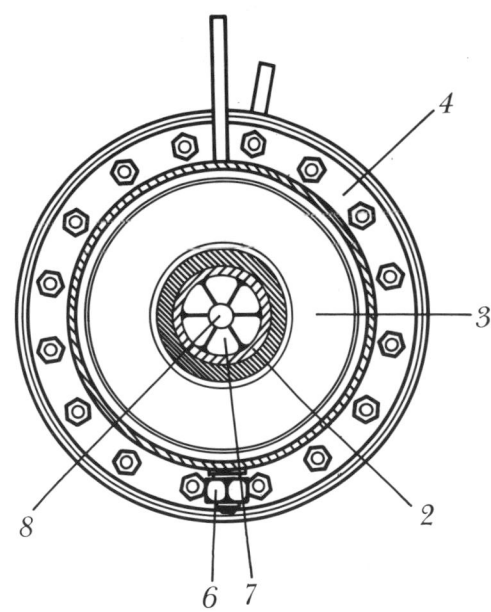

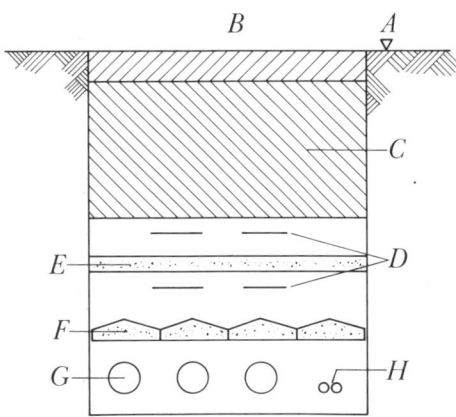

A typical trench cross-section for flexible surface (tarmac)

A Ground level
B Tarmac
C Leau mix
D Marker tapes
E Thick coloured concrete
F Standard cable tiles
G 400 KV cable
H Pilot cables

Right: Stringing the conductors of the 400 kV overhead transmission line between Castle Peak station and Tze Wan Shan where it goes underground

The Cross-Harbour Cable

The Hongkong Electric Company and the China Light & Power Company were once more connected by a submarine cable laid across the harbour in March 1981, and the link was formally opened on 3 April. This first stage of the cross-harbour connection has a capacity of 160 MVA. It has a two-fold purpose for both companies; to enhance supply reliability and to economise generation costs. The first is achieved by one company providing transfer assistance through the interconnector at time of emergency of the other company. The second is achieved by better utilization of the low running cost units in the two systems and by sharing the required amount of spinning reserve between the two companies.

The cable was laid from a special barge on which large drums of the over 9-inch diameter armoured cable were stacked. The barge moved across the harbour by hauling on its anchors as the cable was paid out. The seabed was opened up by high pressure water-jets, forming a trough just ahead of the cable as it was lowered into place.

Two cables were laid, together with a smaller pilot cable, attached in a metal clip through which a steel hauser also runs. When the operation reached the far side, the remainder of the cable was attached to inflatable rubber rings until it could be jointed to the installations on shore.

Previous cables laid on the surface of the sea-bed were eventually carried away by ships dragging their anchors. Tests have shown that the present cable has not been affected by dragging. Opposite the mechanism is shown from above, and in the lower diagram in profile, whereby the cables are laid in a gouged out trough in the bed of the sea. The two cables and the narrower guage pilot cable are fed from the coils on the deck of the barge and clipped together as the barge hauls on its anchors so as to move gradually across the harbour.

The cables, clipped together with a steel hauser running above them, are being paid out over the side. The nearer bunch of tubes form part of the mechanism which conveys a high-pressure water jet to the seabed just ahead of the cables as they reach the bottom

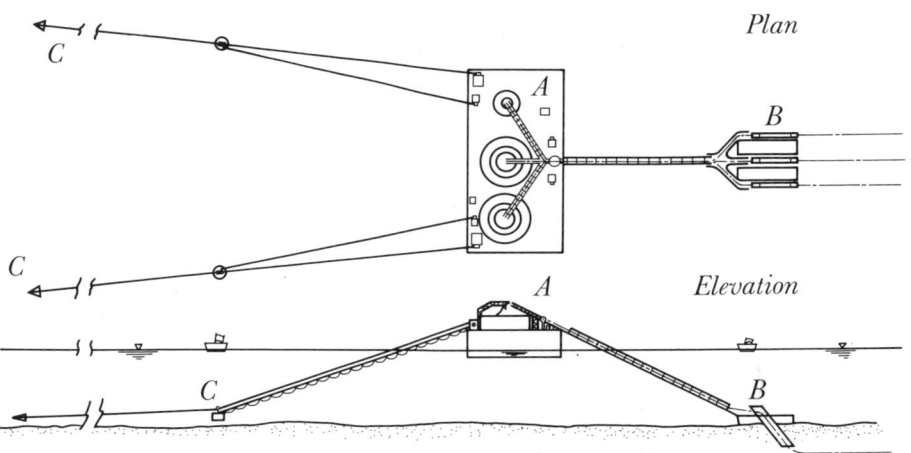

Plan

Elevation

A   Barge
B   Burying machine
C   Anchor

Overleaf: Aboard the cable-laying barge the cable is coiled ready to be paid out across the harbour. Page 235: The tricky job of positioning the huge low pressure turbine rotor for the first 350 MW unit at Castle Peak 'A' station in 1981. Comparison with some of the photographs of earlier generating plant reveals graphically the vast strides that electrical generating technology has made over the past half century. Pages 236–237: The giant Castle Peak site as it looked in the latter part of 1981. To the left of the tall stack, the boilerhouse was under construction for 'A' station. To the right, the jetty for coal ships to berth at takes shape, and in the left foreground lies a small piece of the original shore with its strewn boulders. The site of 'A' station occupies the nearer two-thirds of the photograph, and the site of 'B' station lies beyond. Page 238: At Castle Peak 'A' station a technician works on the boiler tubes for the first 350 MW unit. Page 239: Seen from the air the chimney at Castle Peak 'A' station reveals its four internal flues against a background of construction materials on the ground

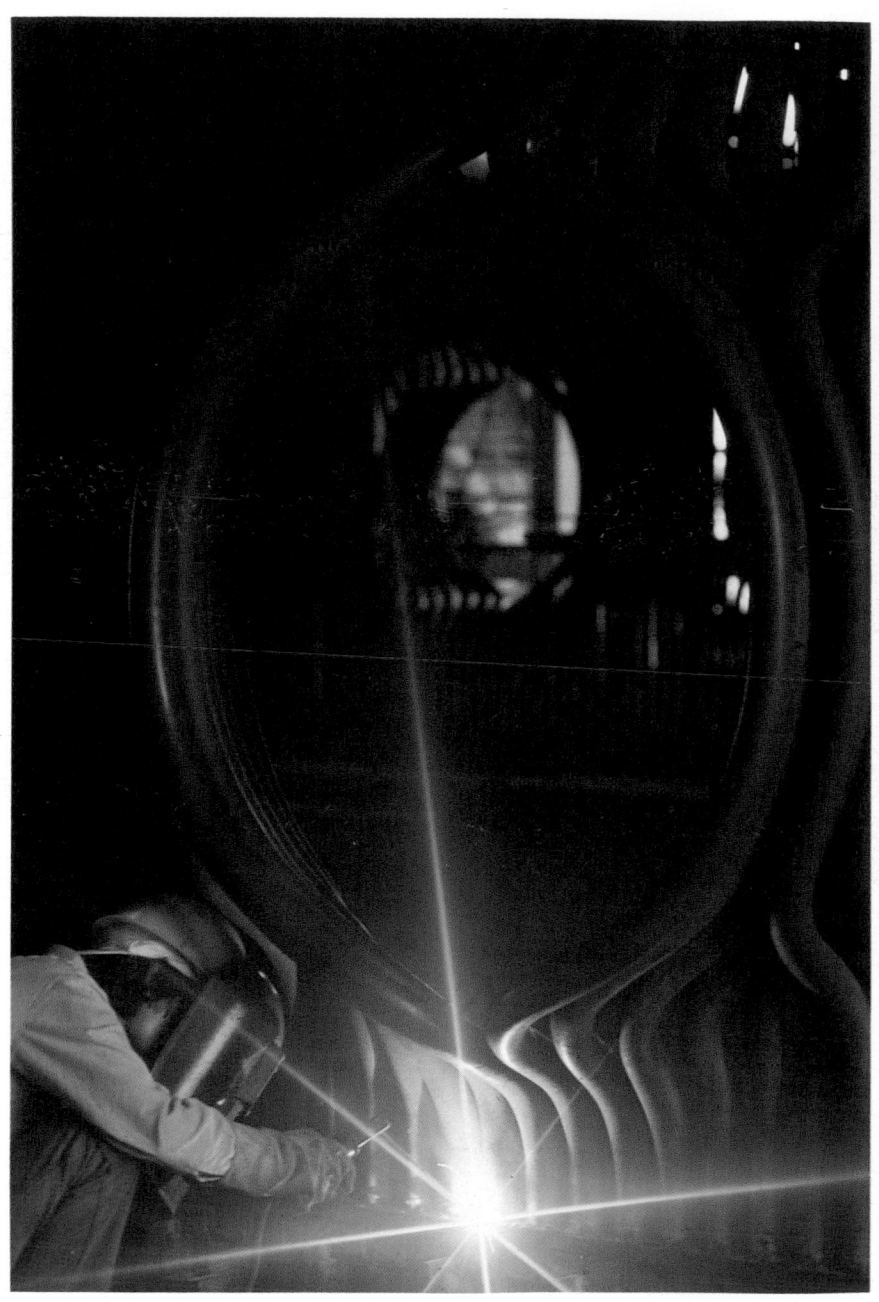

The Board of the Company as at March, 1982. Above: seated left to right – Mr. M.W. Lo, C.B.E., Sir Sidney Gordon, C.B.E. (DEPUTY CHAIRMAN), The Lord Kadoorie, C.B.E. (CHAIRMAN), Mr. H. Kadoorie, C.B.E., Mr. Y.C. Wang; standing left to right – Mr. J.S. Dickson Leach, Mr. W.J. Birkhead, Mr. D. Barrett, Mr. G.R. Ross, C.B.E., Mr. R.J. McAulay, C.A., Mr. Roy W. Smith, Jr., Mr. K.A. Miller, C.A., Mr. C.F. Wood, The Hon. T.S. Lo, C.B.E. and The Hon. Sir S.Y. Chung, C.B.E. Inset: left to right – Mr. A.S.H. Norton, The Hon. Michael Kadoorie and Mr. W.F. Stones, O.B.E.

In 1976, China Light's Articles were amended to permit employees to sit on the board, and at this time Mr. Barrett, the general manager, and also Mr W.F. Stones, deputy general manager, joined the board in October.

Mr. Stones joined the Company from Britain on secondment for two years from a directorship in the Central Electricity Generating Board there. After six months his status was altered and he became a regular Company employee. His appointment was occasioned by the need in a company undertaking vast electrical generating and transmission development for top engineering managerial skills. In this way the financial guidance of Mr. Barrett was complemented by the technical guidance of Mr. Stones. Two more directors, Mr. W.J. Birkhead and Mr. A.S.H. Norton, were appointed to the board in January 1981.

Lawrence Kadoorie was made a Knight Bachelor in 1974.

The sums of money poured into new fixed assets by China Light during this period (1965 to 1979) make any former capital expenditure by the Company look puny by comparison. Something like $2,000 million was spent, more than one quarter of it in the last two years. In the same period of fifteen years, the sum applied by PEPCO for purchasing was about $1,200 million, implying an average of under $670 per kilowatt for the 1,802 megawatts of generating capacity which it owned.

In line with these capital requirements, the authorised capital of China Light was increased in December 1964 from $150 million to $250 million, and by successive stages in 1968, 1973, 1976, 1978, and 1979, until in March 1981 it stood at $3,000 million.

The issued capital in the same period rose from $110.4 million in 1964 to $2,400 million in March 1981. In the past two years alone, shareholders have contributed $900 million to take up rights issues.

Profits and dividends under the scheme of control rose substantially. The 1964 profit was $44 million, which rose to $100 million by 1972 and to $238 million in 1979, and $350 million in 1980. Dividends, which stood at $16.56 million, grew more or less steadily until they amounted to $133 million in 1979 and $160 million in 1980. From 1966, dividends were declared quarterly in place of half-yearly as in former years.

One of the ongoing pre-occupations of the Company in the years after the scheme of control was introduced was getting rid of the 'fateful surcharge,' as it has been called, and the establishment of a fair and rational fuel clause for ordinary as well as bulk consumers.

In 1965, studies were set in motion which, it was hoped, would lead to a revised and up-to-date system of charges. As a result, in 1969, new tariffs were announced. First was the 'general tariff' which would apply to all ordinary consumers from July 1969 – a single meter tariff for both lighting and power with promotional block rates and a low minimum charge, meter rents to be abolished. The general tariff carried a fuel clause. The 'bulk tariff,' to take effect from 1 January 1970, would be available for all consumers using at least 20,000 kWh per month. This was to be a two-part tariff with a low maximum demand element. It also had a fuel clause – for installations with a favourable load factor, the result would be much lower charges than those of the 'general tariff'.

Further changes came in 1974 when higher costs necessitated a uniform increase of one cent per kWh in the energy charge on both tariffs; but at the same time higher thermal efficiency in the station resulted in the fuel charge being lowered, so as to effect an average reduction of 1.6 cents per kWh. While the reduction caused little comment, the increase in basic tariff, the first in 28 years, led to a renewal of the old protests. But the increase, reviewed by the government, was confirmed as being in accordance with the scheme of control.

Distinct escalation of costs led, at the end of 1979, to another (agreed) rise in rates in January 1980. At that time energy charges were raised by 2.6 cents per kWh, and at the same time the fuel clause was adjusted to correspond with a fuel cost base rate of $700 per ton instead of the $100 used previously – the difference being incorporated in basic rates.

The reason for the incorporation was to be discovered in the staggering and apparently irreversible increase in the price of fuel oil following on the 'oil crisis' of 1973. The cost of a ton of fuel oil prior to 1951 was about $90; by February 1952 it had risen to $180. It then fluctuated, reaching a peak in 1957 at a yearly average of $167; after which the price fell to an average of $99 for the year 1967. The same low average was attained in 1973 when the Financial Secretary abolished the Hong Kong fuel oil tax of about $20 per ton.

Following the Yom Kippur War, the Arab OPEC countries clapped on the oil embargo, leading to shortage of supply and sharply higher prices. To cope with this, the government brought in restrictions on the use of electricity and set up an oil policy committee to work on strategy. On this body the electricity companies were represented. Oil supplies, however, were again more readily available in May 1974, and restrictions were lifted.

But oil *prices* did not fall again. By July 1974 they had climbed to four times the former level, $360 per ton, and there were further rises between 1975 and 1978. The following year, 1979, prices suddenly took off into the stratosphere, and by September reached $700. The fuel clause adjustment, for some years past hovering between seven and eight cents per kWh, followed oil prices upward into the threatening skies. In September 1980 the price of oil was $836 per ton, but by April 1981 it had shot up to $1,255 per ton, and the fuel clause adjustment had risen to 34.3 cents per unit.

Underlying the surge in oil prices was, of course, world fear of scarcity of supplies. For China Light and many another power company round the world, the question that had to be faced was finding other types of fuel.

There are only two reliable fossil fuels for a power station – oil, and the old faithful, the nourishment of the original industrial revolution so long ago, and industry's staple food ever since – coal. The other proved motivating power – in place of the steam that comes from the thermal conversion of oil or coal – is of course water. Water thundering down in large tubes from some vast mountain lake, ever supplied by the eternal snows, or by steady and dependable rainfall in the catchment areas.

In Hong Kong there is more or less dependable rainfall in large amounts, a rather small catchment area, natural lakes the size of modest pocket handkerchiefs, supplemented by large but by no means record-breaking dams. And a regulated and dependable supply from China. Nothing like the quantity nor at the right sort of height above power station level required to turn the vanes of a turbine and generate current. The Company at one point considered the possibility of 'pumped storage' (water pumped to a height in off-peak load times and used as a hydro-electric power source when required). Although at that time the idea was set aside, the subject is far from being a dead letter, several apparently suitable sites having been surveyed. The Company is investigating the feasibility of having a joint venture in such a scheme with the Guangdong Power Company.

The sole non-fossil fuel (other than solar power, which is unlikely to be more than a small auxiliary source of localized energy production) is nuclear.

Between 1973 and 1975 the Company made detailed enquiries about the chances for Hong Kong of introducing nuclear power, and considered various reactors – CANDU, the Canadian type; S.C.H.W.R. (British); the Boiling Water Reactor (United States); and the Pressurised Water Reactor (United States or German varieties). In May 1974 a steering group on nuclear power was formed by government with representatives from both power companies. In June a team of three experts arrived from Britain to advise on possible places for setting up a nuclear station, and found suitable sites. In July, Sir Lawrence Kadoorie went to Britain and France to inspect nuclear installations.

The steering group decided in November 1974 to form a Committee on Economic and Financial Aspects of Nuclear Power, and at its request four of its members – two each from Hongkong Electric and China Light – prepared two reports dealing with the economic comparisons of nuclear and oil-fired generating units for Hong Kong use. By May 1975 these reports were in hand, based in part on material from the International Atomic Energy Agency in Vienna.

In that same month, two delegates from the Vienna Agency came to Hong Kong at government invitation to discuss the reports. And with the assistance of both companies' representatives they produced a Nuclear Power Planning Study for Hong Kong. Published in 1977, this covered the relevant economics and listed the sequences of generating equipment which, in the long run and on the assumptions made, would make for the least costly production of power. The steering group had already studied a draft of the document in the previous year, and it had reluctantly concluded that nuclear power for Hong Kong was not going to be more than marginally cheaper than that derived from conventional fuels. Therefore, it was not recommended to set out on such a course, the huge capital costs of which would pose great problems in financing, in a field where the technology was forever changing.

And that, for the time being, was that.

One of the major preoccupations of any intelligent power company must always be the quest for means to produce power more efficiently – and the importance of the activity is underscored, heavily and with the threat of red entering into the balance, by the gigantic appreciation in the cost of fuel since the Second World War. In Hong Kong there has always been in theory one good method remaining untried: a cable link between the generating stations of China Light and Hongkong Electric across the harbour. The Japanese, in entirely makeshift and primitive fashion, made one during the war, simply to get electricity from Hok Un to the Island, which was otherwise in darkness. This was discontinued in due course due to the repeated interruptions caused by damage from ships dragging their anchors.

In 1969, the two companies resumed negotiations for a tie-line, and reports were produced. No real progress was made until fuel costs made the matter one of some urgency. By 1977, the government was taking an interest, and in January 1978 the Financial Secretary's letters to both companies resulted in the 'Working Group' of three parties which was set up and met in that year. A subcommittee was formed and reported in September, using as basis the isolation of each company, and considering several degrees of interconnection.

a) Shared spinning reserve (see glossary)
b) Economic energy transfer – a limited exchange of power
c) System integration – common system planning and bulk energy transfer
d) Corporate integration

The conclusion was that system integration would effect considerable savings. The report was accepted by the 'Working Group' which assumed the title 'Steering Group.'

Agreement on interconnection was reached in 1979, providing for a link of about 12.5 miles of 132 kV cable, 7.5 miles of which would be submarine. The laying of this cable was completed by April 1981, slightly ahead of schedule. The results were that the future capital cost to both companies would be slightly reduced because the spare capacity of the combined systems could be somewhat lower than before the link; and fuel costs would be reduced because of shared spinning reserve.

Late in 1976 an oft-repeated litany of Company requirements was heard once more. Reviewing the history of the Company (indeed of any electricity company the world round) it has clearly contributed one of the main thematic ingredients – the call for more capital to install more generating capacity to meet future demand.

It was deemed inadvisable to place more plant at Tsing Yi station. Therefore a new station would have to be built. The forecasts called for a capacity of 1,400 MW additional to present installed capacity, by 1986. This could be met by four units of 350 MW each; and since oil was expected to become more expensive and less dependable as to supply, the boilers were to be arranged for coal as the fuel of choice, with oil as an alternative.

In line with the Company's policy of buying from historical suppliers when it is cost and design-effective to do so, the Company informed Sir Peter Carey, Permanent Secretary at the United Kingdom Department of Industry, who was on a visit to Hong Kong in January 1977, that it was prepared to order British equipment for the new station if the terms were internationally competitive and export finance were available. This decision was in large part on the advice of Mr. W.F. Stones, director of the Central Electricity Generating Board in Britain, later seconded as we have seen to China Light.

A meeting with Hong Kong government officials confirmed that the idea was generally favoured, and at another meeting in London, with James Callaghan who was then Prime Minister, Sir Lawrence Kadoorie and Mr. Stones (by this time deputy general manager of China Light), British government support was pledged for the plan. The British also offered to form a working party to co-ordinate the matter. Later, Mr. Callaghan informed Sir Lawrence that a package offer was being prepared, and this was made in September. It comprised two 350 MW sets and virtually 100 per cent export finance on favourable terms, with an option on a further two sets of the same size, and the ancillary services of the Central Electricity Generating Board and British Electricity International.

The terms were agreed with the Company's staff after scrutiny by a Swiss consulting firm, Electrowatt Engineering Services Ltd., to ensure competitiveness.

Considering the very large size of the capital investment required for such a power station, both China Light and Esso Eastern decided against further development of generating facilities by PEPCO, and another joint company was formed in which they would both have holdings in the same proportions as in PEPCO. Accordingly, Kowloon Electricity Supply Company Ltd. (KESCO) was formed in March 1978 with an authorised capital of $100 million. (It is no accident that KES in KESCO reverses the initial letters of Sir Elly Kadoorie's name.)

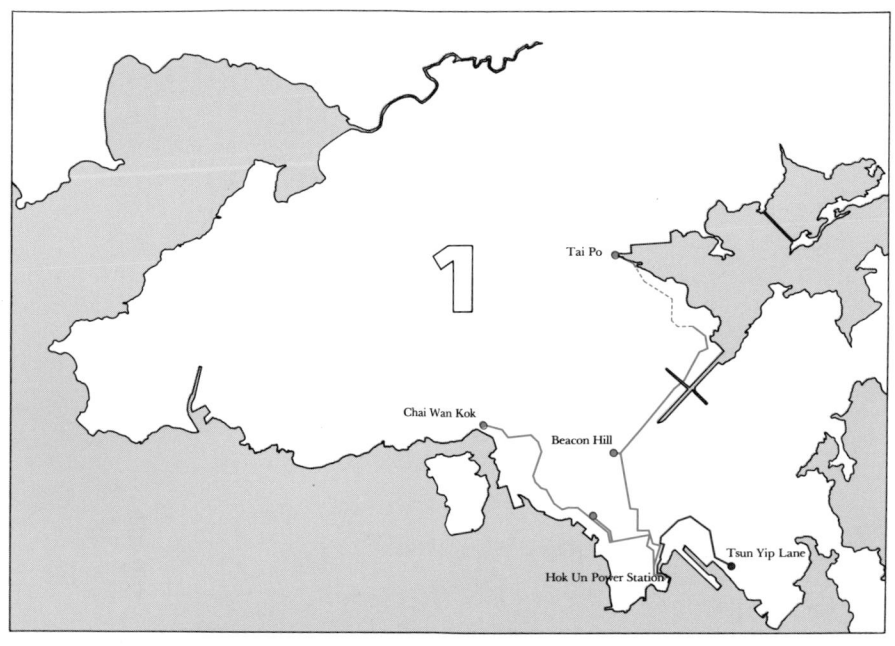

1)   1964 – the 66 kV and 132 kV network (operating at 33 kV)
2)   1982 – the 66 kV and 132 kV system before the 400 kV commissioning
3)   1982 – the actual 66 kV, 132 kV, and 400 kV system

- 400 kV substation
- Power station
- 132 kV substation
- 66 kV substation
— 400 kV cable
------ 400 kV overhead line
— 132 kV cable
------ 132 kV overhead line
— 66 kV cable
------ 66 kV overhead line

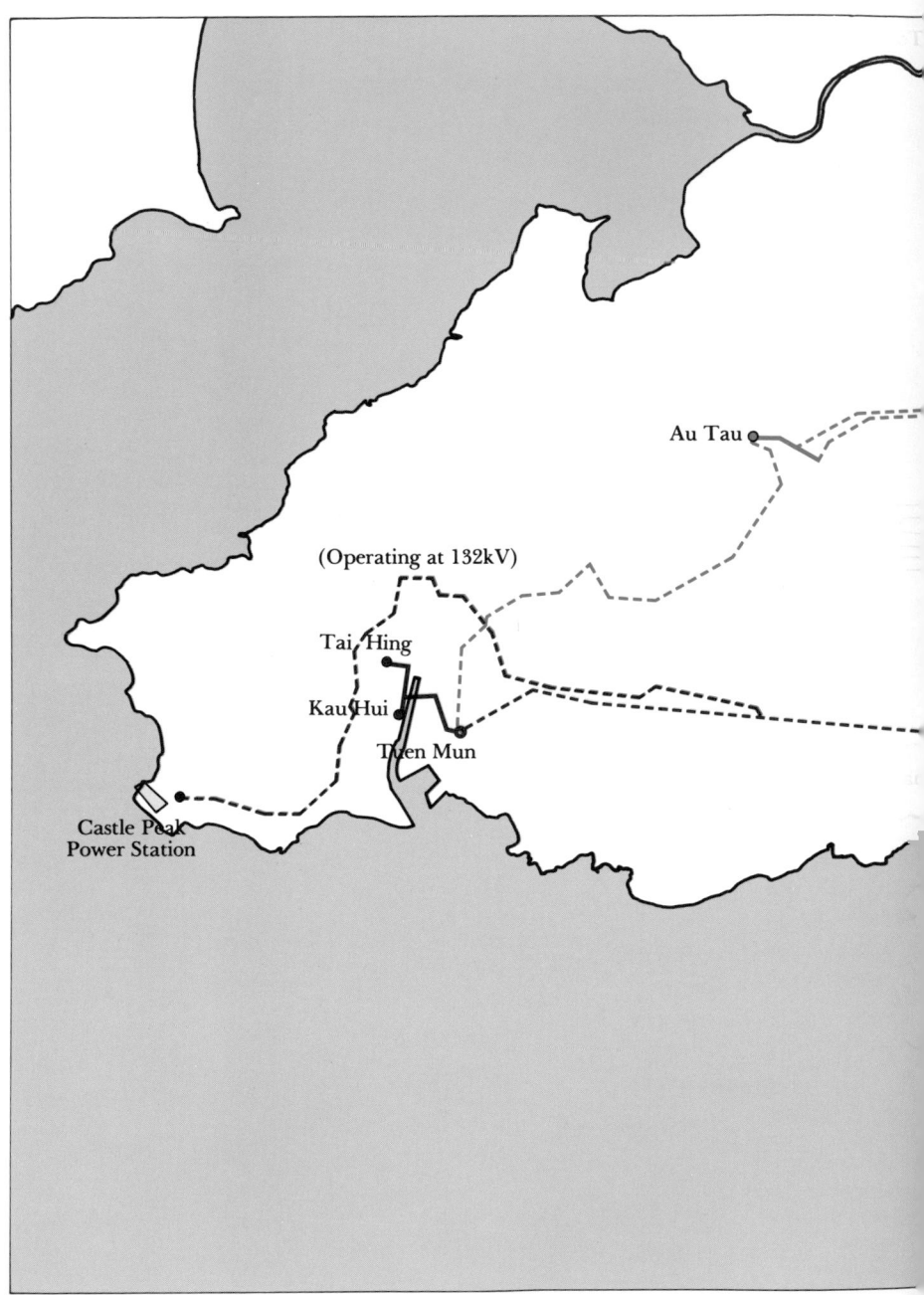

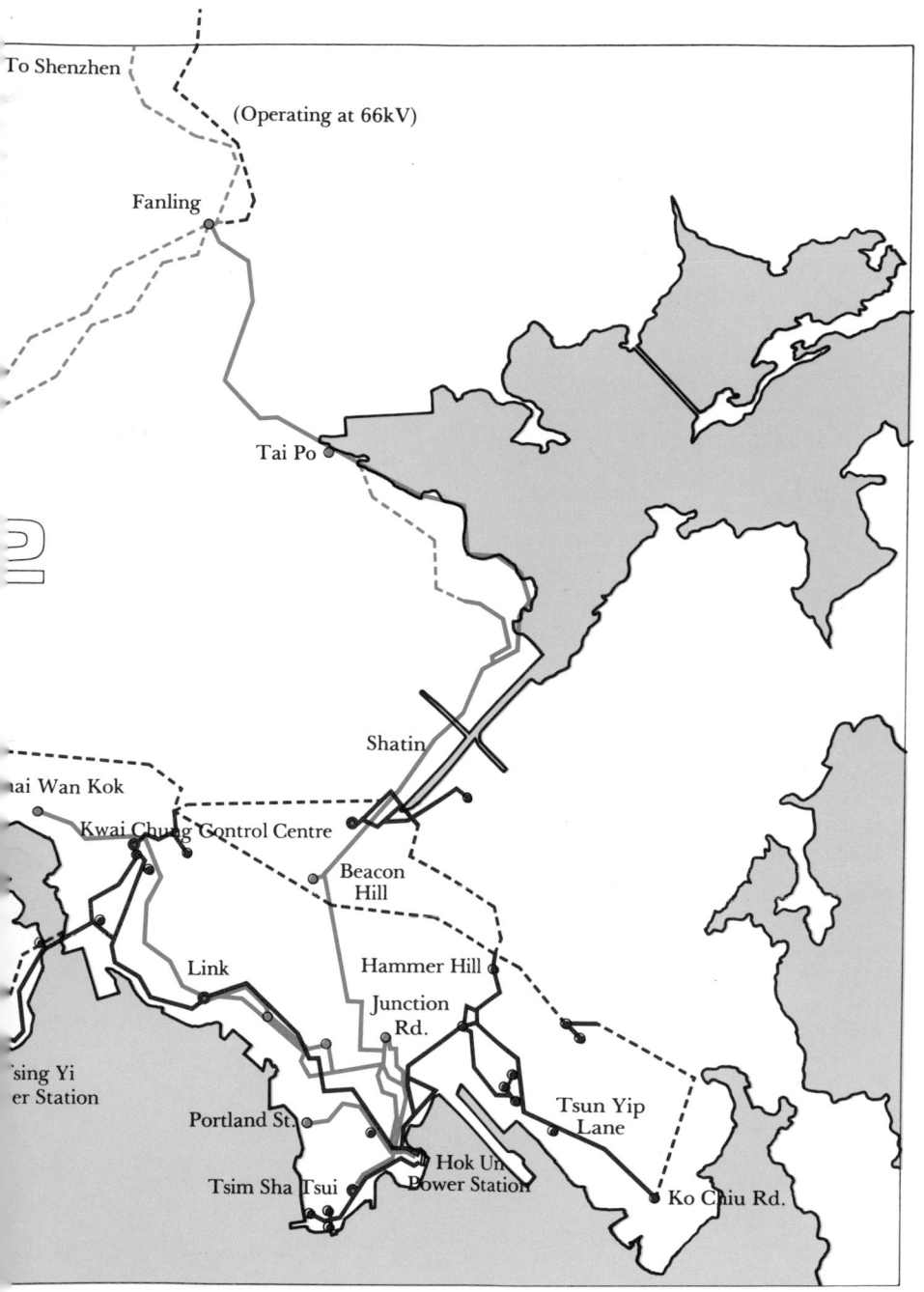

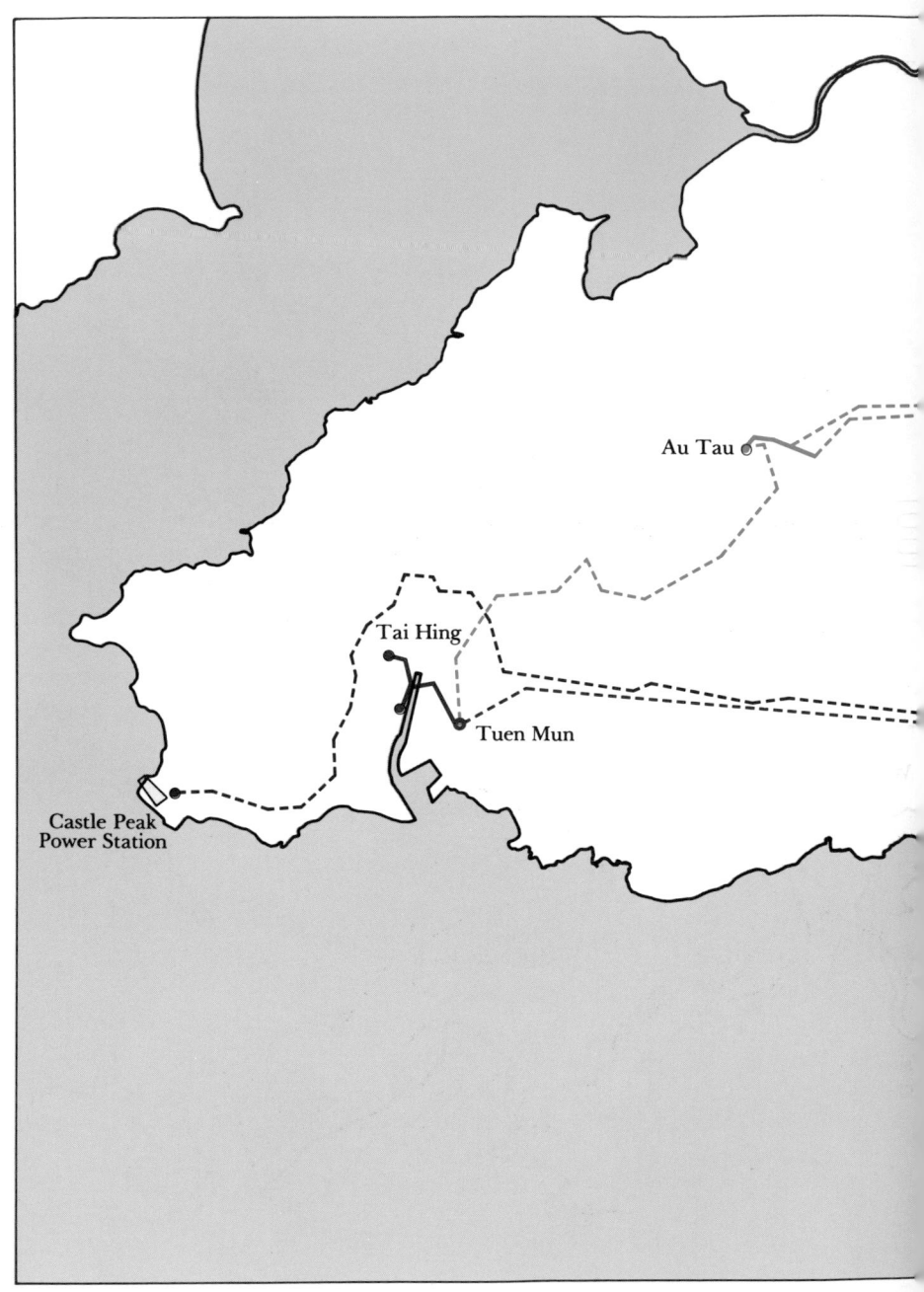

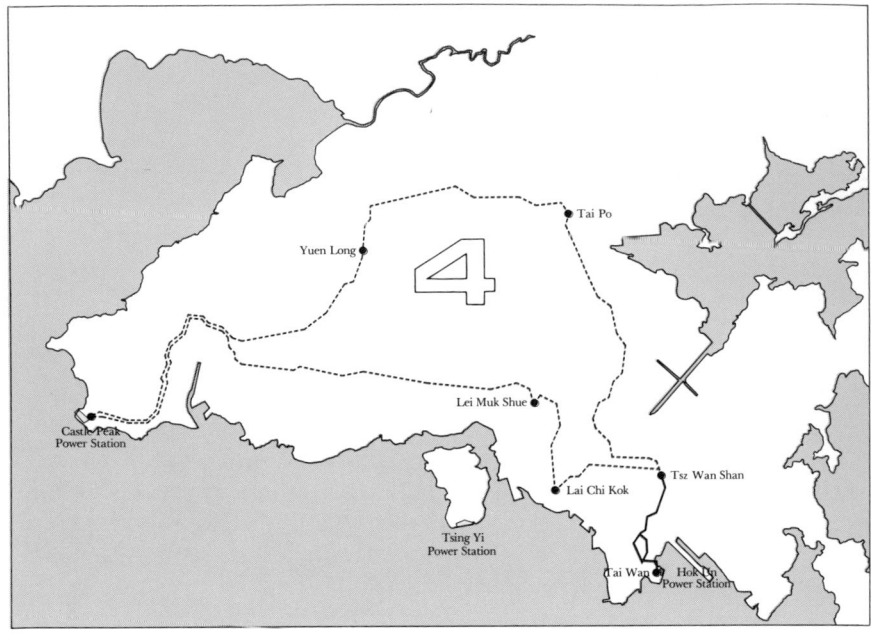

4) 1987 – the 400 kV network

⬚ *Power station*
— *400 kV cable*
------ *400 kV overhead line*
● *400 kV substation*

The fundamental idea was that KESCO should function as PEPCO functions, and that the net return would be shared between China Light, PEPCO, and KESCO in proportion to their respective shareholders' funds.

In April 1978, KESCO signed a contract with GEC Turbine Generators Ltd. for the first two 350 MW units. The British General Electric Company, successor long ago of A.E.I., would in addition act as principal contractors for the project. Another well-tried company, Babcock Power (formerly Babcock & Wilcox) would provide the boilers, and the construction and civil works would be designed and built under the supervision of L.G. Mouchel & Partners. The commissioning dates of the two sets were to be 1982 and 1983.

But once again the anticipated demand factor entered into the considerations and it was decided that KESCO should install 504 MW of gas turbine units to bridge the anticipated gap in capacity until the steam sets had been commissioned. The first, a 56 MW GEC machine, was put up in Hok Un and started to run in 1979; the remaining seven units were commissioned in 1980 and 1981.

KESCO obtained loan financing for two 350 MW units and the gas turbines, to the extent of one hundred per cent of the value of goods and services, from the United Kingdom, with repayment starting in 1983 to extend over eight and a half years. The loan agreement was signed in London in April 1978 with the representatives of a consortium of bankers, J. Henry Schroder Wagg & Co. Limited, and with the British Export Credits Guarantee Department as guarantor of the loan.

In October 1979, KESCO entered into another contract with GEC Turbine Generators Ltd. for a further two 350 MW units. The financing of these units was again arranged through J. Henry Schroder Wagg & Co. Limited and supported by the Export Credits Guarantee Department.

The site chosen for the new power station was Castle Peak, at Tap Shek Kok – Stepping Stones Corner – almost at the western extremity of the New Territories coast. The place was formerly rural in the extreme, a headland trailing down from the solid rocky hills to the sea where a few rocks rise in a disordered scattering from the shallows.

In 1896, it must have looked entirely similar. A small, and at that time probably very useful, publication called *A Tourist's Map of 8 Short Trips on the Mainland of China (Neighbouring Hong Kong) Including The Principal Places Frequented by Sportsmen*, was published in that year by

R.C. Hurley from numbers 12 & 13 Beaconsfield Arcade, and describes a journey in the region.

'Proceed overnight to Deep Bay by steam-launch accompanied by a sampan and a small punt or dinghy. Instruct steam-launch as to destination. Land at Deep Bay on the southern shore as near as possible to the village of San Wai which is situated close to a low hill and is well shaded by banyan trees. The very extensive paddy fields in this neighbourhood afford excellent cover for snipe. . . . Follow the beaten track skirting the many villages . . . and with shooting all the way, you will, in a few hours, find yourself on the shore of Castle Peak Bay, where your steam launch should be in readiness to convey you back to Hong Kong.'

This idyllic sporting picture from more than eight decades ago cannot, alas, be made to correspond with the realities of the present. The terrain is still just as described, although it is hardly likely to contain much in the way of snipe. And the hardy sportsman, at the end of the suggested itinerary (which is perfectly possible even today) would find himself bogged down in the highrise of the new town of Tuen Mun as he descended the ancient slopes to Castle Peak Bay – a bay now stolen from the sea in favour of man and industry. And along the coast to the west the formerly lost little point with its scrub and boulders, the promontory of Tap Shek Kok, is now only a small incident, carefully preserved as a landscape feature in a scene from the future. For here it was decided to build Castle Peak power station. The hills have been scarified, their slumbering rock exposed, cut back at angles, terraced; and the sea has been made to retreat before the dumping of millions of cubic yards of fill.

The old days of haphazard siting of industrial units have gone for good. The new power station has been planned so that, while maximum efficiency in all its processes is taken care of, so too are the visual and human environmental aspects. On the 6.7 million square feet of site the first power station has risen with all its ancillary structures, its wharf where a coal ship will always be tied up unloading, every day of the year, and the skyscraping chimney carrying fumes upward for safe dispersal, pointing gracefully, with the hint of a question, like some rocket to the sun.

The characteristic of the process of installing new generating capacity has always been not only that this must be done but that the respite before more is needed is generally short. And, as Hong Kong ventures toward the end of the twentieth century, that interval has further shortened. Before the first reclamation was more than just under way at Castle Peak, and the 'A' station determined, moves were afoot to secure the wherewithal to build the next station – Castle Peak 'B' station with four 660 MW units – alongside the 'A' station. The purchase of the land and formation of the reclaimed portion of the site had of course been planned with this in mind. But the eventual problem, likewise foreseen, would be the finance. Eight hundred million pounds sterling is a lot of money, even in 1982.

'It was a question of confidence in Hong Kong,' Sir Lawrence Kadoorie says, 'to be able to raise the finance without any guarantee from China Light or Exxon, and without any personal guarantors, for a project that will go well beyond the period of Hong Kong's "lease". The money was raised on the strength of confidence in Exxon and China Light keeping their word.' Sir Lawrence is a man who pauses briefly when he is recounting something, as if to run it through once more in his mind before he goes on. 'It is essential,' he then continues, 'to remember that one can only have what one pays for, and if we incur these debts we've got to repay them, and *show* that we can do so. It is really up to China Light to prove to the Hong Kong government that in its carefully worked out financial forecast up to 1990, the scheme of control, tariffs, and so forth, will allow a margin to meet the obligations we have incurred. In return we guarantee to provide electricity in sufficient quantities to meet foreseeable demand up to that date.

'The situation was a bit like this just after the war. If we had not gone ahead then, Hong Kong would have stopped at that time, and Singapore would have taken over. One reason you have to go ahead is that, from the moment of decision it takes at least four and a half years to give the electricity to the customers.'

The *Financial Times* in London on 31 March 1981 devoted two considerable articles to the deal. 'Great Britain Inc. wins the day,' runs the headline on the major piece by industrial correspondent Hazel Duffy. 'Early on Saturday, January 31, four copies of a 34-volume proposal for the construction of a complete power station arrived at the offices of the China Light and Power Company in Hong Kong. The volumes, which weighed a quarter of a ton and cost £2,500 in airfreight, were the basis of a £550 million deal – the largest single order won by British industry – which was to be signed less than two months later.'

The paper recounts how, for Castle Peak 'B' station, 'Britain was asked to put together a complete project package, including finance. Furthermore it was asked to make its presentation in a very short space of time – the whole process from despatch of the formal request from China Light and Power on December 1 to the signing of the agreement was less than four months.'

'Britain's success was the outcome of a remarkable degree of co-ordination between Government, industry, and the banks – the sort of "Great Britain Incorporated" effort which is frequently extolled ... as the only way to win major export orders....'

The total financing package obtained (again by J. Henry Schroder Wagg & Co. Limited in London) for the construction of Castle Peak 'B' station was the largest ever arranged in the City of London, approximating to US$2,000 million, and, for the first time, a loan of this order was offered to Hong Kong which does not mature until the year 2002 – five years after the expiry of the New Territories lease in 1997.

The total order for equipment from Great Britian, amounting to about £700 million, is the largest power plant export order ever awarded to that country, and one of the largest export orders it has received in any field.

Once more, GEC was the main contractor and Babcock Power won the contract for the boilers. For Castle Peak 'A' station, 'China Light ... turned out to be a hard bargainer on every aspect of the proposed contract – technical, contract conditions, and in the third week of negotiations, price. A separate team appointed by the utility had been evaluating the loan offer which then formed an integral part of the overall formal negotiating procedure.' But the Department of Industry in Britain thought that for Castle Peak 'B' station the negotiations were much tougher. 'The customer had hired a lot of staff to advise on all aspects, and Exxon played a much bigger role in the negotiations. Other power plant manufacturers in the world have been itching to get into the Hong Kong market, and China Light and Power was not averse to telling us that it wanted a very good package as a result.'

A further joint company on the same lines as PEPCO and KESCO – Castle Peak Power Company Ltd. (CAPCO) – was formed in July 1981 to own the 'B' station.

The papers paid tribute to Sir Lawrence, the key to whose thinking 'is that Hong Kong is founded on what he calls a "three-legged stool." The first leg is that Hong Kong must show that it is of some use to Britain; the second is that it must show that it is of use to China; and

Castle Peak 'A' Power Station

This power station will house four dual coal/oil-fired 350 MW units. The first unit (A1) has been commissioned: the remaining three units will be commissioned in each of the three years 1983 to 1985. Steam-to-set for the A1 unit was achieved on 27th February, 1982 – two days ahead of the scheduled date, which had been determined some four years previously. Coal-firing commenced on 19th March and the unit was then progressively run up to its full commercial load of 350 MW. The commissioning of this unit has been achieved in under four years after site formation work commenced in June, 1978. This period is significantly less than the world average of between six to eight years from beginning of site work to commissioning of the first unit at a new power station.

The principal contractor for the supply of plant for the power station is GEC Turbine Generators Ltd. Project management, erection and commissioning of the plant was carried out by China Light with the assistance of experts from the contractors and British Electricity International Ltd

257

the third, that it must show it can give better jobs to the more sophisticated and educated younger generation in Hong Kong.'

'In bearing and behaviour Sir Lawrence is the epitome of an urbane and cultured English gentleman,' the paper continues, after outlining his Jewish Middle Eastern origins and the fact that he was born just after the lease on the New Territories was signed. 'His office is on the top of St. George's Building in the heart of Hong Kong. One wall is full of a large collection of jade. The other affords a panoramic view of the harbour and of Kowloon with the twinkling, if sometimes glaring, lights of the shopping and entertainment area, lit by his China Light & Power Company....'

The article goes on, rightly, to praise the role played since the mid-1970s in the Company by William Stones, now China Light's deputy general manager.

'Logically,' Sir Lawrence is quoted as saying, 'Hong Kong should not exist.' But he is also quoted as adding that 'illogically the international need for the services it renders is essential to the future relationship between East and West.' Sir Lawrence appreciates the delicate political balances. He and his family remember what happened in Shanghai when the Communists took over. Hong Kong can act as the 'free zone of China under British management,' as Sir Lawrence puts it. But Britain must continue to appreciate the importance of the territory, and so must China.

Thus, in an intensive period of furious work, the Company laid the basis for the sure supply of power to Hong Kong's industry in the foreseeable future.

The route to be taken by the extra-high-voltage power lines from Castle Peak lies straight across some of Hong Kong's roughest hill country, very difficult of access. At the instigation of Sir Lawrence's son, Mr. Michael Kadoorie, a director of China Light, a helicopter company was formed on a fifty-fifty basis with the Singapore company Heliservices to facilitate the transport of material to the sites of towers, and to perform other work in areas hard to reach by normal means. The French-made Lama machines are basically flying cranes and the venture has proved time and money-saving.

At this juncture, the Company could contemplate once more the old project that failed before the Second World War – the supplying of power to China from Hong Kong. In fact the supply was established before the Castle Peak 'B' agreement was made. In 1978, Sir Lawrence visited Peking in May and Canton in June, discussing in

THE PRESENT AND THE FUTURE

both cities the requirements for a power supply with the officials there. By early December word came that the Chinese authorities were interested in having about 50 MW of power at Shum Chun as soon as this could be arranged. China Light at once started discussions with the Guangdong Power Company, and these resulted in January 1979 in an agreement under which the Company would supply 50 MW, equivalent to about one million kWh a day, at bulk tariff rates.

A joint team of engineers from China and from the Company then put up a 66 kV overhead line from Fanling to Shum Chun, a distance of about seven miles, in the record time of under three months. The switching-on ceremony took place at the Kwai Chung Control Centre on 31 March 1979, with both Sir Lawrence and Mr. Shih Chao-hsiang, general manager of the Guangdong Power Company, officiating at the ceremony. Chinese officials have indicated that a larger supply will be welcome in the future, and this request has been included in the question of forward planning by the Company.

The old 1964 scheme of control was due for replacement on its expiry at the end of September 1978, and in accordance with its terms, discussions on the future were scheduled to begin three years prior to that date. After long negotiations, agreement was reached between the Company and the government on a new scheme, and the formal document was signed in February 1978.

The Company was released from the close constraints of the former scheme, and could therefore look forward to a future in which it had a larger measure of leeway in which to conduct its business as business sense and the need to supply the demands of the community dictated.

London newspapers, commenting on the Castle Peak 'B' station contract, had touched on the astute political mind of Sir Lawrence Kadoorie. And in relation to a different matter, Sir Lawrence himself demonstrates the incisiveness, but also the flexibility of his thinking.

Five large bound volumes, printed in the offices of China Light, in English and Chinese, represent the labours of a joint team of specialists – likewise English and Chinese – on the question of nuclear power for Hong Kong and Guangdong. They are entitled *The Feasibility Study Report on the Joint Development of a Nuclear Power Station in*

Guangdong Province, and they were ready by early November 1980.
'We gave one hundred copies to the Chinese,' Sir Lawrence recounts the story. 'They said they'd never seen a report like it before,
and that it was of tremendous importance and interest since it set a
standard for the way big projects should be investigated prior to
embarking on them. As a result they asked for another two hundred
copies – that is, another one thousand volumes. We sent them.
'Of course any feasibility study on a nuclear power station has to go
further than this report. You can't say "We'll have a nuclear power
station" from a year's study. But you *can* find out whether you
shouldn't have one at all.'
In a letter to Mr. Shih Chao-hsiang accompanying the volumes
sent to the Guangdong Power Company, Sir Lawrence spells this out:
'The proposal to build a nuclear power station in Guangdong
Province to supply power both to Guangdong Province and Hong
Kong is a project of such importance and magnitude as to remove it
from the level of ordinary commercial enterprise.
'What we have been able to establish at this preliminary stage is
that basically it is a feasible proposition to build a Nuclear Power
Station in Guangdong Province to supply electricity to that province
and to Hong Kong, further that such a project is viable and would be
of benefit to both areas. However, there is still a great deal of work to
be done before we can proceed any further.'
Amplifying this at a later date, Sir Lawrence sketches the field of
problems to be investigated – the seismic, the environmental, the
actual physical feasibility, 'to say nothing of the question of expense.
Four thousand million US dollars (4 billion) removes the project from
the commercial field altogether and puts it straight into the hands of
governments.
'As such, the report has been sent to the People's Republic of
China, to the Hong Kong government, and to the British government, as well as to the authorities in the Guangdong Provincial
government. They now have enough to go on to see that it is a feasible
proposition.'
Sir Lawrence says that naturally enough the reactions from the
Chinese have been tentative up to the present, but that such a vast
undertaking equally naturally requires much careful study by
everyone.
In the protracted discussions with the Chinese authorities – in
particular with the general manager and deputy general manager of

the Guangdong Power Company, Mr. Stones played what more than one other member of China Light has termed an absolutely vital part. On numerous occasions the whole subject was discussed at length in Canton. And it was from the substance of these meetings that the eventual report was compiled. Mr. Stones was fortunate in developing a close rapport with the Guangdong Power Company's general manager, a cordial relationship which naturally greatly assisted in the efficiency of the talks and in reaching conclusions. The China Light team at the talks comprised besides Mr. Stones several other important Company executives: Dr. Y.B. Lee, systems planning engineer; Mr. Stephen Poon, forward planning engineer; Mr. C.K. Ho, manager, financial planning and control; and Mr. Eric Lo, chief accountant.

'The report shows,' Sir Lawrence continues, 'that at today's rates it would be possible to pay for the whole project by the year 2009 out of the cost of the electricity that would be sold by the Guangdong Power Company to China Light, if China Light took seventy per cent of the total generated output initially, dropping to 40 per cent later.' From China's point of view the station would provide not only much-needed power, but also much-needed foreign currency in the form of Hong Kong dollars to pay for the station.

'This projected station,' says Sir Lawrence, 'would be the *first* nuclear power station in China. Now, if you wish to build such a plant in any country you first have to find out what are that country's regulations regarding nuclear power. But China has, so far, none. The result is that whoever builds the first one will in a way set the pattern for the future.'

He goes on to explain the constituent parts of a nuclear power station: 'There is what's called the "nuclear island" – that is, everything directly to do with the nuclear reactor. There you have your own private source of heat, a nice little stove, and once you've made your tea there and steam is coming out – then we come to the "conventional island" which is just like the generating parts of any other power station.

'For political reasons I'm very anxious that a combination of British involvement in the conventional island and French involvement in the nuclear island (the reactor) should come about. Then we would have done something worthwhile indeed.

'My hope is to find some common ground which would involve British, French, and American technology.'

The sites so far considered suitable for a nuclear power station are two, about fifty kilometres distant from Hong Kong on the shores of Bias Bay, 'round the first bump' in the coastline, as Sir Lawrence puts it. But the Chinese have themselves found one more, which may be more suitable.

The whole project obviously has deep political significance of a nature that only the governments of China and Britain are capable of handling.

But, again, says Sir Lawrence, 'It is a matter of confidence, and trust in the Hong Kong dollar. Obviously, if the Chinese were to be paid in our dollars, they would want to be sure that this currency retained its value.'

Such then are some portents of a still undefined but interesting future.

The future is always interesting, if only because we have to imagine it. We can only make projections, which are really assumptions based on known present facts and the probability that certain other intentions will actually become realities in that future time. There is, on that account, an element of hazard in scanning the future. Being as cautious as possible, sticking closely to reasonable plans, not exaggerating or being over-enthusiastic, a number of probable statements can be made about China Light in the year 1990. Perhaps these may be more interesting when compared to electricity generation in other places which are similar in terms of population or contain comparable levels of industrialisation.

In 1990 we may assume that the population of Hong Kong will be at least six million, of which 4.5 million will be in Kowloon and the New Territories and supplied by the Company. This is a figure similar to the population of Scotland (which does not greatly vary). The present load in Scotland (over 5,000 MW) will be about 6,000 MW in 1990. At the same date, China Light will have an installed capacity of approximately 6,125 MW and a load of about 4,850 MW on the assumption that the last 660 MW unit of Castle Peak 'B' station has been installed. However, in the next few years, a decision to construct a 'C' station could be made. Thus China Light will be supplying more power per head of the population than is supplied per capita in Scotland.

Coming to cities, it is hard to find one that fits as regards population. But, taking Glasgow with just over one million people, the load will be about 1,500 MW in 1990. Birmingham, with a population of about two million people, will have a load of about 2,000 MW at the same date. The China Light load at 1990 (about 4,500 MW) will therefore be greater than the combined load of Glasgow and Birmingham – two highly industrial cities. Figures such as these, admittedly with an element of speculation as well as sound projection from known facts, put the China Light operation in something like perspective.

It is now over eighty years since that first ill-managed little power station in Canton was boldly taken over by China Light. Eighty years ago the world was still in the throes of machine-adulation. The machine was seen as a sort of all-powerful but obedient slave by means of which – with man directing it – almost everything could eventually be accomplished. The popular press of the day – not just in Hong Kong but in New York and London and other sophisticated capitals – was full of the wonders of the newest machines. Mankind began to feel itself released from its millennial toil as the obedient machines took it over and, puffing steam, clanking, gorged with inexhaustible supplies of coal, began to do the work for them. It was a happy time of great optimism in the longest interregnum that Europe had ever known between wars. There was no thought of the negative aspect of this new machine age. The word pollution was not heard and the idea would have been laughed at had it been brought up. No one knew that fossil fuels were *not* inexhaustible, and people were only just beginning to think of electricity in terms of the next magical slave. And so it proved to be – but a very demanding servant, not at all easy to handle.

The picture from our world window today is so profoundly different that one can hardly believe we actually inhabit the same planet. There is not now so much carefree thought of technological inventions as mankind's slaves – even though today we have infinitely more efficient and slavish technology at our beck and call. We have learned something the hard way. Sir Lawrence Kadoorie mentioned it: 'It is essential to remember that one can only have what one pays for.' And this is the broad lesson that it took mankind in general such a long time to learn about the consequences of owning and managing the steam-powered slave and his offspring the electric slave.

Optimism, nowadays, has to be laced with extreme caution. But within that framework, China Light & Power continues on its way as an essential partner to the people of Hong Kong in their lives and in their industrial strivings. The partnership may not at all times have been an easy one, and there are still dissentions between industry and the Company over various matters. But, looking back on more than eight decades, a clear pattern of mutual help, mutual and lively response to the challenges that Hong Kong has encountered in full measure, clearly emerges. Perhaps only in the realms of finance in Hong Kong has one single activity been directed so consistently to supplying demands before they were actually made. Facts, not speculation, readily prove it. And the Company is now better equipped both as to technology and as to management and personnel than at any time in those turbulent years past.

At this point in the history of China Light, where at a natural place we may break off the tale of its affairs, and where the involvement of the Kadoorie family in the Company has been fairly minutely detailed – Sir Lawrence Kadoorie became the recipient of a signal, indeed unique, honour.

In the Birthday Honours list of 1981, Her Majesty the Queen bestowed on him a Life Peerage. This in itself was an event of great significance in the tale of the Kadoorie family, and also in the history of China Light. More than that, it was an honour for Hong Kong since in the person of Lord Kadoorie the Colony received its first peerage conferred on a Hong Kong man.

The happy news was received in Hong Kong with considerable gratification, first because Lord Kadoorie is, and has been for many a decade, a well-known and well-liked figure in the public eye; and second because of the honour his elevation to the peerage reflected on Britain's estimation of Hong Kong. The principal newspaper, the *South China Morning Post*, dealt thus with the news on the morning of 16 June 1981:

'There could not be a more fitting recipient of the honour of being our first life peer than Sir Lawrence Kadoorie.'

'Certainly there have been few Hong Kong personalities who have distinguished themselves in so many fields. A glance at the Who's Who of Hong Kong shows an impressive list of achievements virtually without peer, spanning more than sixty years service to the community.'

'Sir Lawrence has always been proud of the fact that he revels in hard work. And his record bears testimony to this. One of our most prominent industrialists and businessmen, he is also renowned for the unflagging enthusiasm with which he approaches every task he tackles, and his unstinting generosity.'

'Born in Hong Kong and raised in China, Sir Lawrence, who turned 82 earlier this month, is a visionary whose planning has kept his companies, particularly China Light and Power, well ahead of developments in Hong Kong.'

Thus, as the year 1982 sees the Company well on its way to its first century, and as its most ambitious project to date, the Castle Peak power station, with all it implies for the future, comes on stream, there is a happy historical coincidence with which to round off the Company's history.

The Company has turned eighty-two, and Lord Kadoorie, its chairman through many of those years, has also attained that age. Few Company histories have the chance to bring their story to the end of the first volume with such a happy combination of facts.

APPENDICES

Names of the Company

The name under which the Company has conducted its business has undergone several alternations both in English and in Chinese.

The original Company was registered on 23 April 1900 in the name of the China Light & Power Syndicate Ltd.

On 27 June 1900, the Company acquired the Canton Electric & Fire Extinguishing Company. This Company was later sold, the transaction being completed on 31 July 1909.

The Chinese name of the Company in 1913 was listed as Chinese Electric Light Company, 中華電燈公司 Jung Wa Din Dang Gung Sze.

The name in English was altered in 1918, on 28 December, after the decision to form a new company to take over the operations of the former one, and the new company became The China Light & Power Company (1918) Ltd.

By 1923, the Chinese name of the Company was listed as 中國電力有限公司 Jung Gwok Din Lik Yau Han Gung Sze – China Electric Power Company Ltd.

By 1935, it was decided to drop the (1918) from the name, which then became The China Light & Power Company Ltd. This remains the name to the present day.

But in Chinese, by the year 1936, the name 中華電力有限公司 Jung Wa Din Lik Yau Han Gung Sze – Chinese Electric Power Company Ltd. – had appeared, and this Chinese name has endured to the present time.

The Chinese characters for the Company's name on the Company seal, still remain in the form that attained official currency in 1923

Members of the Consulting Committee 1901–1927
Directors 1927–1981

R.G. Shewan	1901–1931	Chairman 1901–1931
C.P. (from 1902: Sir Paul) Chater	1901–1926	
H.P. White	1901–1929	
Dr. J.W. Noble	1903–1912	
T.F. Hough	1919–1922	
A.H. Compton	1919–1947	Chairman 1933; 1937
C.A. da Roza	1922–1936	Chairman 1932
Lee Hysan	1923–1928	
Sir Robert Ho Tung	1926–1933	
Sir Elly Kadoorie	1928–1944	
J.P. Braga	1928–1944	Chairman 1934; 1938
J.H. Taggart	1928	
L. (from 1974: Sir Lawrence, and from 1981: Lord) Kadoorie	1930–present	Chairman 1935; 1939; 1955–present.
F.A. Joseph	1931–1937	
C.S. Lo	1933–1934	
M.K. (from 1948: Sir Man Kam) Lo	1934–1959	Chairman 1936; 1940
A. Raymond	1938–1955	Chairman 1945–1955
H. Kadoorie	1946–present	
H.O. Benham	1947–1962	
L. D'Almada	1955–1968	
W.A. Welch	1956–1966	
M.W. Lo	1959–present	
Y.C. Wang	1961–present	
G.R. Ross	1965–present	
F.C. Westphal, Jr.	1965–1971	
K.H.A. Gordon	1966–1976	
M.D. Kadoorie	1967–present	
Dr. S.Y. (from 1978: Sir Sze-Yuen) Chung	1967–present	
R.J. McAulay	1968–present	
C.F. Wood	1970–present	
S.S. (from 1972: Sir Sidney) Gordon	1971–present	Deputy Chairman: 1971–present
C.H. Duncan	1971–1978	
T.S. Lo	1975–present	
K.A. Miller	1975–present	
D. Barrett	1976–present	
W.F. Stones	1976–present	
R.W. Smith, Jr.	1978–present	
J.S. Dickson-Leach	1978–present	
W.J. Birkhead	1981–present	
A.S.H. Norton	1981–present	

Note: Alternate directors and acting chairmen are not listed

Principal Statistics 1919–1980

Financial year	Capacity* MW	Maximum demand MW	Units sold GWh	Thousands of consumers*	Issued capital* $M	Dividend $M
1919	2.02	. . .	2.70	2.7	0.79	0.03
20	2.02	1.06	3.50	2.9	0.80	0.08
21	3.50	1.45	4.46	3.5	1.00	0.09
22	3.50	1.90	5.34	4.8	1.00	0.10
23	3.50	2.50	7.06	6.5	2.00	0.20
24	6.50	2.82	8.69	7.8	2.20	0.32
25	6.50	3.40	9.72	8.9	2.40	0.17
26	11.5	3.85	8.29	10	2.51	0.19
27	11.5	3.97	9.13	11	2.53	0.19
28	11.5	4.20	10.1	12	3.46	0.28
29	11.5	4.75	13.1	13	4.00	0.51
30	11.5	5.45	15.0	15	4.51	0.62
31	14.5	5.60	15.5	18	5.00	0.50
32	19.5	8.15	26.2	20	6.00	0.56
33	19.5	7.57	23.1	22	7.00	0.59
34	19.5	8.03	22.4	22	7.99	0.68
35	19.5	8.38	28.0	23	8.00	0.80
36	19.5	8.44	27.8	23	8.50	0.83
37	19.5	9.53	31.3	24	9.00	0.87
38	19.5	10.9	40.9	27	10.0	0.93
39	32.0	13.0	45.9	30	11.0	1.06
40	32.0	13.8	51.0	31	12.0	1.10
41	32.0	16.2	57.5	33	13.2	—
46	19.5	8.3	18.3	24	13.2	—
47	30.5	14.0	36.1	27	13.2	3.30
48	30.5	18.9	60.4	30	14.9	3.33
49	50.5	27.0	95.8	36	21.0	4.86
50	50.5	37.2	145	40	21.0	5.88
51	50.5	42.8	182	43	42.0	6.58
52	67.5	46.1	208	47	42.0	7.98

* At end of financial year

Principal Statistics (contd.)

Financial year	Capacity* MW	Maximum demand MW	Units sold GWh	Thousands of consumers*	Issued capital* $M	Dividend $M
1953	67.5	50.5	232	52	42.0	8.40
54	87.5	57.2	269	56	42.0	8.40
55	82.5	70.5	319	65	42.0	9.24
56	82.5	79.0	381	80	45.1	9.24
57	97.5	86.8	423	95	55.1	10.1
58	123	99.8	471	112	55.2	12.1
59	183	123	553	132	110	13.8
60	183	145	680	154	110	12.1†
61	183	175	827	180	110	12.1†
62	243	206	982	205	110	12.1†
63	303	247	1161	241	110	14.9
64	363	297	1348	289	110	16.6
65	363	339	1614	345	180	20.0
66	483	400	1831	388	180	22.5
67	603	455	2091	428	180	25.2
68	663	536	2355	468	180	28.1
69	783	617	2755	500	300	33.9
70	870	709	3154	531	300	37.5
71	1110	804	3503	561	300	41.7
72	1250	869	3824	594	420	48.7
73	1370	961	4302	634	420	54.6
74	1612	1005	4316	668	625	62.5
75	1812	1086	4464	699	688	65.9
76	2012	1232	5182	731	688	75.6
77	2212	1380	5770	769	1000	87.0
78	2152	1572	6405	805	1000	100
79	2208	1780	7206	843	1200	133
80	2416	1980	8009	889	1600	160
81	2656	2109	8545	949	2400	245

* At end of financial year
† Restricted by government

Glossary of Abbreviations and Technical Terms

Electrical Measurement Terms

Multiples and sub-multiples

Kilo (k)	$1,000 = 10^3$
Mega (M)	$1,000,000 = 10^6$
Giga (G)	$1,000,000,000 = 10^9$
Tera (T)	$1,000,000,000,000 = 10^{12}$
Milli (m)	$\dfrac{1}{1,000} = 10^{-3}$
Micro (µ)	$\dfrac{1}{1,000,000} = 10^{-6}$
Ampere (Amp., A)	Unit of electrical current. The amount of current sent by one volt through a resistance of one ohm
Candlepower	A unit of light intensity equivalent to the intensity emitted by burning one candle (obsolete). Superceded by Watt (see below)
Volt (V)	Unit of electrical pressure. The electromotive force that will cause a current of one ampere to pass through a conductor whose resistance is one ohm
Mega-volt Ampere (MVA)	One million volt amperes
Watt (W)	Unit of electric power, equal to a current of one ampere at one volt pressure
Kilo-watt Hour (kWh)	One unit of electrical energy
Mega-watt Hour (MWh)	One thousand units of electrical energy
Tera-watt Hour (TWh)	One million units of electrical energy

Technical Terms

Blackout	Complete loss of generation
Diesel, Diesel Electric	Diesel is light distillate fuel obtained by distillation of crude oil and used in the diesel internal combustion engine to produce mechanical energy. Diesel electric refers to electricity generated by a machine set in which the diesel engine is coupled to a generator
Frequency Control	Regulation of power generation to maintain the required system of electrical speed or frequency. 50 cycles per second electrical speed is equivalent to 3,000 r.p.m., the mechanical speed of turbine generators used by China Light & Power
High Tension, Low Tension	High tension refers to a voltage level (normally taken as above 650 volts) at which special design and precautions are necessary for safe and efficient use. Low tension refers to a voltage level, usually less than 650 volts, as in electricity supplied to domestic and small consumers
Installed Capacity	The total maximum continuous rating of all generating plant (usually the nameplate rating of the generators)

270

Load Factor	The ratio of the number of units supplied during a given period to the number of units that *could* have been supplied had the maximum demand been maintained throughout that period. Usually expressed as a percentage, thus:

$$\frac{\text{Units supplied during the period} \times 100\%}{\text{Max. demand} \times \text{number of hours in period}}$$

Load Shedding	Controlled load reduction in order to obtain a required demand relief when there is a shortage of generating plant. This entails voltage reduction of consumer supply which eases the demand; or actual disconnection of pre-arranged groups of consumers until generation matches demand
Plant Load Factor	The ratio of the number of units supplied from a generator or generators during a given period of operation, to the number of units that *could* have been supplied had the plant operated at maximum continuous rating throughout the period. Usually expressed as a percentage, thus:

$$\frac{\text{Units supplied during period} \times 100}{\text{Max. continuous rating of plant} \times \text{number hrs. in period}}$$

Spinning Reserve	The difference between the maximum continuous rating and the actual generated output of running plant. The reserve is usually calculated to cater for frequency regulation, errors in calculation of demand, and sudden loss of generation
Start, Hot; Start, Cold	The starting of a hot turbine when heating of the plant, if any, occurs only at higher loads; starting of a cold turbine where heat is applied during the whole starting and loading sequence
Steam, Saturated	Steam in the saturated state for the specific temperature and pressure. Additional heat will change dry saturated steam to superheated steam
Steam, Superheated	Steam at a temperature above the saturation temperature corresponding to its pressure. Superheated steam can produce more work than the same quantity of saturated steam, making for savings in fuel consumption, and allowing reduction in boiler size. Superheated steam makes for dryer steam at turbine blades, thus minimising blade erosion
Steam Consumption	Quantity of steam that produces one unit of electricity, expressed in lb/kWh
Superheater	Part of a boiler where saturated steam is heated to become superheated steam

Thermal Efficiency	The percentage of fuel heat energy converted into electrical energy (kWh)
	Plant and Ancillary Equipment
Boiler	A means of generating steam by heating water efficiently, the intention being to drive a turbine by steam pressure applied to its vanes
Furnace	Part of the boiler surrounded by boiler tubes containing water, which is heated by the combustion in the area of the furnace where burners produce the fuel for combustion
Generator	A mechanical device which converts mechanical energy to electrical energy
Oil Burner	A device used in the furnace of a boiler to receive oil at pressure and to atomise this fuel so that the fine particles are suitable for efficient combustion
Transformer	An electrical induction apparatus used to step up or step down voltage for various uses
Turbine	A vaned wheel on a shaft, made to revolve by the impingement of a jet of fluid, or (in the case of gas turbines) by the passage of a fluid which completely fills the space. The gas turbine is one using gaseous combustion products of a distillate fuel as its working fluid
Turbo-alternator	A machine set in which the turbine and the generator are mechanically coupled so that the energy of the working fluid of the turbine is converted into electrical energy at the generator terminals
Substation	A building which houses all necessary equipment for the efficient and effective transmission or distribution of electricity in a power system – transformers, switching gear, and the like

PICTURE SOURCES

With the exception of those listed below, all photographs and other illustrative material form part of the Company's archives; the photographs in colour showing the Company's contemporary activities were specially taken for this book by Frank Fischbeck at the Company's instigation:

Babcock Power, London:
Holborn Viaduct to Calder Hall
Archives: endpapers, 8, 10, 11

Steam: Its Generation and Use. Pub. Babcock & Wilcox Ltd., London, and The Babcock & Wilcox Co., New York. 1900. 12

Public Records Office, Hong Kong: 14, 22

Illustrations of China and its People. John Thomson. Pub. Samson Low, 1874. 24 (courtesy Frank Castle, Hong Kong)

Museum of History, Hong Kong: 30

Nigel Cameron (photographs by): 59, 60, 127

BIBLIOGRAPHY

Arnold, J. *A Handbook to Canton, Macao and the West River*. China Navigation Co., Ltd., Hong Kong. 8th edition 1910

Cameron, Nigel. *From Bondage to Liberation: East Asia 1860–1952*. Oxford University Press, Hong Kong, 1975

Hong Kong: The Cultured Pearl. Oxford University Press, Hong Kong, 1978

Cassery, Gordon. *The Land of the Boxers*. Longmans, Green, & Co., London, 1903

Crisswell, Colin N. *The Taipans: Hong Kong's Merchant Princes*. Oxford University Press, Hong Kong, 1981

Coates, Austin. *A Mountain of Light*. Heinemann, Hong Kong, 1977

Endacott, G.B. *A History of Hong Kong*. Oxford University Press, London, 1958

Hong Kong Eclipse. Edited and with additional material by Alan Birch. Oxford University Press, Hong Kong, 1978

Hayes, James. *The Hong Kong Region 1850–1911*. Archon Books, Connecticut, 1977

Hong Kong Government Annual Reports

Hurley, R.C. *Tourists' Map of 8 Short Trips on the Mainland of China (Neighbouring Hongkong) Including the Principal Places Frequented by Sportsmen*. Pub: 12 and 13 Beaconsfield Arcade, Hongkong, 1896

Leeming, F. *Street Studies in Hong Kong*. Oxford University Press, Hong Kong, 1977

Lindsay, Oliver. *The Lasting Honour: The Fall of Hong Kong, 1941*. Hamish Hamilton, London, 1978

Sayer, G.R. *Hong Kong 1862–1919: Years of Discretion*. Hong Kong University Press, 1975

Steam: Its Generation and Use. Babcock and Wilcox Ltd., London; The Babcock and Wilcox Co., New York. 2nd British edition, August 1900

Tregear, T.R. and Berry, L. *The Development of Hong Kong and Kowloon as told in Maps*. Hong Kong University Press, 1959

Twentieth Century Impressions of Hong Kong, Shanghai and other Treaty Ports of China. Lloyd's Greater Britain Publishing Co., London, 1908

Watton, E.B. *Holborn Viaduct to Calder Hall*. Babcock & Wilcox Ltd. No date

Wesley-Smith, Peter. *Unequal Treaty 1898–1997*. Oxford University Press, Hong Kong, 1980

INDEX